Visions of God's Coming Judgments

by Kimberly Vinson-Jackson

VISIONS OF GOD'S COMING JUDGMENTS

Copyright © 1997
by Kimberly Vinson-Jackson

Scripture quotations are taken from the
King James version of the Bible.

Additional copies are available.
You may contact us at
Divinehous@aol.com

ISBN: 0-9662666-1-7

Printed in the USA by Morris Publishing
3212 E. Highway 30, Kearney, NE 68847

CONTENTS

POEMS

SPECIAL THANKS

A very special thanks and honor to
The Father My God
To Jesus Christ The Son
To My Teacher and Best Friend
The Holy Ghost
For your divine presence
and anointing
that constantly guided me,
protected me,
and gave me the
strength and power
to fulfill the will of the Father
to accomplish this book.
For it is finished and I thank you highly.

Your Servant

DEDICATION

This book is dedicated to the unbelievers, who are lost in sin and headed for swift destruction if they don't repent.

To the worldly Christians, who have one foot in the church and the other foot out in the world.

To those who are saved, to continue to live that holy life required of you because we know not the day nor hour Jesus cometh.

FOREWORD

The contents in this book main focus are to let people know that time is whining up and it is time to repent. To reach those whom the enemy has blinded far too long, deceiving them into making sin look good, thinking they are having a good time and making them think they have all the time in the world to get right with God. This book is here to let you know that time is very short and to warn you of *God's Coming Judgments.*

God says in Matthew 16:2 that you can look up in the sky and predict what kind of weather it will be, but can ye not discern the signs of the time?
As for the church world, it's time out for playing church. It's time to stop conforming to the things of this world. It's time to start living by the commandments and laws God has laid before us in His Holy Word. He warns the church world to get your house in order because you know not the day nor hour the Son of man cometh.

God is warning the world to wake up and see the signs. The Lord is coming soon! If you could only feel the urgency He has put into my heart to get this book out. Believe me, it is a strong urgency.

TIME IS DRAWING NEAR

Too many people are going on by their merry way
Not taking heed to warnings from God's people today
Do you think they even believe what the people say?
No, they're just ignoring not realizing God don't play
The devil has people so blind they can't see nor hear
Yet, some hear and see
They rather be rebellious and not adhere
They don't want to listen and they won't even budge
They don't want to give up sin
Especially the nightclubs
What a shame! What a pity!
How the devil got people minds, not only in our city
God is getting tired and that's for sure
He's about to rain down His judgment
And Jesus' coming is drawing near
Why do you continue to hold on to sin?
Is it really worth it?
If you don't repent from your wicked ways
You are destined for the bottomless pit
Destruction is coming, it's coming your way
Oh rebellious child!
There will be no place to run
And there will certainly be no place to hide
Now is the time to repent before it's too late
Or you too,
Will be taking a one way trip to Hell's Gate.

❦

February 14, 1998

AND THE LORD ANSWERED ME, AND SAID, WRITE THE VISION AND MAKE IT PLAIN ON TABLETS, THAT HE MAY RUN THAT READETH IT.
FOR THE VISION IS YET FOR AN APPOINTED TIME, BUT AT THE END IT SHALL SPEAK, AND NOT LIE: THOUGH IT TARRY, WAIT FOR IT; BECAUSE IT WILL SURELY COME, IT WILL NOT TARRY.

HABAKKUK 2:2-3

INTRODUCTION

BEHOLD A MYSTERY OF GOD REVEALED

For nothing is secret, that shall not be made manifest; neither anything hid, that shall not be known and come abroad.
Luke 8:17

But we speak the wisdom of God in a mystery, even the hidden wisdom, which God ordained before the world unto our glory:
But God hath revealed them unto us by His Spirit: for the Spirit searcheth all things, yea the deep things of God.
Now we have received, not the spirit of the world, but the spirit of God; that we might know the things that are freely given to us of God.
I Corinthians 2:7,10,12

Behold I bring to you the revelation knowledge God has given unto me that is about to unfold before our eyes.

The Real Truth........

chapter

1 *The First Vision*

Lo and behold a vision the Lord has given unto me, a globe of the world itself in an array of colors. As I could see, over to the side of it, there was a huge clock, in which I knew in my spirit represented time. As I sat on the passenger side of my car, with the vision off to my right, I turned around to find a woman sitting in the back seat of my car. This woman and I held a brief conversation and if I remember nothing at all we talked about, the Lord did let me remember a question she asked me, and in this question, she mentioned the word *"short."* For some reason, that word stood out more than anything in the conversation. My eyes then became fixed back to the vision with the word *"short"* ringing in my ears. At that point it became clear to me in my spirit that I was viewing the world catastrophe. A world catastrophe will hit this planet shortly and time is whining up!

In other words, to make it plain and clear, it is **TIME FOR REPENTANCE!!!**

2 The Prophetic Three

Lo and behold another vision the Lord has given unto me. I looked up and behold in the northern night sky an object I stared at continuously. I could not figure out what this strange object was. Suddenly, my eyes became glued to the word written underneath this object. The word was spelled like this, *R-O-E-T-E-M.* It was meteor spelled backwards.

As I awaken out of this vision by the Holy Spirit, it was very late in the night. God is a God that likes to talk and reveal things in the wee hours. In as much as it is said in St John 16:13, the Spirit of Truth will guide you into all truth and He will show you things to come.

The Holy Spirit led me to kneel down and pray, and as I finished, I sat on my bed and He began to speak to me. He told me, *"I will show you things to come upon this earth. There will be destruction like you've never seen before. The people must repent. Destruction is coming soon."* Then, the Lord began to bring to my remembrance something I heard about years ago; the mountain rock John saw on the Island of Patmos. You will find it in Revelation 8:8,9. It read as follows:

*8th **And the second angel sounded, and as it were a great mountain burning with fire was cast into the sea: and the third part of the sea became blood:***

*9th **And the third part of the creatures which were in the sea, and had no life, died; and the third part of the ships were destroyed.***

This mountain he saw burning as it fell out of the sky as the Lord revealed and confirmed unto me is a *METEOR.* This mountain rock (meteor) caused all kinds of chaos upon the world. The words like meteor, asteroid, and comet were not used in their vocabulary back then, so John described what he was seeing as a mountain.

I looked up the word *"meteor."* Meteors are tiny pieces of metal or stone, which as they fall toward the earth, most of them burn before they reach the ground. As God was dealing with me about the vision, Hale (hell) Bopp made its grand entrance in the northern sky. I had no previous knowledge from the media, etc., that it was coming. It was strange how it appeared at the same time God was communicating to me about a meteor. I began to question in my mind; by Hale (hell) Bopp being a comet and I am seeing a vision of a meteor, there is quite a difference here, so, Lord, what is the connection? Lord, why am I seeing the word a-s-t-e-r-o-i-d in separate visions twice? What is the connection here?

In my spirit for days, I could hear ringing in my ears *"remember the mountain John saw."* I then looked up the word *comet,* but I didn't get deep into it. I read enough to know that comets are clouds of frozen gases, ice, dust, and rock. They travel around the solar system in long paths. As they travel slowly toward the Sun, the Sun's rays knock particles out of the comet and push them away to make a long tail, which always point away from the Sun. To answer the question, what is the connection of Hale (hell) Bopp and what God was trying to communicate about the meteor and asteroid?

Well, ***comets were once thought to foretell the coming of harmful events, since they appeared so unexpectedly and dramatically.*** For centuries they were believed to have an evil influence on human affairs, in particular they were thought to foretell plagues, wars and death. I found this piece of information to be very interesting because before it came to me, God had already given me a poem concerning Hale (hell) Bopp. In this poem He revealed that it will come back sooner than we think. He said, it will appear out of nowhere and man won't know what to do.

Man has predicted that it will come back thousands of years from now. It is not expected to return to the inner solar system until the year 4300. In all reality, as long as there is a God in heaven and who will always be, man's calculations and predictions don't mean anything because God is in control. He was the one who made the heavenly bodies in the first place. God has the same power He had from the beginning of time to speak things into existence and they appear. The same power He used then will be the same power He will use to speak to those heavenly bodies with their prophetic calling to go forth and accomplish their work.

As Hale (hell) Bopp made the headline for several months until the time of its departure, it shone so brightly in the northern night sky. Its grand entrance was God's way of communicating His coming judgments upon the world. God told me that it would return, but He had not shown me where it fit in scripture until later on. He always confirms things to me with scripture. He is a confirming God.

As I am going to a particular scripture for one thing, God began to show me something about this scripture. I could feel the presence of the enemy, which usually happens, when God is about to reveal something. The devil always shows up.

Matthew 24:29 says, ***Immediately after the tribulation of those days shall the sun be darkened and the moon shall not give her light, and the stars shall fall from heaven, and the powers of the heavens shall be shaken.***

My next chapter talks about stars. Anytime you read a scripture describing the stars falling out of the sky: an astronomical phenomenon is taking place. This particular one is very powerful because the powers of the heavens shook. What in the world took place that caused the powers of the heavens to shake?

As I continue to look at this scripture, I could feel the anointing of God all over me as the words *astronomical phenomena* was flashing across my mind very strongly. My body felt drenched in the anointing as I heard lines of a poem God had given unto me a while back concerning the comet.

Hale (hell)Bopp will return again
It won't take as long as astronomers claim
This comet is Bible prophecy
It's God's judgment on the world
For refusal to take heed

The rest of the poem may be found at the rear of this book. Why did God wait so long to reveal the answer? I don't know. But, He made sure I knew where the comet fit biblically before I finished this book. He is yet awesome!

In addition to Revelation 8, there are meteor showers to take place and there is the great earthquake, rain mixed with fire, darkness upon the earth, etc. I can't say when, only God knows when, for He is in control of all of these things. All I know is these events are Bible prophecy and they must come to pass and if you don't have the seal of God upon your life, you will not be able to escape God's wrath.

Hollywood has already prepared us in the movies, Deep Impact and Armageddon, but they left out one thing and that is the *message of repentance*. There is yet a message to be taken out of Deep Impact for all of God's people. I highly recommend every child of God to see it.

After viewing the movie, you will see there is no time for foolishness and there is no time to keep going in and out of God's will. If you have a calling on your life and you're running, there is no time for running. Here you are shouting you are on your way to heaven and don't have a burden for the people on the streets that are on their way to hell.

As I ride through the streets of Brooklyn my heart went out to those people. I didn't realize until then that there was so much work to be done. So many, lost souls roaming the streets. Something very devastating is getting ready to happen and the saints of God are still within the four walls of the church trying to get delivered themselves. There are some churches that welcome sinners and focus more on sinners getting saved at the altar and there are some churches where you see more saved people at the altar who are persistent repeats mainly because they want let go and let God. Some of them have acquired unto themselves the name "altar addict" meaning you are addicted to the altar. Unsaved people coming in can't even come to the altar and get saved in some churches because there is no room. The altar is full with saved folks who haven't come unto the realization that this walk is about faith and trust in God. God is not slack concerning His promises and everything that goes forth out of His mouth shall not return unto Him void; therefore we need to learn how to wait on Him. Time is running out. Many souls, many souls are in the valley of decision and God is holding His people responsible for these lost souls.

We have concerts after concerts, conferences after conferences, banquets, seminars, anniversaries, you name it, within the four walls. What are we doing to reach the lost? We are so caught up on ourselves. People are dying in the streets. It's time to come out of the four walls and pave the streets. They can't pay two hundred dollars to attend your conference. They can't pay sixty dollars for your banquet. And then you want to charge a dying soul fifty dollars to come in and listen to you give a seminar on the end-time events. You know that time is of the essence and lives are at stake, therefore you should be giving the information away free. Soul winning should be our first priority. In this present day and time, it's all about making that dollar. The dollar that will soon be history. Let's get real saints and wake up!

The words to a song has caught my attention as I am in church and it goes like this:

The Prophetic Three

I love you, love you, love you
I love you, love you, love you
With all of my heart
I'll do what you want me to do,
I'll go where you want me to go
I'll say what you want me to say
I'll say yes   *Repeat*

The Holy Spirit began to speak to me as I listened to the words carefully. I began to look around and observe how others were singing this song from the bottom of their heart. Do we really know what we are saying to God? What we are saying to God is, God if you tell me to go to the rough side of St. Louis, Brooklyn, or Chicago, I'll go. God if you tell me to go to the jungles of Africa, I'll go. God if you tell me to go somewhere I do not want to go, I'll go. Now if He tells you to go to a country stricken with stench, poverty, and disease such as India, a country where they serve over three hundred million gods, will you go? Or are you just singing a lie?

God can't even get some of His people to go to the rough side of their local city to pass out salvation tracks. Some saved folks will tell you in a minute that God didn't tell them to go there. And I can tell you, yes He did. He told us in Mark 16:15, **Go ye into all the world, and preach the gospel to every creature.**

God may have only three words for you to say to that prostitute on the streets and that may be: *Jesus loves you.* God may have only two words for you to say to that homeless person and that may be, *Jesus cares.* God may have one word for you to say to that drug dealer and that may be to *repent.* Is God asking too much from us? The answer is NO.

The name of Jesus is all-powerful by itself. God is really not asking much from His people. God says to go to the house of the lost sheep of Israel. The lost sheep God is talking about is the drunkards, the drug addicts, the homeless, the prostitutes, the gangbangers, and so forth.

We have to go out there and get them. Go out into the highways and hedges, and compel them to come in, that My house may be filled (Luke 14:23). What are we afraid of when God has said in His Word that He is our shield? We are covered under the blood of Jesus Christ. We have power to tread on serpents and scorpions and over all powers of the enemy: nothing shall by any means hurt us. What are you afraid of when you see a drunk coming in your path and you want to cross the street and get on the other side? GOD HELP US TODAY.

There are some that have a misconception of what the work of God entails. Some think they will be behind a microphone all the time, but God's work involves more than being behind a microphone only to be seen. You know how some people in the church are "mike" happy? Don't give them a little position of authority in the church, it goes to their head.

There are some people who are called to be evangelists, etc., who say they have to get a new wardrobe for when God sends them out on the field. Barely do they even realize what that field may end up being. They want a custom made robe for their first sermonette. The work of God is not about being inside the four walls. It is not about making money and it is not a fashion show. It is about SOULS.

You need to take your mindset off of what you're going to wear and how many speaking engagements you are going to have, etc. Here you are fantasizing about putting on a designer suit holding a revival at the DoubleTree with a chandelier over your head standing in front of a podium on red carpet. Those walls are going to be broken down and the revival is going to be in the streets. So, it's best to concentrate on getting some power behind your belt because it is going to be ferocious out there. The closer we get to the end please expect the unexpected when it comes to God and His work to win souls.

God took me to Matthew 10:9 and this is where Jesus told the disciples, ***Provide neither gold; nor silver, nor brass in your purses. Nor scrip for your journey, neither two coats, neither shoes, nor yet staves:*** In other words pack light and your God shall provide the rest. By the time God gets finished equipping you for your calling as evangelists, teachers, prophets, etc., you will not need a new wardrobe for where God is getting ready to send you. The only thing you will need is a pair of sneakers, a jean skirt, jeans and a backpack. So be well aware that you may not get to have the fancy stage, the bright lights and the cordless mike like so and so you see on Christian TV.

Some of the well-known evangelists or ministers of the Gospel have turned their hearts more toward money than souls. Some of them will not preach at your church unless they have an estimated crowd count and are paid upfront. Now where is God in all of this? I don't know. Some have lost their focus on the vision of God to win souls. Now whatever has happened to having a hunger for lost souls and trusting God to make provision for you on your journey? I don't know. What people fail to realize is money will be of no use shortly.

God is raising up a new breed that will be on fire for Him and will not let anything come between them and the vision of God for souls. They know that God equal souls. And when God says Go. They know to go and don't worry about provisions because the way has already been made.

Yes, God is going to send you out on the field, but it may be an open field using what you got and wearing what you got. It's getting ready to get serious out there and God is getting His people ready. The handful of well-known true anointed preachers and evangelists you very seldom see on Christian TV, etc. are His 19th Century anointed ones.

Now God said He is raising up a new breed of evangelists, prophets, and ministers of the Gospel. They are the 21st Century evangelists, prophets, ministers of the Gospel, etc. So, don't try to get what man calls raptured up out of here prematurely. There is a great work to be done. There is a great move of God that has to take place before you are caught up. It has not even started yet. The works that you are going to be doing is far more greater than the works that Jesus did. God is getting His people ready for Daniel 11:32.

Even Daniel the prophet saw you, *saint* of God, doing great exploits for God during the tribulation period. It is in the Bible and it shall in no way fail at coming to pass. That's why the devil fight you very hard because he knows that you have a divine calling on your life to tear his Kingdom down. The devil will throw an I don't wanta do it spirit on you. He will have you asking God, why me Lord? Pick someone else. You'll be doing one of Moses numbers, using every excuse imaginable. God says to open up your mouth and He'll speak for you.

If the devil isn't pitching you a fit then you need to go recheck yourself. Every saint of God should be on his hit list. If he isn't bothering you then that means you don't oppose a threat to him whatsoever.

If he's picking at you all the time, then it is obvious that you got something inside of you that's going to tear His Kingdom down.

He has another list called the *"Most Wanted List."* This is the one God revealed to me that I am on, but He let's me know that He has my back. Everytime the devil sees your name on the *"Most Wanted List,"* he trembles but he knows he got to work against you every chance he gets. But know this, that no entity in hell or out of hell can destroy you. God has a work to birth out of you. So don't let the devil have you running.

Where are you running to? I don't know. Where are you going to hide? Where are you going to go? David very clearly states in Psalm 139 that you can't hide or run from God.

1ST **O, Lord, thou hast searched me, and known me.**

2ND **Thou knowest my downsitting and mine uprising, thou understandest my thought afar off.**

3RD **Thou compasseth my path and my lying down, and art acquainted with all my ways.**

4TH **For there is not a word in my tongue, but, lo, O Lord, thou knowest it altogether.**

5TH **Thou hast beset me behind and before, and laid thine hand upon me.**

6th **Such knowledge is too wonderful for me; it is high, I cannot attain unto it.**

7TH **Whither shall I go from thy spirit? or whither shall I flee from thy presence?**

8TH **If I ascend up into heaven, thou art there: if I make my bed in hell, behold, thou art there.**

9TH **If I take the wings of the morning, and dwell in the uttermost parts of the sea;**

10TH **Even there shall thy hand lead me, and thy right hand shall hold me.**

11TH **If I say, Surely the darkness shall cover me; even the night shall be light about me.**

12TH **Yea, the darkness hideth not from thee; but the night shineth as the day; the darkness and the light are both alike to thee.**

You see even David knew that God was omnipresence, omnipotence and omniscience.

Here is an excerpt from a poem you will find in my upcoming book poem book, *Hidden Treasures*:

You can run but you can't hide
You are the called of God
You have been set aside
Why are you running?
God has His eyes on you
He has plans for your life
A great work to do
So humble yourself
And let God have His way or else hear
Depart from me, I never knew you, on Judgment Day
Who is he that feareth the Lord?
Then, why does disobedience rule your heart?
For you know not the Lord and neither His ways
If you did you would surely obey
You can't run from God, you are in His hands
Now what part of your calling do you not understand?

Many are trying to duck, hide and run from their calling. If you don't let go and let God, you're going to find yourself hearing Him say, Depart from me I never knew you when Judgment Day comes. We all will have to give an account to that which God has called us to do. I highly recommend that every child of God go see the movie, The Prince of Egypt. There is

24

a very strong and powerful message in it. Very strong and powerful. God is very serious when it comes to His work and He is being taken very lightly by the I don't wantas and why me, and I can't spirits. We must let the devil know that he is not our master. God is our Master and King and we are His servants. We have been bought with a price. Our mind, body and soul belong to God. We are no longer our own.

Let us be reminded that the wrath of God does fall upon the children of disobedience. Know that in these last days that this thing is not about you at all. It is about God trying to use you to reach souls blinded by the devil, headed for swift destruction if they don't repent, and it is our responsibility to reach them before it's too late. Something very devastating is getting ready to happen that involves a comet, a meteor, and an asteroid. It is time out for playing hide-n-go seek with God.

Saint of God you may read this more than once, but God told me to tell you, when you see these things come to pass, Don't be afraid, for I am with you. So what does that let you know? All I can say is God is real, He does exist and He is no one to play around with. He holds all power in His hands. He is a caring God, in that He is letting us know what's ahead beforehand, giving the world a chance to repent. He could have destroyed us a long time ago. The people in the Bible days were destroyed in a heartbeat. When the people didn't hearken to the voice of God in those days, God took them out in one stroke.

Sodom and Gomorrah were set forth as an example to the world today of the price they'll have to pay for being wicked and rebellious. And that price is suffering the vengeance of eternal fire. God's desire is that no man perish, but have everlasting life. Time is running out people and God is getting tired of watching you in your sin, even the church world.

One day I read where a movie star gave his view concerning his belief in God. He said, "I don't believe God gets angry and zaps someone." My response to that is he doesn't know God. He needs to read the Old Testament and perhaps have a talk with the children of Israel, Noah, Pharaoh (Ramses), the people of Nineveh, Lot, and many more. Psalm 7:11 says *God judgeth the righteous, and God is angry with the wicked everyday.*

12th *If he turn not (if the wicked don't repent), he (God) will whet his sword, he hath bent his bow, and made it ready.*

Now all that God has in stored for the wicked is in that sword and I personally do not want any parts of it. As I said before God is not playing around. When He says, *"repent"* He means what He says!

Yes, God is a loving God and there's another side of Him that some preachers don't touch on, therefore God is going to hold them responsible. They are too busy trying to ordain themselves as bishops and apostles and trying to get popularity. They done swept the vision under the pulpit carpet. Some of them don't preach on the wrath of God that will fall down upon the children of disobedience if they continue to reject Him. There is a side of God that will get angry and will allow bad to happen.

God has given unto us all a freewill to choose between good and evil. If you choose evil then you are walking in disobedience to God. Keep on ignoring Him by not turning from your wicked ways and He will show you who He is. They mocked God recently in a movie on national TV. Hollywood twisted the story of Noah and Abraham. They portrayed things that happened in the Bible falsely and look what happened? Seventy-two tornadoes touchdowned in the Midwest.

You see God is no one to be mocking. The movie was a deception from the very beginning. Lot's time was after Noah. Noah had nothing to do with Sodom and Gomorrah or with finding 50 righteous men. This movie started out lying and to think of all the people that didn't know the Bible and got deceived. God is not happy with that at all. The devil himself was behind the scenes concocting this deception through atheistic minds that don't have respect for God.

When you mock someone in authority you cause his or her anger to lash out. Ask the wise men and Herod. They mocked Herod and Herod got angry and killed all the children two years old and under in Bethlehem and in all the coasts around. As I have said before it is a dangerous thing to keep rejecting God and God is not playing around. When He says to repent and get your house in order He means just that!

To continue on with the vision, as I get a view of Hale (hell) Bopp, high in the sky. The mountain John saw continues to run across my mind. God being the all knowing God that He is, knew my every thought and question, gave me another vision in the wee hours of April 4,1997.

3

The Two Stars

Lo and behold another vision the Lord has given unto me, two stars seen visible in the northern night sky. One star stood out from the rest because it shone so brightly. The other star was red and it was moving in slow motion, easing over to the bright star as to cause some type of disruption.

As I awake, the Spirit of the Lord was very heavy on me. He led me to do some research; what I call a spirit-led research. I looked up the word *"star"* and it gave the meaning that in the Bible *"star"* is used as a generic term for all the heavenly bodies including stars, planets, comets, and meteors, etc. A star represents God's power exhibited in judgment. I looked up the color *"red."* Red is the color of blood and the picture of the carnage of war. The word *"carnage"* means, massive slaughter; massacre. This doesn't sound pleasant at all. Then the Lord brought me back to Revelation 8 again. I requoted verses 8 and 9 but now the main focus here is verses 10 and 11. Revelation 8:8 again reads as follows:

8th **And the second angel sounded, and as it were a great mountain burning with fire was cast into the sea: and the third part of the sea became blood:**

9th **And the third part of the creatures which were in the sea, and had life, died; and the third part of the ships were destroyed.**

*10th **And the third angel sounded, and there fell a great star from heaven, burning as it were a lamp, and it fell upon the third part of the rivers, and upon the fountains of waters;***

*11th **And the name of the star is called Wormwood: and the third part of the waters became wormwood; and many men died of the waters, because they were made bitter.***

In verse 8 and verse 10, here you have two astronomical phenomenas taking place in these scriptures. To add to those two, take a look at verses 6 and 12. Earlier I stated that there would be more than one cosmic disturbance to take place soon. God spoke to me and He said, *"Many things, many things are about to come upon this earth."*

I recall a vision God had given to me before He began giving me visions of the meteor and asteroid. I saw a humongous rock coming toward me very fast and all I could do was open my eyes very quick. But little did I know that God was giving me a sneak preview of what's to come and that I must put it on paper and get the word out. I highly commend John for being able to sit there and record something like that. This thing is real! When God gives visions of things pertaining to the solar system, it feels as if your spirit is out there in space!

It's quite an experience and as I sit here and write, I can feel the anointing of God as I think on the awesome power of God to create everything about the universe. Man has the audacity to this day, to ponder on how the world came into existence. It is now, going on year 2,000 and they still haven't figured it out and the answer is in Genesis 1. God said in Genesis 1, "Let there be" and there it was.

As you read this chapter, you will find that God created day and night; He created heaven and earth

30

and He created you and me. Genesis 1:16 tells us that he made the stars also. Now that is a lot of power to simply speak things into existence and they appear.

Let us go back to the definition of star. As I cross referenced Genesis 1:16, it led me to an interesting scripture out of Isaiah 40:26 and it reads as follows: *Lift up your eyes on high, and behold who hath created these things (stars), that bringeth out their host by number: he (God) calleth them all by names by the greatness of his might, for that he is strong in power; not one faileth.* This scripture alone let's us know that God is in control. He controls the stars; every move they make. Psalm 147:4 tells us that, *He telleth the number of the stars; he calleth them all by their names.* Isaiah 42:5 reads, *Thus saith God the Lord, he that created the heavens, and stretched them out; he that spread forth the earth, and that which cometh out of it; he that giveth breath unto the people upon it, and spirit to them that walk therein:* Now you see it in scripture, God being the Creator of all things. He spoke it out of His mouth into existence and there it was.

As you may have well noticed, I chose to put scriptures throughout this book simply because some people will not pick up a Bible and read it.

There is a spirit of atheism that has swept across this country. Atheism has plagued the minds of some of our scientists, astronomers, and just people all around. The Bible has given the truth concerning the creation? Why can't you believe? It's time out for the big bang theory. It's time to stop believing in Darwin's theory of evolution. The wisdom of this world is foolishness with God. Therefore, it's time to start giving credit to whom credit is due. It all goes to God.

As we go back to Revelation 8, it referenced to Jeremiah 51:25 saying, **Behold I am against thee, O destroying mountain, saith the Lord, which destroyest all the earth: and I will stretch out mine hand upon thee, and roll thee down from the rocks, and will make thee a burnt mountain.**

Even the prophets of old had visions of future end-time events. God says in this verse that He will stretch out His hand and allow this thing to do some damage.

As you can see, God is in control. He got His hands on these things. Like I said before, one of these events will creep up out of nowhere and people won't know what to do. Men's hearts will fail them for fear, for the things that will take place on earth. The Bible speaks of men in high power; the kings of the earth, and the great men, and the rich men and the chief captains, and mighty men, and every bondsman, and every free man, will hide themselves in the dens and in the rocks of the mountains; and will say unto the mountains and rocks, fall on us, and hide us from the face of Him that sitteth on the throne, and from the wrath of the Lamb: for the great day of His wrath is come: and who will be able to stand?

This is what you call the desperate actions of the people when cosmic disturbances began to take place. Those men that the Bible speaks about in high power, etc., are your everyday politicians, presidents, princes, the rich and famous; people of high rank and then the average everyday people will totally freak out trying to hide from God.

As I read men's hearts will be failing them; it sounds as if heart attacks, strokes, blood pressure rising, and everything else will be taking place. The saddest thing about it is, people shall seek death; they will try suicide, but death shall flee from them. They'll just have to suffer. Isn't that something? Death will not want to have any part with them; for death itself will run from them.

God is calling people to repentance because these things are near upon us and Jesus is soon to come. They've been saying this for years I know, but those years have turned into anyday now, anyday.

As we look at Revelation 8:10, it mentions a great star. Again, let's go back to the definition of star. In the Bible, a star is used as a generic term for *all* the heavenly bodies including stars, planets, comets, and meteors, etc. Also remember, a star represents God's power exhibited in judgment. In verse 11, this star has the name Wormwood. It means bitterness, sorrow, and calamity. Wormwood is any of several aromatic plants that yield a bitter, dark green oil. It is mentioned several times in the Bible. It had a bitter taste and strong aroma.

In the Bible and in this verse, *wormwood* is used symbolically to refer to any calamity or bitter experience. In other words this particular disaster described in Rev 8:10 will indeed be a bitter experience. This star will effect a third part of the fresh water supply of the earth causing it to be unfit for human consumption. It will cause many to die. This star that God, being the all-knowing God that He is, has revealed and confirmed unto me is indeed an *ASTEROID.*

According to the Bible, God named this particular star and has given it a prophetic judgment to carry out. Let us remember Isaiah 40:26, says that God calleth them all by names by the greatness of His might.

There are other interpretations of what Revelation 8:8-11 is talking about and what these two stars represent. The word star is mentioned several times in the Bible. There are passages in which stars represents angels but in the scriptures I have mentioned it is not so.

Psalms 3:32 let us know that the secret of the Lord is with the righteous. He reveals things to them that are intimate with Him, them that reverence Him and fear Him. Too many people got their heads stuck in the Book of Revelation and God hasn't told them to go there. Therefore they go there on their own coming up with their own interpretations, opinions, etc., misleading people for filthy lucre gain. Beware: Don't believe everything you hear, go to God for the truth.

Earlier, I mentioned that God had shown me the word "asteroid" in two separate visions. He led me to look up the word *"asteroid."* It gave a very interesting definition as being countless thousands of tiny planets left over from the time when the Sun and planets were being formed. Most of them can be found in the wide gap between the orbits of Mars and Jupiter. There may be a collision between a comet and an asteroid or a comet and Jupiter. After reading the next chapter on Jupiter, you may understand why I made this statement.

It is amazing as God is revealing things to me, I recall hating science in grade school. But now, looking and learning from God's viewpoint and not man's, makes it all the more interesting! I love it! God is the revealer of all truth.

However, there will be a lot going on and whatever way God chooses to make any of this happen, it will, I guarantee you have a devastating impact on the world. It will be felt worldwide.

As I sit and watched Armageddon, I noted quite a bit of deception in this movie. First, you will find Armageddon in Revelation 16. According to the Bible, Armageddon is the site of the final battle of this age in which God intervenes to destroy the armies of satan into the bottomless pit. In this chapter there is no mention of a word that fits the description of an asteroid nor is there mention of a meteor shower as it was portrayed.

There is mention of a hailstone shower in verse 21 and these stones weighed from 50 to 100 pounds. However there is still a difference between a meteor and hailstone shower. That's why I stress sticking with the Bible and not man's wisdom and knowledge. They portrayed this event as though they can stop it from happening. They made it look as if man defeated God's plan. When in all reality, no matter how many fine astronauts Nassau sends up there; they will not be able to save the world. The Bible tells us the devil is defeated at Armageddon. God won the battle.

As for the asteroid, it is Bible prophecy. Man can't stop what God has already ordained to happen. So don't let Hollywood deceive you. Man can pray all they want, but it's going to happen. The only prayer God wants to hear is the prayer of repentance. Who knows what Nassau keeps going up into space for? They may be going for one thing and telling us another. An asteroid or a meteor could be fifteen days away from us and they're not telling us.

In the movie they did try to keep it hush hush from the world. As I sat and watched, I could hear the word *"death"* ringing in my ears. Many shall die. Then I heard it again *"death"* and again. When I arrived home I was led to Revelation 8:11 and it said many men shall die. Just another confirmation, the Lord has given to me.

No matter how Hollywood tries to portray these events. They haven't come near the actual impact that these events will cause. It would cost them trillions to do so.

Remember the asteroid that hit the headlines on March 12, 1998? That week I had been hearing in my spirit, the word *"asteroid."* Then I could hear God's coming judgment ringing in my ears. On the morning of the 12th, as I awaken, the newspaper was brought to my bedside and the headline read as follows, "Asteroid in the Neighborhood," and then another heading "Too Close for Call." What gets me is that scientist knew that this object was up there since December 6, 1997, and they waited till three months later to mention it. It makes me wonder what else are they observing that they are not informing us about.

What the Lord began to drop into my spirit was don't put your trust in man. God said that one of these events will pop up out of nowhere, which lead me to believe that scientists and meteorologists will get no pre warning at all. I recall in memory of a tornado that hit Georgia on March 20, 1997, the amazing thing about it was it didn't even show up on the radar. They had no warning whatsoever, that it was on its way.

However, you, have a warning that Revelation 8 is well on its way. You have it right here, a message from the Throne Room of God, right here in this book brought to you in plain and simple language. God is not keeping you in the dark. He is letting you know ahead of time, so you can make amends with Him right now. You'd rather put your trust in man because man has a degree behind his name and therefore he knows it all. You must realize that if it had not been for God; they would not have the ability to think, or those degrees. If man tells you not to panic, then you won't. You are then somewhat relieved. If God tells you to do something you won't do it. You won't even budge. The point I am trying to make is God knows all things.

James 3:17 tells us that the wisdom from above is first pure. Luke 8:17 tells us, ***"For nothing is secret, that shall not be made manifest, neither anything hid, that shall not be known and come abroad.***

Some things have been coming abroad and as you can see, Bible prophecies are unfolding before our very eyes. You must recognize God is trying to warn the world beforehand and the world must respond through repentance.

The asteroid that appeared in the headlines was estimated to be as large as a mile in diameter. The impact of an asteroid this size would have devastating global effect, including tidal waves, continent size fires and eruption of dust that could cause global cooling and long-term disruption of agriculture. Now this sounds like a cosmic disruption to take place out of Revelation. In all reality when these things hit earth, the world will not be the same.

On the following day, May 13ᵗʰ just to let you know not to put your trust in man, another article read as follows, "Scientists disagree on peril of asteroid." They said, "Our *guess* is that, it's going to miss earth by a big distance."

Now they must have gotten a lot of hysterical calls because they changed their story quick. It was like a new game being introduced to the market called, "The Asteroid Guessing Game." Spin the arrow and whatever it lands on will determine, will it hit or will it miss.

As you read further into the article, this asteroid will be added to the PHO list, which is a list of 108 known potentially hazardous objects. It looks like more game pieces to be added. With objects like these hanging over my head, not knowing when they will fall out of orbit, should make you want to live right and get under God's divine protection. This article was so unbelievable. To top it off they made the statement, "We simply don't have sufficient knowledge of this object to be sure."

Once again, I will show you in Psalm 118:8, *"It is better to put your trust in the Lord than to put confidence in man."* Then too, how can they put trust in someone that they have already shown they don't believe in? Some don't even believe that there is a God. However, if they would recognize God as being the Supreme Being, the Creator of the universe, as being omniscience (all knowing) and would seek His face, He would supply them with first hand sufficient knowledge concerning some things. God says in Jeremiah 33:3, *Call to me, and I will answer you, and I will tell you great and mighty things, which you do not know.*

What the world fails to realize is God's Word is truth. Everything in it and about it comes from God. Just a word of caution: Man doesn't know everything. However, they know some things and will not warn you. The news media will tell you what you want to hear, for instance, things like, there is no immediate cause for alarm or there is nothing to be alarmed about, just to calm you down.

I was commissioned by God to write; to push every alarm button, to sound off every siren, to flip the emergency switch light on, to make your hair stand up on top of your head, to awaken those who are asleep and to proclaim the acceptable year of the Lord.

When God says something is going to happen, He means it and it will not fail at coming to pass. He is a God that cannot lie (Titus 1:2) for it is impossible for Him to lie (Hebrew 6:18). He demands that you clean up your act and repent. He is sending out His warning signals in the skies. He's warning the world in so many ways and people ignore Him as if the world will be here for years and years to come.

Some bible scholars are asking as they see things unfold, what is God trying to communicate? The answer is staring them right in the face. God is trying to communicate His coming judgments on the world. It is as simple as that. He has allowed some of them to surface, but He says it's not time for them to carry out His prophetic judgment. It's getting close!

All of these strange weather patterns we've been having, for instance El Nino as they call it and his sister name La Nina, I must say there is no such thing of the two, however man will throw a name on anything. The truth of the matter is all of these strange weather patterns going on across the world are nothing but a wake up call from God. The earth is slowly, but surely deteriorating. Matthew 24:35 says that heaven and earth shall pass away but my Word shall not pass away. He will not continue to let wickedness rule this earth and it must come to an end. It must. What is God going to do with it? He's going to destroy it. There will be a new heaven and a new earth and it will be sinless. He's loving and caring enough to give you a chance to repent. Time is running out, it's running out!

Even though they had a disagreement with the calculations and the size of that asteroid, remember that God knows all and He knows when it too shall return. God is in control.

The devil has people so blinded. The sad thing is, when these things happen, people will not repent, but instead they will get angry with God. They will harden their hearts even worst as the people in the Bible days.

It's time for the preachers to not only preach that God is love, but it is time for them to start preaching the other side of God. The side of God that hates sin and because of it, He is going to pour down His wrath upon the ungodly. It is time for them to stop sugarcoating the Gospel. It is time to stop preaching what the people want to hear: avoiding certain subjects for fear of losing members. It is time for the people to know who God really is. It's time to instill fear into the hearts of the people. They don't fear God at all. It is time to stop playing church. It is time to get the people spiritually prepared for the destruction that is on the way. I know you are planning on being raptured out of here before any of these things take place. But believe it or not, some of these things you will see.

If your heart is right with God, Revelation 8 will not bother you. You have nothing to worry about because you are covered under the blood of Jesus. God made promises of divine protection for His people (the obedient). He says to the obedient to not let your hearts be troubled, neither let it be afraid. He also says to the obedient. When you see these things happen, don't be afraid, for I am with thee. So, God's people live by faith. Faith in the promises God has spoken in His Word unto them that obey His Word.

Bible prophecies are unfolding before our eyes and the more that unfolds let me know that we are even closer to the coming of Jesus. However, there is a work to be done and that is to warn others of the things to come and to pass along the visions.

As I write about this asteroid, God reminds me of a poem he gave me titled, The World is in Trouble with God. In this poem He said, *"Many things, many things, shall come upon this earth. Sin, Sin, is tearing this world apart. They must repent from the bottom of their heart."* On another occasion He said, *"There will be destruction as never before seen on mankind."*

As I finished my spirit-led research on stars, the Spirit of the Lord was very heavy on me. I've never experienced nothing like this before in my life. I was led to my knees to pray. I started out singing slowly the Lord's Prayer. I really didn't know what to say and what to expect next. I knew something was different, I could feel. As I finished singing, something hit me in my spirit, I felt as though I wanted to cry.

I knew my spirit was in the presence of Almighty God. I said Lord, please have mercy on this world. The response He gave to me was, *"I have been lenient with this world long enough."* I could hear His voice way off in a distance. He told me, *"Fear not for I am with thee. Don't worry and don't be afraid. These things must come to past."* He went on to say, *"He that keepeth Israel shall neither slumber nor sleep."* Then something dropped in my spirit as He began to say, *"The world is in trouble with God. God has extended His mercy long enough."*

Like in the days of Noah, they refused to take heed to God's warning to repent of their sins. As in the days of Sodom and Gomorrah, they would not turn from their wicked ways.

The world is in trouble with God and must repent now. They have provoked God to anger with their rebellious acts. They are doing those things that are an abomination in My sight and are sentencing themselves to God's wrath. The world is in trouble with God and must repent while they have the chance. Something dropped even lower in my spirit; as I could hear, *Judgment is coming very soon.* They must repent now. *Judgment is coming; it's coming, coming very soon!*

There are no words to describe this experience. When God was finished saying what He had to say, I had to lay flat on my face onto the floor for a few minutes. I can truly relate to the aftereffects Daniel felt after each vision he received concerning the future. When I came out of this, I had a different perspective on God. I had a fear for God, I knew God was a God to respect and He is serious and is no one to play around with. Sin, hell, and God's wrath should be emphasized more in the church today.

As the scripture says in Matthew 10:28 **don't fear them that kill the body, but are not able to kill the soul: but fear him (God) which is able to destroy both soul and body in hell.** The problem with the world today is they don't fear God. After God spoke these things unto me, He gave me a message for His people. You will find it in the seventh chapter titled *A Message to the Godly.*

So, here we have a comet that has already announced God's coming judgments upon the world. Then, there is a meteor and an asteroid that play a role in the end-times with their prophetic calling. I thank God for our scientists and astronomers and this is not to put them down, but they don't know everything. They and the news media will play the cover-up game as to not alarm you.

I am here to relate a message from God Almighty who knows what, when, and how concerning all things. God told me, it's coming and there is everything in the world to be alarmed about if you have not repented and are not living according to the principles of His Word. What's in the dark shall come to the light. Remember that there is nothing kept secret, that it shall not come abroad, neither is nothing hid that shall not be made manifested.

4 *Jupiter*

In December 1997, I had a vision of a planet. As this planet was before me, the Spirit of the Lord let me know that I was viewing Jupiter. I saw something that appeared to be reddish yellow melting off this planet. As I awaken I asked myself, why am I seeing a vision of Jupiter? God, what are you trying to communicate to me?

I read a little about Jupiter and to my surprise, the picture of Jupiter shown, was the same colors of Jupiter I saw in my vision. Therefore, I was on the right track. As I read information about this planet, they didn't seem to know for sure whether Jupiter was hot or cold. Astronomers believe that most of it is made of hot hydrogen. From what I could see in my vision, something extremely hot was melting off this planet. Do any of what I read truly answer my question, why are you showing this to me, Lord? Well, I believe it answers the question whether Jupiter is hot or cold, but, there is more, there is more to this. Only God knows.

So, I told someone about the vision that same day and that person called me later and told me they saw Jupiter on the World News and told me to watch for it on a later taping that night. As I watched the news, they were saying the reverse of what I had seen as though Jupiter was cold. So, I say, okay Lord, talk to me. I then knew I had to wait on God for an answer and not lean on my own understanding. So, my mind slipped away from the vision for a while, but God had a way of bringing it back to me. January approaches and my answer came on the 29th. Why God waited so long to reveal it, I don't know, however, there is some things you just don't question Him about.

I am not the type to read every book on the market, because every book is not of God. I have to be led by the Spirit as to what books to buy and read. I can count the books on my hand that the Holy Spirit has led me to read and believe me, it's not many.

So let us be careful and beware, because many false teachers and false prophets with false doctrines have plagued this country and our bookstores. When in all reality, all you really need to read is The Holy Bible.

God inspired men to write the Bible as a guide for you and me to live by. It has everything you need in it for everyday living. It provides answers to your questions and problems. You don't have to sit there and question God because His Word is truth.

Some of you know and have heard that God works in mysterious ways. Well, anyway I recall coming home from my shop one evening and my son met me at the door. He said, "Mom look what I've got, a book on the universe." My first thought was God. I knew God had something to do with him bringing this book to me.

As he opened this book, it was like reliving my visions again. I was amazed at what I was seeing because it looked so real. At that moment, I could feel the presence of the enemy. I knew immediately there was something in this book that God wanted me to read. As I rushed to get dinner on, I had my son to thumb through chapters as I prepare dinner. He showed me individual chapters on meteors, comets, and then asteroids.

Last but not least, I asked him to look up Jupiter. The same colors I saw in my vision were the same colors of Jupiter in this book also. At last I was to the point where I could sit down and take a break.

As I began to read about Jupiter, it was one of the most interesting planets to read about. Jupiter is highly praised among all the planets. Jupiter is the King of the Planets. Although, as of early 1998 they have discovered an even bigger planet outside the solar system that is three times larger than Jupiter. Jupiter makes up about 318 of Earth. Earth is a little dot compared to this big planet. Jupiter's gravitational force is so great!

Get this, **many comets are eventually pulled close to the orbit of giant Jupiter and there they stay.** Jupiter has captured many comets and has its own comet family, as do some of the other planets. Comets have been known to collide with Jupiter. I was so amazed at what I was reading. Out of all the planets in the solar system, Jupiter was the only planet God showed unto me!

There's the answer to my question, why was God showing me a vision of Jupiter? It all goes back to the comet Hale (hell) Bopp. God had revealed the whereabouts of Hale (hell) Bopp at that time! And in chapter 5 He has also brought to light the term "Jupiter" and its relations to the ancients of old and future endtime events. There's nothing like digging back into history and finding some missing pieces to a puzzling future. History is good information. Let us remember; there is nothing secret that shall not be made manifest. God has His hands on this particular comet, but He's holding it back to give people a chance to repent.

Time is running out! I tell you, this comet is so evil, I truly believe it is filled with nothing but evil spirits. Whenever I began to write about it or even mention it to someone, as I am doing right now, I can feel the presence of evil. They know God has given me the revelation and will stop at nothing to keep me from going forward with it. God lets me know to keep on writing and know that He is by my side. I can sit and write another book on the experiences I have encountered while putting this book together, which will let you know that these things God has revealed are real.

Even the people in the cult knew something about the comet, but they got information from the wrong spirit realm and got deceived out of life eternity. I hope and pray that God will allow the catching up of the saints to take place before this comet comes back because once it hit nothing but evil spirits will be lashed out upon this earth. I'm not talking about little imps. I'm talking about satan's chief captains and lieutenants, etc. That's why it's wise to get as much of God as you possibly can now.

After absorbing all of this information in amazement, I began to walk through my house. The Holy Spirit put a song in my heart and I began to sing it out. I had no control over the words that were coming out of my mouth, which was not unusual for me. He usually communicates to me through songs as well. As I began to sing, the words that came out of my mouth were, *I am with thee, I am with thee.* Then I remember singing out these words, *"For God knows all things."* God does not hide anything from His people.

48

There is a spiritual message to be taken from this quite interesting planet. As I think on how Jupiter is highly praised, it reminds me of how Jesus is highly praised. Jesus is King of Kings and Lord of Lords. He is much greater in power. You will never find anyone one greater than Him except the Father and they are One.

Yes, Jesus has a strong spiritual gravitational pull. Once you have become rooted and grounded in Him, nothing can pull you away from His love, grace, and mercy. As you become a part of Jesus gravitational pull, you become a part of the body of Christ. You are a part of God's family.

Yes, the devil will try to collide with us by sending his shooting stars, meteor showers, asteroids, etc., which represents his fiery darts, obstacles, and hindrances with the ultimate goal of trying to knock us out of orbit and destroy us. He's trying to pluck us out of God's hand. But, that strong gravitational pull full of God's love, grace, and mercy keeps us going strong. For, we are strong, determined and victorious in Christ Jesus.

Some things have already surfaced, but God said, it's not time yet! I have some lost sheep on earth that I want to give a chance to find their way back to Me. He said that in the last days there would be signs in the sun, and in the moon, and in the stars. Truly He has been giving us many signs lately in the heavenlies.

chapter

5 *The Cashless Society*

For over a course of two days I could hear Psalm 3:32 in my spirit. The secret of the Lord is with the righteous. I could hear the scripture wisdom from above is first pure. Wisdom is more precious than silver and gold. Wisdom is sweet to behold. It's like a treasure. I could hear these things ringing in my ears not realizing God was about to open up my understanding and give me a revelation. And did He drop a bucket full of wisdom and knowledge on me. It was as if I had found precious hidden treasure that filled my heart with joy.

On August 30, 1998, God gave me a revelation dream. In the dream, I was conscious of what event had taken place. My family and I were driving along what was once a busy street. I was observing and taking note of closed down businesses. Even I have a business located on this street. Everything was different as if not one thing on earth had life. The sun was not shining; it was gloomy outside. We had gone several blocks down before I even realized we had passed my shop.

All of a sudden my subconscious kicked in. I knew I was in a dream and I knew that if we could turn around to go to the shop, I could see what type of display was in my window. Yes, that would be the key to a couple of things God did not want me to know or see. The dream became a three-fold revelation. For some reason we could not turn around and go back, so the car kept going. It was as though the driver himself had no control over the steering wheel. As I think about that particular moment, it just lets me see how amazing our God is! He is yet in control of our dreams!

I recall looking in the mirror and I appeared to be pregnant, even though I didn't feel like I was pregnant. I saw men in uniforms and I knew to stay out of their sight. At one point in the dream we began running so these men in uniform could not catch us. All of a sudden as I was running, it became pitched dark. I thought I was blind. We managed to get away somehow. We ended up in a room with a few people inside and I recall looking down to find a wallet full of money and credit cards on the floor. What use was it for now? We were now living in the cashless society.

As I came out of this dream, I could hear myself saying two lines of a poem. God gave me that poem about two days later titled *The Cashless Society.* I could see the Holy Spirit off in a distance, not clearly, but just enough to see a figure in the shape of a dove in the midst. As His usual way of letting me know that yes, this is a message from God.

A day later as I meditated on the dream I could hear Genesis 6:3, ringing in my ears. ***My spirit shall not always strive with man.*** The mere fact that things looked different, gloomy and lifeless outside was something to read into. God brought to my understanding that He had taken His Spirit off of this earth. The glory of the Lord no longer shone upon the face of the earth. The Day of the Lord had come.

The Day of the Lord is a lengthy period in time beginning at the tribulation through the millennium.

When it looked gloomy and when I thought I was blind, God brought to my understanding these were just astral effects that took place during that period. And He revealed what had happened in Chapter 2.

As I hear other interpretations of what God meant when He said *His Spirit would not always strive with man,* I questioned God in my mind. People's minds have been conditioned for years to believe it to mean that when God takes His Spirit away, we the church will not be here. And God told me that is not so. God brought to my understanding that when *"His Spirit no longer strive with man"* it is referring to His grace and mercy being taken out of this world.

As in the days of Noah when God's grace and mercy was available unto them, they rejected the message of repentance. Rejection will cause the wrath of God to fall upon you. God being the long-suffering God that He is will not continue to let sin abound. Noah was righteous in the sight of God. God instructed him to build an ark for him and his family. The ark was their protection from God's wrath. Noah warned the people a flood was coming and told them to repent. They mocked him and didn't believe. Just like the world today they don't appreciate God's grace and mercy. They continue to reject the message of repentance, therefore sentencing themselves to near future judgments to be poured out because of their sin.

I asked God concerning His coming judgments upon the wicked. Lord, what about your people? What about your people during the time when you will be pouring out the judgments and the plagues, etc. All I could hear in my spirit was the word "*seal.*" A seal is a stamp of recognition. A seal represents possession and security. The only scripture that struck out at me was Ephesians 1:13 and it reads:

In whom ye also trusted, after that ye heard the word of truth, the gospel of your salvation: in whom also after that ye believed, ye were sealed with that Holy Spirit of promise.

Do you remember in Exodus 12 when the children of Israel were in captivity and God instructed each family to slay a lamb? They were to take the blood of each lamb and post it on their doorposts. The blood was like a protective covering for them. God was going to pass through the city to execute judgment upon the land because of the king's hardened heart to let God's people go.

As God passes through the city with this plague and He sees the blood on the doorposts, the plague would not come near them. He said, *"when I see the blood I will pass over you."* It goes back to the scripture that says, God knows who is His own. This event is an illustration of the human sacrificial shedding of blood on the cross for us today. Jesus Christ was that sacrifice. Upon the day of redemption we become the sealed of God. God recognizes us as His own. When God sends His wrath down, those who have repented of their sins and are living according to God's Word are covered under the blood of Jesus Christ.

As I mentioned before there are people that are hopping in and out of God's will. This is not the time to be doing that. Take a look at Exodus 8:22. It talks about the Israelites and how God protected them from all the plagues that He sent upon Egypt. The key was they had to stay in Goshen as God had instructed them to. That was the will of God for them in order to be saved from these plagues. They obeyed and did so.

What is the will of God for us today? His will for us is to serve Him and to obey His commandments.

When we disobey and fall outside of His will we are no longer covered under the blood of Jesus. And guess what that means. When those bowls of judgments that are mentioned in Revelation are poured out upon this world and you are out of Goshen (God's will), you will be too through.

Psalm 145:20 says, **The Lord preserveth all them that love him** (the ones that keep His commandments) **but all the wicked will he destroy.** God says if you love Him, you'd keep His commandments. If you love Him you would obey Him. Now is the time for God's people to obey Him and stay in Goshen because that is the will of God for you. It is a terrible thing to be out of Goshen (out of God's will) when these bowl judgments and plagues come upon this earth. I agree that there are some things God's people will not be here to see and there are some things they will see. However, my word of caution is to STAY IN GOSHEN in the meantime.

Take a look at Revelation 9. In this particular chapter we see the word *"star"* being referred to as an angel. God placed limitations on these creatures mentioned in the third verse to only hurt those men who did not have the *seal* of God in their foreheads. If orders were given unto them to hurt only the unsealed, then who were left that they couldn't hurt? It sounds like saved folks were around after all. He said don't kill the unsealed, but just torment them for five months because they refuse to repent. Even with the 144,000 Jews, the angel commanded, don't hurt the earth and the sea until we have sealed the servants of our God in their foreheads. You see it's all about that seal. Revelation 6:16 should be enough to make you want God's seal on you. It says that people are going to be crying out to the mountains and rocks to fall on them and hide their face from God.

As the Lord is still confirming Genesis 6:3 to me and about His seal. He gave unto me another dream. As far as God is concerned Genesis 6:3 is all out in the left field being very misinterpreted like so many other scriptures. And now its time for it to take its position in the right field and be perceived correctly.

In this dream my companion and I were outside and again it was gloomy. You could tell things were quite different. The time in which we were living had changed. I took notice of a gray cloud moving around the city. It hung very low to the point that if it came near you, you had to lie low. You knew that this gray cloud meant serious business. As we watched this gray cloud move around the city it finally made its way toward us. The closer it got to us, we laid low to let it pass over us. I knew that the wrath of God was in that gray cloud. It proceeded to pass over us because we were covered under the blood of Jesus. We had the seal of God upon our lives. Amid the plagues and judgments that God is about to send this way, the judgments cannot come near you because you are the sealed of God.

People are so busy trying to get raptured up out of here, they don't believe they'll be here to see certain things. Teachers are out there teaching that we won't be here when God pours out His wrath. I questioned God about that. God took me to Psalm 91:8 and it says that only **with thine eyes shall thou behold and see the reward of the wicked.** When the wicked are cut off thou shalt see it. In Psalm 58:10, it tells us that **the righteous shall rejoice when he seeth the vengeance: he shall wash his feet in the blood of the wicked. So that a man shall say, Verily there is a reward for the righteous: verily he is a God that judgeth in the earth.**

That's why it is so important to stay in God's will. There is no time to keep turning God on and off. People treat Him like the clap on clap off light. Some of God's children keep going back and forth in God's will one minute and out of God's will the next. When you get out of God's will you are stepping back into the kingdom of darkness. The devil can put on you whatever he wants. He can have a field day on you because you are no longer under the protective shield of God. When God pours out those judgments mentioned in Revelation you will need the seal of redemption. We know not what hour Jesus is coming, but in the meantime we need the seal of God upon our lives.

There is yet a message that God is trying to relate to His people through this. Let's go back to the times when it was gloomy outside. I actually felt and saw what it was like when God takes His Spirit away from this world. You could tell that something was different. You could feel it in the air. The Spirit of God is what gives life. You could no longer see His glory burst through the rays of sunlight. It felt as though He was not here. You could actually look around you and see.

God brought something to my attention. You know how we as children of God go through a trial and all of a sudden it feel as if something is missing. It feels as if God is not there. It feels as if He has forsaken you, leaving you with the question, Lord where are you? You send your prayers up and they seem to bounce back off the wall. Well, it is in those times of trials, etc., that God wants us to be confident in knowing that He is right there by our side. It is in those times that when all hell breaks loose upon this earth, God wants us to remember His promises that He is always with us and will never forsake us. We must maintain our faith and trust in Him. It is in these trials that we are experiencing today, God is preparing us for when He takes His Spirit away from this world. We got to know with all confidence that He is right there by our side. We've got to maintain our faith in Him and know that we are seated in heavenly places. We've got to know who we are and what we have in Christ. If we don't know now then we won't make it through the tribulation. It is highly important that we begin to have faith and trust in Him now.

There is a reason for God leading preachers to preach faith and trust sermons today. God is preparing us for the future. He also led me to Isaiah 55:6,7.

6th **Seek ye the Lord while he may be found, call upon him while he is near:**

7th **Let the wicked forsake his way, and the unrighteous man his thoughts: and let him return unto the Lord, and he will have mercy upon him; and to our God, for he will abundantly pardon.**

Saints of God we better get a hold of God like never before now, while His Spirit is still here. It is time to stop tripping over little petty stuff. Sometimes I can't believe what God allows me to see and hear when I am around other saved folks.

You have saints that are trying to be impressive of their leaders. There are those that want recognition and want a pat on the back. There are the follow-the-leader folks. Instead of keeping focus on God, they are focused on the leader. And then there is the competitive spirit in the church. Who do you think is jealous of your position in the church? We all serve the same God within the body of Christ who gives according to His will and purpose for our lives. And let's not forget the want-to-be center of attention spirit. They always want to be in the spotlight. Your focus is all out of wack. It is time for the people to give their pastor and first lady a breath of fresh air and concentrate on what God is calling you to do. The only face he called you to be up in all the time is that of the lost souls that are on their way to hell. We are to pray for our leaders and support them on the vision that God has given him or her for the church.

Whatever happened to having that mind set to please God. Where is God at in your salvation? Man can fail you, but God won't. We need to take our eyes off man, because if we don't we will keep missing God. The Bible already let us know that the righteous shall scarcely make it in and all our righteousness is as filthy rags. Time is short and we as righteous people are just barely making it in ourselves.

Some people are too easily moved or knocked down by every wind, trial and storm that comes their way. You give in to the devil. Instead of running to God, you run back to your old habits. We need to get rooted and grounded in God. We need to have that determination that no matter what comes our way nothing can pluck us out of God's hand. You are on a sure solid foundation to the point where you are unable to be moved. You are like a tree planted by the waters. You shall not be moved. We need to wake up and start proclaiming the year of the Lord. God is in the soul saving business. We need to keep our focus on God and focus in on what He is focusing on and that is souls. That is His main concern.

So, let us begin to hide His promises in our hearts now, because they will come in handy in worst times ahead. Pretty soon we may not have access to Bibles. If you don't have time to read the Bible you better make time while it is available to you. The future is going to be so bad, it don't even want itself. We must remember those scriptures in Revelation chapter 2 and chapter 3 of the promises God made to those who overcome.

You maybe saying in your mind, this sister is talking as if we will be here during the tribulation period. When God gave me the visions concerning cosmic disasters, He told me to tell His people, "*when you see these things come to pass, be not afraid for I am with you.*" That statement alone was enough to let me know that the saints will be here during the tribulation period. So much for the pretrib, the midtrib and the partial rapture theories. By the time God finished with me all of those theories got washed out. The truth, the whole truth and nothing but the truth is in the posttribulation view.

Many people think they will be caught up out of here before the Antichrist appears. I began to talk to God and I mentioned to Him that for years man has been teaching that the saints will be raptured out. I said Lord there is so much diverse information and theories concerning the end-times. Prophetic books are plaguing the bookstore shelves.

God began to reveal more and more unto me. He began to open up my understanding. When God enlightens you with something it is as though you have found a gold mine. He led me to a scripture pertaining to false teachers and false prophets. They are the ones that mislead the church. God says He is not the author of confusion. He is not in the midst. So if God isn't, who is? The devil is in the midst. He is the author of confusion.

God brought to my attention that His people are reading too many books. They are leaning on man's wisdom and knowledge and not relying on God's.

They get caught up in these fiction books believing events will take place exactly how the book portrays them. Not even discerning the fact that God has an appointed time for the order in which these events are to take place. God is in control and not man. Fiction is not the way to go to increase your knowledge in the things pertaining to God. The Bible tells us that the anointing teaches you. I John 2:19 *But the anointing which ye have received of him abideth in you, and ye need not that any man teach you: but as the same anointing teacheth you of all things, and is truth, and is no lie, and even as it hath taught you, ye shall abide in him.*

There are two wisdoms, godly wisdom and worldly wisdom. Godly wisdom is truth and is here to help you. Worldly wisdom is here to gain from you by aiming for what's in your wallet. With godly wisdom you can obtain knowledge straight from the Spirit himself and through others He has placed a special calling upon. Ephesians 4: 11 tells us *And he gave some, apostles, and some prophets; and some, evangelists; and some, pastors and teachers;*
12th *For the perfecting of the saints, for the work of the ministry, for the edifying of the body of Christ.* The Spirit has placed the anointing upon these people in this scripture so that we don't become victims and fall into satan's deception.
14th *That we henceforth be no more children, tossed to and fro, and carried about with every wind of doctrine, by the sleight of men, and cunning craftiness, whereby they lie in wait to deceive.* A lot of teachings out there are not the work of the ministry of God. That's why He has given the anointing because the anointing helps you to distinguish the truth from error. Don't believe

everything out there because everything is not coming from God.

The book of Daniel tells us that many shall run to and fro and knowledge shall increase. People are going to be hungry for information. They want desperately to know what the future holds. And my, oh my, is that not what is happening today? Who lies in wait, to deceive these people? Who takes advantage of these people? Money hungry false prophets and false teachers are the ones.

The Bible tells us that the spirit of antichrist is here and true enough it is. Even now there are many antichrists whereby we know that it is the last time. They are the deceivers of this world. They counteract the word of God making it ineffective. They endorse antichristian teachings and activities.

II John tells us **that many deceivers are entered into the world, who confess not that Jesus Christ is come in the flesh. This is a deceiver and antichrist.** This is not the only issue that they talk against in the Bible. Preachers and teachers are on the airwaves teaching things they ought not. They say there is no Trinity. They preach you don't have to tithe. They teach against the coming of Jesus. And the list goes on and on. But God tells us in II John 8, **Look to yourselves, that we lose not those things which we have wrought, but that we receive a full reward.**

9th **Whosoever trangresseth, and abideth not in the doctrine of Christ, hath not God. He that abideth in the doctrine of Christ, he hath both the Father and the Son.**

10th **If there come any unto you, and bring not this doctrine, receive him not into your house, neither bid him God speed:**

11ᵗʰ *For he that biddeth him God speed is partaker of his evil deeds.*

What in the world does a Christian look like standing side by side participating in religious events with another that distorts and confuses the doctrine of Jesus Christ as taught in the Holy Scriptures? The scripture tells us don't even receive him into your house. Don't even waste your time on people that teach anything other than the Word of God. Don't even entertain them or let them in your house. For some of you pastors, etc who have such a soft spot and who speaks out to defend these type of people you are just as much a partaker in the evil deeds of such people who insult God and distorts the doctrine of Jesus Christ.

Sure enough this is free country. But who does it belongs to? Who created it? Who gave you the voice to speak? And the nerve of people to get on somebody else's territory, which happens to be God's and speak heresies, lies and insults concerning the things of God. You've forgotten that the earth is God's and the fullness thereof and all power is in His hands. God has the power to shut off anything that blasphemes His name and talk contrary to the things of the Bible. You think your local utility company has power: their power can't touch God's power and ability to shut off. God didn't have to be trained to shut on and shut off. He is power.

Many were looking for the rapture to take place on January 1, 2000 while others were looking for the Apocolaypse. And there were those who were fine tuned to God with the least bit of worry awaiting the millennial blessings to be poured out from God himself as He promised in His Word. And there were those who just didn't and still don't know what to expect. Looking for the rapture to take place on the

1st was showing how selfish people are when there are yet thousands upon thousands of lost souls on their way to hell. We should know by now that He's coming when we least expect. That why He tells us to watch, pray and be sober. Why look for the Apocalypse when we haven't even seen the great move of God take place yet. Here you are looking for the worst to happen when you haven't even reaped your Jubilee yet as God has promised. When God makes a promise He will in no way fail to bring it to pass. Some will reap theirs while others won't because of their disobedience. God's people will reap the good before the worst comes.

That's why it's important to maintain a close relationship with God in these times. If you do then you won't have to sit back and wonder what's next. There are too many deadbeat preachers, teachers and prophets out there that can't even get a revelation from God to be able to stand on the mountain top of God and proclaim what thus saith the Lord. They themselves are so busy trying to gain riches and popularity seating themselves in positions God didn't tell them to fill. Half of them can't even lead the people and let them know what's going on and what to expect.

Where are the Elijahs of this age? Where are the Jeremiahs of this age that can hear from God? Where are the Abrahams and Moseses who were able to go into the presence of God and receive instructions from Him for the people? They walked upright. They were righteous in the eyes of the Lord. God walked with them. It's awkward for God to walk with you when you're walking a crooked line. Where is he that walketh upright in the eyes of the Lord? Who can stand on the mountain of God and proclaim what the future holds?

Nowadays you got to listen for the voice of God for yourself. About a week before we embarked on the new century the Lord spoke to me. A lot of people did not know what to expect but if we get on our knees and talk to God He will lead us and guide us? In the midst of hearing stuff concerning the New Year arriving I began to take note of what the teachers and prophets were feeding the people versus what God was already speaking to me. Everytime you pick up the paper there was articles that could scare you or make you think. After the Lord had spoken to me it looked like the news articles increased heavily and people were on the radio jibber jabbering, getting their last seminars in and selling all kinds of surplus for personal gain. Amid the rumors, headlines, etc., the Lord spoke unto me on December 23rd and December 31st.

Man is only allowed to do so much. I am the beginning and I am the end. The planets in the sky, they obey my voice. Be not concerned with daily headlines. Man cannot destroy this world. At my hand shall all things be fulfilled. I am in control. Many things must come to past but I am with you. If you could only see into the spirit realm that which surrounds you. Man cannot put an end to something I've created. I am the beginning and the end. Don't become distracted. Stay focused on God. Do not get caught up in the hustle and bustle of the crowd as they prepare themselves for January 1st. Take no thought for tomorrow. It will take care of itself. The New Year brings nothing but blessings for you. Whatever comes upon this earth, know that I am with you. Calamities will come in the near future as you already know to be true. In any calamity I am with you. Look back on the years how each century rolled in smoothly. So will the year 2000 roll in just like any other century.

Man took the year 2,000-bug situation and turned it into a moneymaking venture and some of the church folks got caught up in it. It's bad enough that the church is already sleeping only to be awaken by and distracted by scare tactics that the enemy put in position to deter people's attention away from what time it really is. Instead of having survival seminars they should have been having soul winning seminars and get your house in order seminars. But no they had other plans to get you scared and get your money.

That's why I highly stress throughout this book how important it is to maintain a close relationship with God. Maintaining a close relationship with God will not allow you to fall prey to any type of endtime scams and lies brought on by a bunch of greedy liars. The false teachers and false prophets had people panicking, stacking up on food, and going through their bank accounts like crazy. Now that the century has rolled in like any other century, where are the false prophets and teachers? Who profited well from all of this? They got rich and are now somewhere vacationing off of your money while you are working 9 to 5 and overtime trying to put back what the devil stole out of your wallet.

Some of God's people forgot that He said in His Word that He has not given us the spirit of fear and to take no thought for tommorrow. God shall supply all my needs according to His riches and glory. Fear not for He is with you. They forgot to *trust* and have *faith* in God while others held on and encouraged one another with the promise of His sayings. We must believe that God will do what He said He will do. In the book of Malachi He said He will rebuke the devour for our sakes, being that we follow the principle of tithing and giving. He will keep the devil from sucking you dry. A lot of people got juked and deceived listening to man and his wisdom instead of seeking the counsel of God.

God warns us of false prophets and false teachers and preachers leading the people astray in the Bible. Prophets are referred to as messengers of the Lord, servants of God, shepherds and watchmen. If what they prophesy does not line up with the Word of God then you need to give a deaf ear to what they are saying. Isaiah 56:9-11 gives the characteristics of a false prophet. It says that the false prophet is blind and ignorant. They are dumb dogs that cannot bark and they love to slumber. They are greedy dogs, which can never have enough. They are shepherds that cannot understand. They all look to their own way, every one for his own gain. The same goes for the false teachers.

II Peter 2 gives a good description of the false teachers. The false teachers rail at things of which they are ignorant and will perish in their own corruption. They live in constant disagreement when the Bible tells us to live in harmony. They are high-minded, proud boasters. They are right in their own eyes and have entangled their followers into the yoke of bondage with their false doctrine. Proverbs 26:12 says, ***Do you see a man wise in his own eyes? There is more hope for a self-confident fool than for him.***

Their hearts are trained in greed and lust. They hire themselves to do religious work for personal gain. They speak evil of things they don't even understand. They are well-educated professionals who have attended some type of schooling. Some of them have gone to seminary school, Bible College or Regular College. They've taken courses in speech, miracles, psychology, mind control, etc. Just to name a few. People are easily persuaded and lured unto them because they speak with great swelling words. They will take the scriptures from the Bible and define them in whatever way they see fit or pleasing unto them.

These false teachers are the devil himself who comes and take the seed (Word of God) out of people's hearts and cause the people to err by taking heed to their strange doctrine. They yoke the people up in bondage with their ungodly practices. The false teachers have forsaken the right way. Scripture says that it would have been better for them or anybody who has erred from the Truth to have not obtained the knowledge of the way of righteousness than having obtained it and turn from the holy commandments, which was delivered unto them. The false teacher is likened unto a dog that returns to his own vomit again and the sow that was washed to her wallowing in the mire. God sends out a Woe unto the false prophets and teachers throughout the Bible.

Now concerning prophetic issues, focus is given more on the time of the fulfillment of things than the reality; ruling out the fact that God is in charge of all things. Just because events don't take place when we think they should does not mean the Bible is inaccurate. You just need to stop leaning on your own understanding and put your mind under the subjection of God. I bought a book about two years ago on the rapture and I couldn't understand why I could never get pass the third or fourth chapter. Now I realize it was because God does not want His people to go that route. God wants us to seek His face for revelations. He said in Jeremiah 33:3,

Call unto me, and I will answer thee, and show thee great and mighty things, which thou knowest not.

68

It's amazing how people are making money off the end-times. They are dissecting the Book of Revelation as if it's some kind of science project and God hasn't anointed them to go there. Some of these writers have strange religious backgrounds. Some of them don't even know God. Some of them don't even have a relationship with God. Some of them don't have an understanding of the scriptures and the mysteries of God that accompany them. They are teaching and writing from their own understanding and going after their own fleshly desires. They don't care about misleading people. It's all about that dollar. The Bible instructs us to cease from thine own understanding.

I am reminded of the song that says, what the world needs now is love sweet love. I hear the Spirit of the Lord telling me that what the world needs now is the Truth. We need to shoot an arrow through the heart of deception. The devil is busy. He got people thinking they are right and got all the answers when they are wrong. Yes, he got his false teachers, false prophets and false everything else at work in these last days. There is too much false information out there and guess who's eating it up? Some of God's people are eating it up! That's why it is important to maintain a close relationship with God. It is through that intimacy you will be able to discern that which is right from that which is wrong. That which serveth God from that which do not.

I am reminded of Matthew 7: 22 and 23 that says, ***Many will say to me in that day, Lord, Lord, have we not prophesied in thy name? And in thy name cast out devils? And in thy name done many wonderful works? And then will I (God) profess unto them, I never knew you: depart from me, ye that work iniquity.*** As you can see it is a dangerous thing to mislead the children of God. Man

69

has come up with his own interpretation of the end-time prophecies. Man has even come up with formulas to calculate Jesus' Coming. You simply cannot do that. Man has charted out Revelations, but they don't know what order in which events will occur because God is in control of them. The scripture clearly tells us that no man knows the day or hour the Son of man cometh. The angels in heaven don't even know when Jesus is coming. If you read the scripture carefully, it says only the Father knows. Instead of trying to figure out when He will return we should be waiting patiently in expectancy and occupy till He comes. Share the gospel of Jesus to others.

God then shed even more light on the dream He had given me concerning the cashless society. He led me to Matthew 24:29. He let us know that there will be astral disasters that will lead up to the coming of Jesus. God then led me to II Thessalonians 2. I found it very interesting. I do not recall ever reading this before. The title heading in my study Bible reads, *Correction Concerning the Day of the Lord.* It was a correction for the Thessalonians back then and it still stands as a correction for us today. There is just too much conflicting information out there and God is not the author of conflicts and confusions.

In this chapter Paul is talking to the Thessalonians because they received false information about future end-time events. The false teachers taught them that they were already living in the Day of the Lord. If they thought they were already living in the Day of the Lord back then, can you imagine how much more closer we are to it today?

This chapter refers to the church age today. As we already know false teachers and false prophets are on the widespread throughout this country. The first verse instructs people not to be disturbed by false teaching concerning future events.

The third verse goes on to say, **Let no man trick you in any way for the Day of the Lord shall not come until there be a great falling away first and the man of sin is revealed.**

Here it is plain as day! Why in the world is the church ignoring this scripture? The man of sin is the Antichrist. This great falling away leads us to I Timothy 4:1. The spirit of apostasy is already in the world. These things are happening right now. People are steadily rejecting God and the teachings of Christ. With these things already happening, the Antichrist's appointed time is not far away at all. His spirit is already in the world. Look at how those two things that must happen first follow each other.

A teacher was on TV interpreting this *"falling away"* and he or she was all out of wack in their interpretation. The Lord told me to place it in order. This same teacher frequents the radio airwaves, so can you imagine those that are eating up what he or she is dishing out? Let's look at *"falling away"* in which the teacher explained was the rapture of the church taking place. This is very untrue.

As I look at these words *"falling away,"* these are negative action words. *"Fall"* means to descend downward and *"away"* means out of place. Rapture means *"transport," "lift."* This is an act of ascending or raising from one place to another. From the Latin for *"caught up"* comes the term *"rapture."* The scripture did not say for the Day of the Lord shall not come until there is a great catching away first and the man of sin revealed. If it had mentioned that then we could have said the rapture had taken place but it didn't. The scripture says until there be a great *"fallen away"* first.

71

Common sense will tell you without having to look up the word *"fall"* that it means the act of going down. You see a lot of people don't want to accept the truth, so they condition their minds to believe how they want to believe.

What happened to cause this great falling away? A lot of people became offended, stumbled and fell away. Just like I explained before a lot of things will be happening. Troublesome times are on the rise and people are going to wonder where is the promise? Where is Jesus? These people are like unto those in which the seed fell on stony ground. They hear the word and receive it with joy. They are not rooted, but last for a little while and as soon as afflictions and trouble (tribulations) comes on account of the Word he falls away (stumble) and begin to distrust and desert (forsake) God. They cast away their confidence. They lost courage and patience (steadfast endurance). It's not like they haven't received the knowledge of the truth and yet they willfully sin. The Bible tells us that those who endure unto the end the same shall be saved. The scripture again says that day will not come until there is a great falling away first and the man of sin is revealed. These people are going to lose their faith in God and take heed to seducing spirits and doctrines of devils to include being caught up in miracles, signs and wonders done by satan himself.

The Antichrist can show himself on national TV today, even as you are reading this book and a lot of God's people will freak out! Why will they freak out? Because some of them have been conditioned for years to believe things were going to happen such and such a way. Jesus is coming and that is no lie. To say the church will not have to go through some things is a deception just to catch you off guard.

In this falling away, distrust or deserting of someone has occurred. Here you have saved folks all pumped up to get off of this earth before certain things occur and when it doesn't happen at a specific time in which they have been conditioned by false teachers to believe it will happen, they will then become angry at God. They will be angry with God because they are still here. If you've never gone to an ice skating rink and seen some falls this is it. If you've never attended a circus or gone to a gymnastics tournament, well this is it. They will start flipping out doing emotional cartwheels and splits. They will become scattered abroad. They will be angry with no one other than God.

You know how in your trying times the devil will ask you where is your God now? Well, he's going to sing that tune to you again. As it has been said many times before, *"You've got to know that you know."* Yes, you got to know who you are in Christ and know that God is always there and will never forsake you as He has promised in His Word. When the Antichrist appear on the scene he will be convincing, charming and will speak with great swelling words. If you are one of those whose trust level in God has descended then you will become easily deceived. The Antichrist is going to have you believing he is God.

We must remember Hebrews 10:37 tells us that for yet a little while and He (Christ) that shall come will come, and will not tarry.

38th ***Now the just shall live by faith: but if any man draw back, my soul shall have no pleasure in him.*** 39th ***But we are not of them who draw back unto perdition; but of them that believe to the saving of the soul.***

If you go on down to the 8th verse of II Thessalonians 2 this scripture tells it all.

And then shall that wicked be revealed (Antichrist), and I'll pause right there because God says that right after that comma many things are going to take place. The rest of the scripture reads, **whom the Lord shall consume with the spirit of His mouth, and shall destroy with the brightness of His coming.** The Antichrist cannot be destroyed until He has fulfilled the scriptures. He will be destroyed with the brightness of Jesus' coming, which is the Coming of the Lord, and is the same event described by man as the *rapture.* And this event takes place towards the end of the tribulation period. Here it is plain as day in scriptures, the rapture taking place after the Antichrist has fulfilled his calling on this earth. Take this information and run with it because this is how God gave it to me.

Around about now the companies that make ziplock bags' stocks should be reaching an all time high if you get my drift. These preachers, false teachers and false prophets need to stop spreading lies telling people what they want to hear to keep members or to make million dollar profits. God is going to rain His anger on you on Judgment Day.

So, what is keeping this Antichrist from revealing himself? The Holy Spirit has a restraint on him. When that restraint is lifted off, look out, we are now embarking on a time where the true test of our faith is tried. It is in this time you will experience the gloominess I speak of. It is right here in these times that you better have the scriptures of God's promises in your heart. You better know who you are in Christ.

As I refer to the dream concerning the cashless society where things seem different, gloomy and lifeless, yes, in the dream the Holy Spirit had released the Antichrist and the one world order had begun. And Jesus had not come to get His church.

Many teachers have taught for years and preachers are on the airwaves today preaching that the saints will not have to go through the tribulation period. They are giving the people a false vision.

God gave me a poem concerning the dream He had given me. When God gives me poems He speaks in rhymes.

Never in my life had I found money before
There was a wallet with money inside,
Lying on the floor
No need for it now, cashless society was in affect
Jesus had not even come to get His people just yet

God wants His people to get out of the mind set that man has put them in for years, that Jesus is coming before the Antichrist. Leading them to believe that they will be out of here before these events occur. I have already shown you in scripture that the day shall not come until the great falling away come first and the man of sin is revealed. We all shall know who this man of sin shall be.

God brought to my attention that if we don't prepare our minds now we are going to fall weak in spirit. When the Antichrist appointed time does come and we find ourselves still down here on earth, it will be like a future shock to many. A lot of people are going to be mad with God.

The first thing that will happen is your spirit man will become weak and you really can't afford that during this time. The first thing that will go through your head is God has forsaken me or God lied. And I must say unto you that NO, God did not lie. It is impossible for Him to lie. Those books you've been reading lied to you. Those end-time videotapes that God didn't lead you to buy lied to you. Those end-time seminars you sat in on lied to you. We must stop following man and lend our ears to hear the voice of God concerning all things.

For days I could hear the word *"persecution"* and I am lead to Revelation 12 discussed further into the chapter. I hear the Spirit of the Lord telling me to write about the persecution of the saints. As He awakens me out of my sleep one night. I could hear, *"write it plain upon the tablets."* He first takes me to Matthew 5:11 and it reads:

11th **Blessed are ye when men shall revile you, and persecute you, and shall say all manner of evil against you falsely, for my sake.**

12th **Rejoice and be exceedingly glad: for great is your reward in heaven: for so persecuted they the prophets which were before you.**

Saints want the easy way out. The easy way out for people is the rapture taking place before the worst comes. Jesus suffered many things and so will God's people. Jesus taught that the prophets of old suffered persecution and so will His disciples. What is a disciple? A disciple is a follower of Christ. A person who has the witness of Jesus in them. And may I ask, "What are you today?"

Hebrews 11:35 describes some of the sufferings of the prophets of old. Some were tortured, mocked, whipped, imprisoned, stoned and sawn to pieces.

Matthew 24:9 tells us, **Then shall they deliver you up to be afflicted, and shall kill you: and ye shall be hated of all nations for my name's sake. And then shall many be offended (fall away) and shall betray one another, and shall hate one another.** Your best friend may betray you, the person you sit next to in church may betray you, your husband may turn against you, and your son or daughter may turn you in. The false teachers and prophets led the people into error. The love of many waxed cold because of iniquity and lawlessness. People strayed away from God's standards to follow other doctrines. They deserted God. When you abide in Christ the love of the Father is in you. Their love waxing cold is a sure enough sign that they no longer abided in Christ and the love of the Father was not in them. They kicked the teachings of the Bible to the curb. Here you have the abounding lawlessness of the apostate church.

I looked up the word, *"persecution."* Persecution is the hatred and affliction that follows the witness and holy life of God's people in a hostile world. We think the little trials, temptations, and persecutions we go through now are unbearable. God says we haven't seen anything yet. You may be going through something with your family, on your job, financial matters, etc., but it's nothing compared to what we must face in the trying times ahead. He that endureth unto the end the same shall be saved.

The Bible already tells us we are overcomers. We overcame the devil with word of our testimony and by the blood of the Lamb. We have the power of God inside of us to withstand anything that comes our way. We will need that same power to help us endure until the end. The key is to stay focused on God, stand on His promises and you will come out on top. There is a light at the end of the tunnel. We might not be able to see it with darkness around us but we must believe its there.

There is a reward at the end of the tunnel for those who endure. It's going to cost you to be able to obtain it. You've got to go through something to receive the crown of life. You've got to through something to receive your new name. You've got to go through something to be able to eat of the tree of life.

God has things in store for us that haven't even entered into our hearts. The devil will stop at nothing to keep us from reaping the promises of God. He will try hard until the very end to keep us from getting eternal life.

The Bible says that the devil is a deceiver of the world and an accuser of the brethren. Everyday he goes before God to accuse God's children about something. He likes to work with blindfolds. Romans 8:37 says we are more than conquerors in Christ.

The troubles we face now are to prepare us for what lies ahead. And God wants the church to wake up to reality and get your minds prepared spiritually because this thing is real. There will be a persecution of the church in the near future.

Even Paul tells us in II Timothy 3:12, **Yea and all that will live godly in Christ Jesus shall suffer persecution.** That's why we simply have to get the revelation from God for ourselves instead of listening to a bunch of Bible scholars who have not fallen flat on their faces in the sight of God and cried out to God and asked Him for the revelation.

As God is dealing with me concerning the persecution of the church, He gave me three dreams and a poem. What I love about God is He will not lead His people wrong. If they are in the blind about something, He will make certain the truth is revealed. Revelation 3:10 reads, **Because thou hast kept the word of my patience, I also will keep thee from the hour of temptation, which is to come upon the world to try them that are upon the earth.**

No where in this scripture did God say that before trouble comes upon this earth, the church would be caught up. The rapture is not your deliverance or way of escape. Many are misinterpreting this scripture and misleading God's people.

This scripture is clearly stating that in any trial, test, temptation that we face today and during the tribulation period, God will deliver you in a sense that He will keep you from falling. He will keep you from giving up. He will keep you from missing out on His promises.

The tribulation period will be very troublesome times and a lot of God's people will become weak in spirit behind what they will see happening and will feel like giving up. You will need something inside of you to sustain you when these things come. Just like in our tribulations today, who delivers you when you become tired and feel like giving up? Who delivers you when you think to go back to your old ways? Who delivers you when you are tempted to do something contrary to God? Do you get the picture?

The final test of your faith is coming during the tribulation period in the hour in which you are told to denounce your faith in Jesus Christ. If you don't denounce your faith in Jesus you may be persecuted for Christ sake. We will be tried until the end. Whatever your test may be, whether its some type of persecution, imprisonment, mocking, etc., you got to have sustaining power. If you don't have the infilling of the Holy Ghost now, you better get it! The Holy Ghost is power.

I was lead to go to Matthew 4:1 where Jesus was tempted of the devil forty days and forty nights. Even Jesus was faced with temptation. Look at how He handled satan and came out victorious. We definitely need to take notes. Temptation is not a sin until you give in to it. It's easy to say you will not denounce your faith in Christ now, but when that hour comes and they hold a chainsaw to your neck, what will you do? When that final hour comes, will you love your life more than Christ? It's easy to say, No, now. Will you deny Christ or not? It's easy for you to say, No, now. Some people are so foolish in their thinking, especially compromising folks, they figure they can hold on to the world a little bit and when it comes to taking the mark, they are convinced they will not take the mark. I must say it won't be that easy.

Jesus told the disciples in Matthew 26:31, *All will be offended* **(fall away)** pay close attention to that word, *because of me this night: for it is written, I will smite the shepherd, and the sheep of the flock shall be scattered abroad.* Peter told Jesus, *"Yet will I never be offended."* Refer back to Matthew 24:10 and then check out the *"falling away"* in II Thessalonians 2:3 to take place.

In Matthew 26:34, Jesus warned Peter that before the cockcrow, he will deny Him three times. Peter was the first one to say, not I, Lord. You see how easy it was for him to say that. Then Jesus and the disciples went to the Garden of Gethsemane, which means *"oil press."* Jesus knew He was getting ready to be persecuted, so He prepared himself by going to the oil press to pray. This is something we all need to do and that is to prepare ourselves and go to the oil press since we know that there are things that are getting ready to take place and persecution is near us. You will need all the oil you can get to help you endure. You will need power to resist the temptation of denouncing your faith in Jesus Christ.

Jesus then tells His disciples to sit while He goes to pray. He took Peter, James and John with Him. I wondered why He took Peter knowing that he would deny Him three times. It became clear to me later as to why. Jesus instructed those three to tarry (remain) here, and watch with me. This means to stay awake, be alert or be cautious. These are the same instructions God is telling the church to do today.

At that point the scripture describes Jesus' soul as being very sorrowful and very heavy even unto death. This is the description of many during the tribulation period. Jesus went farther ahead to pray. When He finished, He found them all asleep. Just like the church today *"asleep."* The 41st verse is so important. ***Watch and pray that ye enter not into temptation: the spirit indeed is willing, but the flesh is weak.*** That's what we must do today is to watch and pray because the hour is coming. Prayer is power. Power that will help sustain you in the hour of temptation. The more Word you get inside of you the more power you will have. Peter is a prime example of the church today. Jesus took Peter with Him because Peter needed to pray. He should have been praying to God to help him not give in to the temptation of denying Jesus.

So what happened? Peter fell asleep. Peter didn't watch and pray like Jesus told him to and look what happened. Temptation came and he gave in to it. Jesus did warn him that it was coming. Just like today, God warns us of things so that we can prepare ourselves in prayer and fasting before they come. Even Jesus being flesh could have easily backed out of suffering on the cross for our sins. But He didn't. He went to the oil press to prepare himself for the things He knew He must face.

Take a moment and look at Peter's background. Peter walked with Jesus physically and spiritually. We today walk with Him spiritually. He was chosen as you and I are chosen to carry out a mission for God. He was a disciple and later an apostle who broke ground that the church would later follow. It doesn't matter what title you hold or how highly you are spoken of, if you are not watching and praying like the Bible tells you to, then it will be easy to fall

81

into temptation. It will be easy for you to denounce Jesus in the hour of temptation. Peter fell asleep, just like the church and this is no time to be falling asleep knowing the troublesome times we will face ahead. The church is caught up in fiction books, videos, etc., concerning the end-times. It's all about money. These writers, etc. don't care who they are deceiving. They figure if they give you what you want to hear verses the real truth, then there is money to be made. Man and his teachings has kept you more focused on a so-called partial rapture instead of preparing you spiritually for the persecution of the church. II Timothy 2:12 says, *If we suffer, we shall also reign with him: if we deny him, he also will deny us.* First, you got to go through something to reign with Him. A lot of things got to come to pass before we are caught up into heaven. Yes, we are to watch in expectancy for the coming of our Lord. But we are also to win souls and wake up to reality and prepare ourselves for the worst things ahead.

Again, I've heard some people say with their mouth; I'm not going to take the mark of the beast. Yes, it is easy to say that now. Watch your tongue because you will be tried. Ask Peter how easy it is to deny Christ. They are going to use every means of persecution they can think of to get you to deny Jesus and you will need that something deep inside of you to keep you from denying Jesus. Some will deny Jesus and some will hold on to the faith. We need to stay prayerful and watchful so that we may not be another Peter.

As I go back to Revelation 3:10 again, *Because thou has kept the word of my patience, I also will keep thee from the hour of temptation.* I recall in one of my dreams I appeared to be on top of something that resembled a maze. As I am on top of this maze, I could look down and see the spaces in between that were very deep. Some of them were large and some of them were small. I remember trying to get from one point to another, but it was hard because knowing the deep spaces in between existed, I knew that if I slipped I would fall.

As I am trying to cross over from one point to another, I saw a woman with her arms stretched out in my direction signaling me to grab a hold of her hands. But the key was to stay focused on her and trust her to help me to get to where I was going. This woman in my dream represented God. No, I did not say God is a woman as someone falsely said that God was both man and woman. The truth is, God is a Spirit. God helps us and keeps us from falling during our trials and times of trouble. We got to keep our eyes on Him. Trust Him and believe on His promises. We are all trying to reach the light at the end of the tunnel. You will find every promise that God made to us in His Word is at the end of this tunnel but we got to go through something to get to it.

Another dream I recall having in which God let me know that He was in the process of getting me ready for something He promised me. He informed me in the dream that the enemy was setting a trap, so that He could have something to accuse me of, so I could miss out on my blessing. I awakened out of this dream about 5 a.m. I tried to go back to sleep but God wouldn't let me, so I opened my Bible and it went to a certain subject and I stared at it and said, "Lord is this what you want me to read?" So I kneeled down to pray and God confirmed what I was reading. God let me know exactly what the temptation was going to be. He told me that when that hour of temptation come, He would deliver me. He instructed me to stay focused on Him and to keep a praise on my lip. Later that evening on that same day, that hour of temptation came just as God said it would. I remembered the instructions God gave me. I did exactly what God told me to do and I came out victorious. Just like Jesus informed His disciple Peter beforehand, God warned me so that I could prepare myself by staying focused on Him and keeping a praise upon my lip. He has informed us in scriptures concerning persecution ahead and has given us instructions to prepare for these things so that we don't give in to temptation. Because of the witness of Jesus Christ in you, you will suffer persecution. When that hour in which the test of your true faith comes, know that God is with you and He will keep you from falling in those troublesome times ahead. Even Daniel saw the saints in more detail in Daniel 7.

As God is speaking to me on the subject of persecution, He leads me to Revelation 12. And He also gave me a poem titled; *The Power of God is In You.* We will certainly need it in the troublesome times ahead. We must begin to go to the oil press and get it. Fast also to keep the flesh under subjection to our spirit man. We must indulge ourselves in His Word because there is power in the Word. An excerpt from the poem reads:

There is power in the blood of Jesus
And it started on Calvary
All I've got to do is believe
And know it is inside of me
The devil is real and he isn't playing
He has but a little time left
He will not cease to leave God's people alone
And besides, you haven't seen anything yet
Daniel 7:25 says.....

84

And I'll stop right there and let you refer to the back of this book for the rest.

As the Lord brings back to my remembrance about the woman who gave birth to a man child who was caught up unto God. I begin to read about it in Revelation 12. This whole chapter is just confirmation of the suffering and pain not only Israel will have to face, but the church as well.

This chapter main focus is on Israel who gave Christ to the world and the church that gave Christ to the world. And because of the witness of Jesus Christ, the church will suffer persecution. The devil hates the witness of Christ in us, so he has to act the fool. And he did just that throughout this whole chapter because now he knows his time is short.

As I look at Revelation 12:7 it reads, ***And there was war in heaven; Michael and his angels fought against the dragon; and the dragon fought and his angels,***

As I read this verse, I'll never forget a dream I had years ago as a child. Even at a young age God gave me dreams of things that would happen in the future but only this one I didn't understand until now. Being raised up in the church at a young age I always thought Revelations was out of place in the Bible. I went to it one time and it scared me. It was scary to read about creatures, a mountain falling out the sky, earthquakes, war and blood. And my young mind wondered why God would put such a book in the Bible. The only thing I could deal with was the last two chapters concerning the New Jerusalem. Yes, that sounds real good. Even as I got a little older I didn't touch Revelations until God told me to. In my younger years I had no idea that it was the revelation of Jesus Christ and it represented the future. I had no idea that it was a book of symbols that could only be understood and interpreted through divine enlightenment from the Holy Spirit himself. I had no idea that God would some day anoint me to go there. I don't see how people today so casually go to the Book of Revelations and interpret it off of their own understanding and that's not good.

In this dream, I was outside of my house and I so happen to look up towards the sky. I noticed some type of commotion was going on and someone was actually fighting. I could see figures moving back and forth battling it out. There was something like a shield over the sky, which made it hard for me to see the objects clearly. You know how when you hold a thick enough piece of plastic in front of you and it will make objects difficult for you to see? Well, that's what God did. I guess as a child that would have been too hard for my eyes to behold and my mind to fathom. God knew exactly what He was doing. And I thank Him for that.

So Michael whipped the devil real good and cast him out onto the earth. The devil is already angry from the first time he was cast out of heaven like lightning and every since then he's been walking to and fro messing with God's people. And now being cast out a second time, can you imagine the anger he'll have then? That's why we haven't seen anything yet. It only gets worse as we approach the end.

The Bible describes two things the devil did in which he is doing now and will continue doing until he is cast into the lake of fire and that is deceiving the world through whomever and whatever means that he can and accusing God's people day and night. Coming up with all kinds of strategies and plans to keep you from gaining eternal life and all the other promises God has made unto you. But God did not leave His people defenseless. We overcome the devil now and we overcame him then by the word of our testimony. That's why when we hear the preacher say, watch, pray and be sober, the church need to stop taking those instructions lightly.

The 12th verse tells us, **And when the dragon saw that he was cast unto the earth, he persecuted the woman.** This woman whom I said represents Israel will suffer severely during the tribulation period, but she won't be alone. I've heard bible scholars say that persecution will go no further than Israel and this whole thing is about Israel only. But that is a misconception. Please don't believe that. Sure enough the Antichrist headquarters will be set up in Jerusalem. But don't think for a minute that he's not going to have mini headquarters around the world.

I remember in dreams God had given unto me, running from men in uniforms, seeing helicopters over my head, monitors up everywhere, seeing piles of ashes of people who didn't take the mark and seeing darkness all around. So it can't be said that Israel only or the Jews only will face persecution and will have to face the Antichrist alone.

Take a look at the 17th verse. And the dragon (devil) was wroth meaning angry with the woman, and went to make war with the remnant (rest) of her seed, which keep the commandments of God, and have the testimony of Jesus Christ. The remnant of her seed are all those who are a part of the family of God. The devil is an angry camper, very outraged, so he persecuted those that have kept the commandments of God and who have the witness of Christ in them. And who are these people? The people are the Church. You and me. That's why these preachers who are not in line with God better form a line and get in line so they can get the flock going in the right direction. Some of them are doing a shabby job of leading God's sheep. Some of them are walking a crooked line in the sight of God. Some of them are not even called. Some of them need to sit down and let someone else see about God's people. God is going to hold the preacher responsible.

Persecution of the saints will reach worldwide. The devil is going to be on the saints of God like white on rice. That's why you got to know who you are in Christ and know what you got in Christ. Read Daniel 11:35, Daniel 7:21 and 25. Daniel saw it all.

Daniel 7:21 reads, *I (Daniel) beheld, and the same horn made war with the saints, and prevailed against them.*

Verse 25 reads, *And he (the Antichrist) shall speak great words against the most High, and shall wear out the saints of the most High, and shall think to change times and laws: and they (the saints) shall be given into his hand until a time and times and the dividing of time.*

This will not be the time to get mad with God because things didn't happen the way those fiction writers portrayed them to happen. By now it will have become reality to you that fiction and God don't mix. It will now be a time to hold on to God with all you got. There are some countries where Christians are already being persecuted and it's only a matter of time before it will reach the states. In the meantime we need to keep them in constant prayer. God promised us eternal life but we must go through something to get to where He is taking us. Remember to stay focused on God. That can't be stressed enough. Keep your head up, stay focused on God and stand on His promises. Remain faithful to God and God shall remain faithful unto you until the end.

As we make our way back to II Thessalonians 2 let us refer farther back to the paragraph that speaks of the *Correction Concerning the Day of the Lord* and come back to this next paragraph below. Again, this scripture spit out the truth. It is vital to stress it. Some kind of way it has been ignored by the church. The church has been brainwashed far too long and its time for the truth to come out. And we know that the Word of God don't lie.

Look at II Thessalonians 2:8 *And then shall that Wicked be revealed, whom the Lord shall consume (destroy) with the spirit of his mouth and shall destroy with the brightness of his coming.* The scripture says that Jesus will destroy him. Okay, but first the Antichrist has to carry out the prophecy first. Everything the Bible says he will do has to be fulfilled. If Jesus destroy the Antichrist before he is able to carry out his work, then he won't live to do his work. So therefore, the Antichrist must come first and carry out his term and then Jesus will destroy him with the brightness of His coming when He returns.

The Bible says, *He who readeth, let him understand.* It's simple and plain in the scriptures. Satan himself will form an unholy trinity, the devil, the beast (Antichrist), and the false prophet imitating the Father, the Son, and the Holy Ghost. This Antichrist's lieutenant (false prophet) will be given authority and power from satan to do counterfeit miracles, signs and lying wonders. And because unbelievers refused the message of salvation, God will cause them to believe in those miracles, signs and lying wonders. We as God's people must stand firm in the faith and be not deceived. The false prophet's works will be deceptive works appearing real just like in today's world.

89

Yes, the devil himself can perform miracles, signs and wonders, but they don't last. He has his people at work even in today's world deceiving people.

Matthew 24:24 tells us that **For there shall arise false Christs, and false prophets, and shall shew great signs and wonder;**

Some of these people are doing these works in the name of Jesus Christ and guess what, the scripture goes a little further to say, **insomuch that, if it were possible, they shall deceive the very elect.** If I am going to pray a miracle into your life in the name of Jesus and by the power of God then why should I turn around and ask you for money. That same power should have already provided all that I need to accomplish the work that God has given me to do. By faith my every expense is already paid for. Everything I need to carry out God's work, God has already gone out before me and taken care of it. A lot of people are going to be saying on Judgment Day, Lord have I not prophesied in your name and in thy name cast out devils? And in thy name done many wonderful works?

The devil can imitate the Holy Spirit having you thinking it's the work of God when it is a spirit, not holy, doing great works to the point that he has the very elect (saved folks) fooled and deceived. That's why it's high time to get as close to God as we can. We truly need the spirit of discernment right now.

Since we are on the subject of miracles and signs we must remember that an evil and adulterous generation seeketh after a sign. According to Matthew 12:39, the only sign this world is going to get from God is the sign of the prophet Jonah. The warning of the judgments to come. The natural disasters and weather patterns are signs. There shall be signs in the stars and moons. These things are happening right now! What more do you need?

There are people that are caught up in religions that have given accounts of supernatural phenomenon that they believe to be signs from God. You have your sightings of Mary. There are statues and pictures of Jesus crying tears and blood. There are statues of Mary crying. Images appearing on rose petals. These things are not of God's doing. God doesn't have to prove himself to nobody. You believe on Him through faith. True enough, Jesus did miracles, he healed the sick and so did some of the apostles and evangelists. These signs shall follow them that believe. Lay hands on the sick and they shall recover. Restoring sight to the blind. Setting the captives and oppressed free. Those are some ways in which God manifests himself.

If you're seeking a sign, the devil will have no problem trying to imitate the things of God. He's a big showoff actor himself. He has no problem with trying to disguise himself as Jesus Christ. The Bible already tells us that he can disguise himself as an angel of light. He has no problem making statues cry tears and blood. He has a certain level of power. His profession is deception. He has no problem drawing images on rose pedals, on walls and floors. He's an artist too. He trains his little imps and they go to work in your house and in your church faithfully.

Satanic forces are what you are dealing with here. The devil is at work in these days and he is playing on people's minds. That's the first thing he goes for is the mind. If he can get to your mind then he can make you believe anything he put out there to deter your mind from God. You think you are on the right path to God but you're not. People who are always looking for a sign will easily fall for the Antichrist.

After the false prophet suckered the people in through his great wonders and miracles he said unto the whole earth, "let us make an image to the beast." You see, people who are off into their world carrying around images (small figurines) and having all these statues in their homes, churches and pictures lining the walls paying homage to these things will have no problem at all worshipping the image of the beast. If you pay more attention to that figurine you just bought or that statue you have sitting in your living room more than you do God, then that figurine or statue is your god.

Remember that God is a jealous God. God has already commanded us in the Ten Commandments that thou shalt not make thee any graven image, or any likeness of anything that is in heaven above, or that is in the earth beneath, or that is in the waters beneath the earth and worship them.

So, when you bow down to pray unto God, you do not need candles: for Jesus is plenty enough Light himself. You do not need a picture, image or statue of Mary in front of you. Neither do you need a picture or statute of Jesus, God, nor any angel in front of you. All you need in front of you when you bow down to pray is some faith. Faith in knowing that God is right there and your belief in Him is not through figurines and objects that try to portray His image or any other image. Scripture tells us, For no man has seen the Father, so why do you gaze into a piece of artwork that depict the Father or His Son looking for and praying to Him through these objects?

You will not find Jesus in a picture. You will not find Jesus in a statue. His Spirit is supposed to abide inside of you. People got these statues of Jesus still hanging on the cross. And then you got Him hanging around your neck hanging on the cross. Don't you think that's enough hanging? Why continue to persecute Him? According to the Bible Jesus is not on the cross anymore. He is resurrected and now sits at the right hand of God. It's time for you to take Him off of your cross and rejoice. In Revelation 13:3, the devil himself imitated the resurrection of Jesus Christ by healing the wound of the Antichrist and resurrecting him back to life. Even the devil knows that Jesus is not on the cross anymore!

As I am on the subject of images and the beast. I am reminded of a vision I once saw of a brass image. This was one of those vision type dreams I tried to fight my way out of and couldn't. I recall seeing this image of a person beyond identifying and it had the ability to move its head and arms as it stood in place.

The Lord is bringing to my attention that man has made a replica of the beast when he created the computer. Everything seems cool with it now, you know how the enemy is he will slide in there real smooth and make things look good for a moment only to sucker people in and then kaboom.

The computer is man's doing. It is getting people in training for the future. People worship it and don't even realize what's going on. They spend countless hours in front of it. Once you get on it, it is hard to get yourself away from it. If man could put God in the place of the computer spending countless of hours in His presence, then we wouldn't have to deal with the foolishness of this world because in God's presence there is peace, love, joy, happiness and protection. But we know that what happens must happen. Bible prophecy must fulfill itself.

When you put more time into or spend more time with something or someone then something else becomes neglected. The computer is easy to get hooked on. Man has become so dependent upon this man made equipment. It is enticing in that it has so much to offer. All of your needs are somehow fulfilled through the many services offered on the computer. You can shop on-line for groceries, clothing, etc. You can make travel arrangements, get all kinds of advice, bank on-line, go to school on-line and pay your bills, etc. The list just goes on and on. You can practically live off of the computer. Man has made things so convenient through his creation. Last but not least, it talks. You can buy voice activation software to add a little personal touch.

There was a time when only businesses had computers. But now they are in just about every household in the country. They went on sale like hotcakes during the holiday season. If you could only see what's going on in the spirit realm. The enticing sales rebate offers that came with such purchase is nothing but the enemy's way of making sure everyone could afford to have one in their homes because pretty soon it will become mandatory for you to run your life through the computer with a certain code. The 666 code. Whatever work you need to get done for the Lord through the computer and through the satellites you need to do so while you have free access. Man with his lazy self has taken the ability that God has given unto him to think and has in turn taken that ability and built another god.

All of these images and statues you got in your homes, churches, etc is doing nothing but getting you ready for the false religion out of Great Babylon. The Babylonian religion is linked to astrology, psychics whom are linked to the New Age religion. They worship images (idols). An idol can be anything that stands between you and God or something substituted in the place of God. Mythology and legends dominate the Babylonian literature.

If the ancient of old would have seen the Saturn like star that trailed Hale Bopp for a minute, they would have given you a background on Chemosh mentioned in Judges 11:24, a national god of the Moabites associated with the heavenly bodies. Chemosh is identified with Baal of Peor, Baal-Zebub, Mars, and Saturn, as the star of ill omen. Omen is a phenomenon, which is thought of as a sign of something to come in the future.

A *sign* is something that points to or represents something larger or more important than itself. The most important use of the word *"sign"* is in reference to the acts of God. A sign can appear for a moment just to get a message across. No matter what type of scientific explanation astronomers or scientists comes up with bottom line is Hale Bopp carries an omen. Yes, Hale Bopp comet C/1995 01 is a sign of the endtimes. Yes, it is a fulfillment of Bible prophecies. God used it to communicate His coming judgments upon the earth and yes, God is going to send it back but only next time it shall fall out of the sky.

You may call it ignorance and superstition, but you are in for a real surprise. God said that there shall be signs in the stars and in the moons. And sure enough there is a sign all around comet C/1995 01 and God wants the world to know it. You can get on the defensive all you want concerning this comet but nobody owns it but God. God created it. No matter how much you try to discredit information surrounding something, know that God will use the foolish things of this world to confound the wise. The *"wise"* refers to those who think they know it all and don't consult God for godly wisdom.

Take a look at I Corinthians 1:27 and 28. ***But God hath chosen the foolish things of this world to confound (confuse) the wise: and God hath chosen the weak things of the world to confound the things which are mighty;***

*28th **And base things of the world, and things which are despised, hath God chosen, yea, and things which are not, to bring to nought things that are:***

*29th **That not flesh should glory in his presence.***

Quite interesting isn't it? Here you are boasting about your expertise in a certain field, your degrees, awards, discoveries, etc., and then you look down on others because they don't have the knowledge that you've obtained over the years. Then here you are getting the glory off of something that belongs to God anyway and He isn't having that. Man has the audacity to put their name on something that belongs to God. You indulge yourself in the "I" syndrome. You boast and you brag by saying I did this and I did that. God says He shares His glory with no man. Every heavenly body in the sky shows forth God's glory and magnificent power. To God be the glory and not man.

So God sends along someone of less importance in your eyes. God will use that person whom you pass bad judgment on, whom you view as foolish, weak, unknowledgeable and of no importance to convey a message. As with the preparation of this book, God took a nobody like me with no title, except to say that I am a child of God and a rightful heir to His kingdom, to reveal things as He gave them to me. He assures me that it will leave some mind boggling and confused. It will definitely confound the wise. But no weapon formed against me shall prosper and every tongue that rises up against me in judgment I shall condemn.

Flesh and blood did not reveal to me everything in this book. God did. Therefore, God will get the glory and not I. What God wanted to see get accomplished, did so, by a nobody who is SOMEBODY in the eyes of God. In a believer's life, God calls and qualifies. You don't have to have credentials to be able to write a book. You don't have to be a professor, a preacher or take writing courses to write a book. I am living proof of that!

You see, when a nobody beats the devil to the punchline the devil gets angry. It leaves the devil wondering, how did you get so smart all of a sudden, you're not experienced and you don't even have a degree or hold a title. And all you can say is, so what, but God does. God knows all things.

So, somebody out there saw a saturn like object in the sky and all they did was reported what they saw and they in turn got scrutinized, persecuted and hung to the ground. Somebody got beat to the punchline. This piece of information confounded the wise. It confused them. They immediately started looking for a scientific explanation. You can blame it on improper setting by the user and call it a diffraction effect all you want, but bottom line is, it was a sign. Remember in the definition of a sign that a sign can appear for a moment just to get a message across and then disappear.

Just because you so called discovered something does not make you any better than the next person that comes along who happens to have no credentials or experience in your line of work and discover something also. God will cause you to be brought to embarrassment to show you that you are a nobody until you come unto the acknowledgement of Him and receive Jesus Christ as your personal Savior. God is God. He creates and in His own timing brings things to the forefront for all to see for a specific reason.

Man is looking at everything that goes on in the heavenlies from a scientific viewpoint instead of from a biblical standpoint. You can't mix God and science. God is cutting through all of this scientific blah blah and is revealing truths in these last days. The Bible has already told us that there shall be signs in the heavenlies. A sign is God's way of communicating to us. The world is full of deceit and it is high time for some truths to start coming out. We are running out of time! God is unveiling the cover-ups. Again there is nothing hid that shall not be revealed.

As I am near the completion of this book the Lord gave me a dream mid October of '99 and commanded me to put it in this chapter. In this dream I was outside and as I looked towards the sky there was this object in the sky. It was a beautiful sight to see. This object had a ring around it. Even with the naked eye, this object with it rings was very visible for all to see. As this object kept its position in the sky I could see great commotion going on here on Earth. Need I say what had happened? You should know that by now.

All I could hear was people running to and fro trying to figure out whats what and which way to go. You could barely distinguish between day and night as though a power outage had occurred. When I came out of this, God brought back to my remembrance of the Saturn like object. I then knew immediately that an astronomical disaster had taken place. The comet had hit planet Earth. As I've said before a "sign" is something that point to or represents something far more larger and important than itself. And boy, oh boy is not the star with its rings pointing towards the comet, which is far more larger and important than it? And need I mention again that an omen is a phenomenon, which is thought of as a sign of something to come in the future. My, oh my is God not an awesome God to yet reveal and confirm?

God used the heavenly bodies to communicate back then and He is still the same God that is using them today. God allowed for such a phenomenon to take place in Joshua 10:14 in which the sun and the moon was commanded to stand still just so that Joshua's forces could complete their victory before the enemy had a night for rest and regrouping. What makes anybody think God can't position this comet by the sound of His all-powerful voice and command it to move? Heavenly bodies had an influence on future events then and still do today. Amen.

The heavenly bodies have no problem obeying the voice of God, however I can't say the same for man today. Demons in hell obey the voice of satan faithfully, but do man obey the voice of God? What man fail to forget or don't realize is God is in sovereign control. Some of them who think this is all ignorance and superstition don't even believe in God anyway.

The things of God are foolishness unto this world. The carnal mind cannot perceive the things of God. God says He will destroy the wisdom of the wise, and will bring to nothing the understanding of the prudent. God created this universe and everything about it is a mystery, however He reveal things to His people by His Spirit and only to them do God reveals the hidden. God is not going to come off of His throne and go knock on Nassau's doors and convey His message. God uses signs, visions and dreams to get

His point across. God is a giver of gifts and therefore gives accordingly the gifts of wisdom and knowledge and the ability to interpret things.

A lot of things happening today are signs. If we look at things from a biblical standpoint and consult God, a lot of unanswered questions will become answered and the mysteries before our eyes will become solved. As you do research and as God is leading you in your research, you will find a lot of things leads back to the Roman Empire. Terminology and history is important information. Sometimes God will take you as far back to the Ancient times and you will find some very interesting information.

Even after God had given me the vision concerning Jupiter, I began reading about how in ancient times gods were associated with the planets. Zeus was associated with Jupiter; He was the King of the gods, the ruler of Olympus and what caught my attention was, and He was the patron (supporter) of the Roman State. His father, Kronos was associated with *Saturn*. He represents struggle and bad fortune, which is what this world is getting ready to experience. Kronos represented *"time"* to the Greeks, devoured his children and thus brought an end to all that begun. Even today, *"time"* is of the essence and God will devour the earth by fire therefore bringing an end to what He begun. II Peter 3:10 tells us, **But the day of the Lord will come as a thief in the night, in the which the heavens shall pass away with a great noise, and the elements shall melt with fervent heat, the earth also and the works that are therein shall be burned up.** This scripture is definitely an end to all things.

Romans celebrated Kronos' festival which took place in December and was called Saturnia, known to us today as Christmas. Rome imported and absorbed many religious ideas and pagan gods from Greece. Roman gods were used and identified with the gods of the Greeks. As you can see terminology and history is important. No matter which direction you go in, everything points back to the Roman Empire where the little horn (the Antichrist) arise out of and the false religion (Great Babylon) is birthed and is later destroyed by God. Daniel 7:7,8,24 and 25.

II Thessalonians 2:4 tells us how the Antichrist will exalt himself above all that is called God and will seat himself in the temple of God saying he is God. Lucifer tried to exalt himself above the Most High when he was in heaven and got thrown out. He will try one more last time. He will not succeed in this kingdom. Read Revelation 19:20 and Revelation 20:10. This scripture referenced me over to Matthew 24:15

When ye therefore shall see the abomination of desolation, spoken of by Daniel the prophet, stand in the holy place, and let us stop right here because He gave specific instructions in verses 16-22. He says, Let those who are in Judea flee to the mountains. If you're on the rooftop, don't come down. If you're in the field, don't even go back to get your clothes. He sends out a warning to those who are pregnant. He says, Woe! Pray that your flight be not in the winter neither on the Sabbath.

That scripture took me back to my dream when I appeared to be pregnant. The mere fact that I looked pregnant in the dream was a lot to be read into. There will be tribulation such as not been from the beginning of the world until now. The dream itself unfolds in this very chapter.

101

When the abomination of desolation takes place, look out. This is when the Antichrists' army will destroy the Jewish sacrificial altar and replace it with a heathen altar. This is where he breaks the covenant with Israel and demands that they and the world worship him. This is where you will see the ugly side of him come out.

You think you've seen ugly in your days, well, he puts the letter *"u"* in ugly. He will have no conscience. He will be unkind, cruel and inhumane. He will have no respect for religious heritages. If you don't worship him you will face some type of persecution as mentioned in Matthew 24:9. Just like the movie, Enemy of the State, we the church is the enemy, a threat to this one world government. The church is a threat to the Antichrist and his kingdom. Daniel 11:32 says, ***And such as violate the covenant he shall pervert and seduce with insincere compliments, but the people that know their God shall prove themselves strong and shall stand firm*** (shall be strong) ***and do exploits for God.***

What caught my attention in this verse was, the *people that know their God* shall be strong. They will see right through the Antichrist's deception. Take this moment to think about who the people are that know their God. Who are they? These are those who have spent quality time with God in prayer and in getting to know Him through His Word.

When a sinner repents, he doesn't know God. He only knows of God. As he or she goes along their Christian walk he grows into the knowledge of God. A person on the airwaves said that a person does not grow in Christ. He went on to say; it's that teaching the charismatic Pentecostal folks are spreading. You see, just another false teacher on the radio. Teaching things he or she ought not. There are deeper depths and higher heights yet to be explored in God. God has secrets that are immeasurable.

As we take a look at Daniel 11:32, so much for the partial rapture theory. We can't say that the saints will be raptured out and the lukewarm Christians and sinners will be left here even though there are many who so selfishly say that. A lukewarm person falls under disobedience because they lack the courage to follow God's ways. God is going to give all a chance to repent even to the end, therefore nobody is going to be *"left behind"* but those mentioned in Revelation who after seeing all the judgments poured down, they cursed God and still repented not.

According to Matthew 15:14 how can the blind lead the blind? We are dealing with blind folks here, the lukewarm and the sinner. If the blind try to lead the blind they will both fall into the ditch. Who is the devil going after during this prophetic time Daniel saw? He's not going after the lukewarm and sinners because He's got them right where he wants them. The sinner man and the lukewarm man do not oppose a threat to the devil. So who does? The saints oppose a threat to the devil and his kingdom. He can't stand the ground that you walk on. If he isn't on your trail now then you need to go re-examine yourself. If you're not on the devil's hit list you better try to get on it. Being on it is a sign that you are on the right track. The Antichrist is going to be hot on somebody's trail that opposes a threat to his kingdom. Somebody is going to have to be here to help others get through and to instruct them on what is going on. Saints will lead others to the truth during the Tribulation period.

Take a look at Daniel 11:33: ***And they that understand among the people shall instruct many:*** People this is what God is equipping you for now. There is a great work ahead!

Daniel 12:3 reads, ***And the teachers and those who are wise shall shine like the brightness of the firmament, and those who turn many to righteousness like the stars forever and ever.***

It all goes back to them that are strong and know their God. Daniel the prophet saw you. He saw the saints who are now going through trials that come to make them strong for those things ahead. Those fires that God takes us through to burn out some things in us are to prepare us to achieve His purposes now and during the tribulation. That's where the exploits in verse 32 come in at. Exploits being deeds or acts that are remarkable. Again, there's a great work ahead! You remember when Moses parted the Red Sea and Jesus turned the water into wine? Well, what more can I say other than greater works shall we do! For some of you finding all of this hard to believe I pray that the power of God will break your mindset and that you will not miss out on God.

Read further down. John also saw the saints in Revelation 13:7. ***And it was given unto him (Antichrist) to make war with the saints, and to overcome them:*** John is giving the same account that Daniel did in Daniel 7:21.

As I read this scripture, I could hear the Spirit of the Lord ask me, *"What is a saint?"* I then knew it was time to do a little research. And may I ask you do you know what a *saint* is? I'll take the time to tell you that a saint is a person leading an upright life. Saints are people who have been separated from the world and consecrated to the worship and service of God. Now, may I ask, "What are you today?"

Amidst all the wickedness and turmoil that will be going on, how will they (so-called left behinders) have time to grow into the knowledge of God as you (saint) did or lead an upright life? It takes time to develop a close relationship with God. You don't become a saint overnight. It takes getting into His Word with fasting and prayer.

We may one day be forbidden to pray or our Bibles may be taken away from us. But God said the Word is inside of you (saint). Those of you who took the time to study the Word and allowed it to get deep inside of you. You may say you don't have time to study, well, I must encourage you to find time to eat the Word, for it along with prayer is power.

That's why it's important to let God be God in our lives. Submit. He is trying to equip us for the things ahead. I found Daniel 7:25 to be a very interesting scripture. It says that the Antichrist shall speak words against God and *shall wear out the saints* of the most High. Those words alone, *"wear out the saints"* lets me know that I better have some power. And He will think to change the time of sacred feasts and holy days and the law: and the saints shall be given into his hand for a time, two times, and half a time which is three and a half years.

Daniel said he heard one saint say to another saint, when will these things end. Like I said before we better get some power under our belts because like I heard someone say, "We are in for the long haul." That is a long time, saints. There are some saints that the devil is already wearing out, so this shouldn't be something unfamiliar to you. God wants you to see how serious this thing is. He says the church is sleep and need to wake up!

As you look further down in Daniel 11:33 which says, **yet they** (God's people) **shall fall by the sword, and by flame, by captivity, and by spoil, many days.** In this scripture you will see what Matthew 24:9 describes as being the time when some shall be persecuted and tormented and will be hated for My names sake and many shall betray one another and hate one another. You may get mocked or scourged. You may get imprisoned. Those that betray you will think he is doing God a service.

You think Hitler was bad. No, Hitler can't even touch the gruesome acts to be carried out by this Antichrist and his army. If you don't submit to this man and his New World government, you may become a martyr. He is infatuated with power. He wants control. He is against anything that serves the true and living God. Therefore, he will try to get you to denounce your faith in Jesus Christ. You must hold on to your faith in Jesus.

Under this New World leader, you may lose all ownership to your possessions if you choose not to be under his rule. His lieutenant, the false prophet will enforce the worship of the Antichrist by performing miracles. As the Bible says, they both will deceive many.

Revelation 13:16 reads, **And he causeth all, both small and great, rich and poor, free and bond, to receive the mark in their right hand, or in their foreheads:**

17th **And that no man might buy or sell, save he that had the mark, or the name of the beast, or the number of his name.**

Why did he choose to mark up the right hand? The Spirit of the Lord brought to my attention through scriptures that the right hand represents a place of honor, a place of power and a place of righteousness. Ecclesiates tells us that a wise man's heart is at his right hand. When you come out of the tribulation victoriously, there will be a separation to take place. The goat will be placed on the left and the sheep on the right, which is your place of honor. Your place of honor is at Jesus right hand. God says in Isaiah 41:10, I will uphold thee with the right hand of my righteousness. He says in Psalm 20:6 that He will save his anointed with the saving strength of his right hand. (power) Your blessing to inherit the kingdom is at Jesus right hand and the devil knows that.

We must remember that he too once lived in heaven. He's not going to mess with the left side or left hand because he knows that it represents everything about him. Even the goats (the unsaved) that belong to him will be placed on the left. He knows that marking up your right hand with his number 666 (the number of man) would forfeit all of what God has promised unto you. You taking the mark in your right hand will indeed forfeit your inheritance. You will be stripped of your place of honor, power and righteousness.

Let's not forget the stamp in the forehead. Why the forehead? Simple. It is the closest to your mind. The devil wants control of your mind. If you take the mark, he will not only own your mind but your soul also. Once again the devil is imitating the things of God. We become sealed of God at the very moment we receive Christ in our life. Revelation 6:17, 7:3 speaks about the servants of God having the stamp of God in their forehead. It's a sign of ownership.

If you take the mark either in your forehead or hand the only power you'll have is being able to buy or sell and even that is temporal and not promising. I don't really look at it as power I look at it as deception. You think you will have freedom, it too is deception. It may look good at first but if you don't know the devil by now to know that he always polish up his deception to sucker you in, then you are going to fall into his trap. You will end up nothing but walking zombies. Tricked and deceived by the devil himself. But if you don't take the mark there are everlasting promises given unto you by God.

When the Bible speaks of the great and the rich, it will be hard for them to give up their worldly possessions. It will be hard for people who have fine cars, million dollar homes, yachts, etc., to simply give them up. That's why God tells His people not to set their affections on earthly goods. You may have to give it up someday. It's okay to have a year 2000 Mercedes or Lexus. You just have to be in a place in God wherein if someone pointed a gun to your head and said denounce Jesus or lose your house, car, etc., that you are rooted and grounded in Christ. No matter what the cost, you will not allow anything in this world come between your faith in Him. I Timothy 6:7 says, **For you brought nothing into this world, and it is certain we can carry nothing out.** Know this that if you do take the mark of the beast (666), you will be damned for eternity.

The scripture says, And he causeth all both small and great, rich and poor, free and bond, to receive the mark in their forehead or right hand. The people in this scripture are like unto those who received seed among the thorns. Yes, they heard the word but something stood in the way of them believing in God. For the rich it was the lust for the things of this world. The scribes and the wise and the disputers of this world were caught up in worldly wisdom. Then there are those that wanted to hold on to God and the devil at the same time. Being conformed to the things of this world when God instructed in His Word not to. Then there are the spiritually blinded whom satan has blinded their minds from believing the gospel truth. These are some of the ones that will easily fall for this Antichrist. They have no root in them to start with.

Some will make it and some won't. Some will adhere to false prophets. Some will lose courage and will weaken, but this is to try them. This is to test their faith, to purify and to make those among God's people white to the time of the end. Blessed is he that waits patiently; who endures without wavering to beyond the period of tribulation and comes to the 1,335 days.

Daniel saw the great time of trouble. He said this tribulation was something never before seen on mankind. Daniel 12:1 tells us that everyone whose name was found written in the book was among those who will be delivered in the end.

2nd *And many of them that sleep in the dust of the earth shall awake, some to everlasting life, and some to shame and everlasting contempt.*
Even Daniel saw people being raptured up. This scripture is identical to I Thessalonians 4:17 of what man describes as the Rapture. It reads, *And the dead in Christ shall rise first: Then we which are alive and remain shall be caught up together with them in the clouds to meet the Lord in the air: and so shall we ever be with the Lord.* In the Bible, you will not find the word "rapture." Again from the Latin for "caught up" comes the term "rapture." In all reality if you read the scriptures carefully with wisdom and understanding from God, you will see this is one big event that takes place toward the end of the tribulation period and is the Coming of the Lord.

109

As I reflect back on the dreams God had given me and how it was gloomy and things were different outside. This let's me know that we better enjoy the sun all we can now and appreciate it because one day she will not give her light. In the prophecy of future desolation Joel describes the gloominess I speak so much of in Joel 2:2, ***A day of darkness and of gloominess, a day of clouds and of thick darkness, as the morning spread upon the mountains: a great people and a strong: there hath not been ever the like, neither shall be any more after it, even to the years of many generations.*** As you look at the part that says, a *great people and a strong* during the day of the Lord, take a look back at Daniel 11:32 to the part that says *and them that know their God shall be strong.* You ever hear preachers preach that God is raising up a great army of people. Well He's raising them up for such a time as this. Joel 2:11 read, ***And the Lord shall utter his voice before his army: for his camp is very great: for he is strong that executeth his word: for the day of the Lord is great very terrible: and who can abide it?***
Like I said before there are some things we will be here to see and there are some things we won't. But whatever part of the gloominess we experience, you better know that you know that God is right there with you. It is bad enough when the sun don't shine nowadays; the gloominess seems to change ones mood. A gloomy day affects one's energy level. Some people may experience depression from it and it makes some people drowsy and sleepy. And God knows the church is doing too much sleeping already.

Can you imagine what it will be like when the Day of the Lord is upon us and the saints of God find themselves still here? They will go into a state of shock. Some will fall back into perdition. Some will cleave to the false prophets who speak perverse things. Remember that God did not feed false information into your mind. Man did it. The truth was in the scriptures all the time. When actuality finally kicks in know that this is not the time to be spiritually unprepared. This is not the time. You didn't listen to the true teacher; the true prophets and you didn't believe the contents of this book, and instead you listened to man's wisdom that brainwashed you with false teachings. We need to get spiritually and physically prepared for the things ahead. As you read a little further down to Joel 2:12-16 God is calling for personal repentance from the heart along with fasting and a national repentance and fasting as He is calling for today. From the church house to the sinner house God is calling for repentance and fasting.

As God reveals the truth to me concerning end-time events, it left me thinking, Lord will I make it? God being the all-knowing God of my thoughts and questionings answered me with a dream and then confirmed it in a poem with a scripture. You see God is so awesome all the time. In this dream God gave unto me, I appeared to be on this icy mountain holding on to something that resembles a pointed iceberg and I began to feel myself lose balance as to slip. We all know how easy it is to slip and fall on ice. I began to feel myself falling. As I felt myself falling, all I could do was look up towards heaven and cry out to God, "Lord lift me up." Immediately when I cried out, both of my arms erected straight up and I could feel myself going up toward the skies. The

111

experience of going up towards the clouds was the best feeling ever! That feeling was so real! Do you think I wanted to come out of that dream?

As I looked toward heaven I could see a man on a white horse coming with clouds. The description of these clouds could not match the clouds as we see them today. Neither can the color white be matched with the color we see as white today. The only two words that can describe the color are *"heavenly white."* God gave me a poem titled, Rider on the White Horse. This poem in its entirety is in the back of this book.

The man on the white horse
Faithful and True
He was the one that delivered you
He lifted you up through the heavenly skies
He was taking you to the place where you shall abide.

God is so awesome He gave me two confirming scriptures that back up the dream.

Revelation 19:11 says, **And I saw heaven opened, and behold a white horse; and he that sat upon him was called Faithful and True, and in righteousness he doth judge and make war.**

He told me to look back at Daniel 11:35. And it reads, **And some of them of understanding shall fall, to try them, and to purge and to make them white, even to the time of the end: because it is yet for a time appointed.** Some will come to their weakest point and will be tempted to give up. This is where your deliverance comes in at. God shall deliver you out of the hour of temptation.

As I am hanging off the edge with my hands gripping onto a piece of ice: it represented the fact that I went through something for my stand in Jesus

Christ. That part of the dream put me in Daniel 11:33 which says, **Yet they shall fall by the sword, and by flame, by captivity, and by spoil, many days.** Some will either suffer or die for their belief in God.

The way that God brought this to me was so awesome and so beautiful. Whether I fell by the sword, by flame or entered into captivity, I don't know, but the most important thing is confirmation in knowing that I embraced the light at the end of the tunnel. Faithful and True delivered me. He was with me all the while, just as He promised in His Word.

When you go through your trials now and you feel as though you can't go on and you feel like giving up, who delivers you? Jesus comes to rescue and deliver you just in the nick of time. The same is here in the dream with scripture to back it up. I had suffered and came to my weakest point and I cried out to God and I looked up and behold with clouds came my prince and shining armor Jesus to deliver me out of my hour of temptation.

We will be tried and tested to the end. It is scriptural and can't be overlooked. Again, the Bible says that they overcame him by the blood of the Lamb and by the word of their testimony; and they loved not their lives unto death.

Revelations 15:2 and 3 says, **And I saw as it were a sea of glass mingled with fire: and them that had gotten the victory over the beast, and over his image, and over his mark, and over the number of his name, stand on the sea of glass, having the harps of God. And they sing the song of Moses the servant of God and the song of the Lamb, saying, Great and marvelous are thy works, Lord God Almighty; just and true are thy ways, thou King of saints.**

Will you be able to stand firm on your faith in Jesus Christ when the persecution of the saints begin in the United States? Will you be able to hold on to your faith in Christ or will you deny Christ?

Like I said before I hear people say, "I'm not going to take the mark. It's easy for you to say that now, but when the final test of faith faces you with a chainsaw to your neck or your baby's neck, what will you do? Let's say you've had five miscarriages and finally for once in your life you conceived. That one and only child you've wanted so badly finally came. I will leave you with something to think about.

Matthew 10:39 says *He that findeth his life shall lose it: and he that loseth his life for my sake shall find it.* I will never forget the courageous young lady who was a victim in the Colorado high school massacre. The gunman asked her, "do you believe in God"? She courageously said, "Yes." Even if she would have said no he still would have killed her and she would have spent eternity in hell. She lost her earthly life at the hands of her assassin, but she has found life again in her eternal state. She gained something far more better by saying YES, I do believe in God. She stood firm on her faith in God and is now resting in peace.

What do you have to lose by saying yes? Life is but a vapor, that appeareth for a little time and then vanisheth away anyway. A lifetime of eternity you will surely gain. God set her forth as an example for the churchworld to wake up and realize the price they will have to pay for their belief in Jesus Christ. Like the scripture says, for all who live godly in Christ Jesus shall suffer persecution.

May I ask how is your walk with God today? Are you spiritually, physically and mentally prepared? Many calamities will befall us, therefore will you have enough power to sustain you through all of what's about to take place here on earth? Will you have the power to say "No"?

If you are feasting on negative things that do not edify your spirit man for instance: the soap operas, garbage talk shows, demonic movies, etc., than you are in trouble! You will feed right into the devil's end-time trap. That's why it is important to get as much of God as you possibly can. There are deeper depths and higher heights to explore in God. God is never-ending. Seek Him while He may be found. Remember His Spirit will not always strive with man. He is about to snatch His grace and mercy away from here.

So, you may wonder how do I go about acquiring that power I'll need to be able to stand? The answer is by feasting on His Word on a daily basis, fasting as the Spirit lead, and maintaining a consistent prayer life. Know that whatever persecution you may have to face, it is better to die for Jesus than take the mark and go to hell. You must remember the promise of eternal life after this earthly life. Keep in mind: *FOR GOD I'LL LIVE AND FOR GOD I'LL DIE.*

God says to watch and be sober. We are about to embark in on the cashless society. The stage is already set. We already know what is holding the Antichrist back. Let's allow God to endorse His seal upon our lives now, while the restraint is still on the man of sin.

Who knows maybe when the computers do go down as I have seen in a dream for six months what will be the outcome? When they go back up things may be entirely different. I seen them go down for six months and the number six is the number of a man. I remember in a vision of being outside and it was gloomy. I remember seeing the computers in the midst of this gloominess but they appeared to not be working. The screens were blank. I knew in my spirit they had gone down and the number six rang in my spirit. One thing for sure is God was letting me no that yes, the computer will play a major part and it is a replica of the beast. The creation of it is man's doing and Bible prophecy fulfilling itself.

As I feel the anointing of God, I can hear in my spirit the word *"prepare."* God wants His people to prepare. He wants His people to be spiritually prepared for the future. As far as getting physically prepared, be lead by the Holy Spirit as to what you need to do. He will guide you. Many calamities shall befall us but we need to be lead by God as to whether or not we need to store up surplus. In times like these God does not want us to make haste decisions. We must consult Him first. They used scare tactics with the supposedly year two thousand calamity and had people preparing out of fear. Fear is not of God. The world prepares out of fear. You are to use your God given wisdom and common sense. II Timothy 1:7 tells us, **For God has not given us the spirit of fear, but of power, and of love, and of a sound mind.**

People have lost focus on what time it really is. It is time to repent. While the world is going around pulling their hairs out about the future I tell you there's nothing like having the feeling of peace in your mind when you hear about future calamities. That peace comes from God. God says for His people to use practical wisdom. God commands His people to lead a worry free environment.

In all actuality the world should have been pulling out their hairs four years ago because according to the Jewish calendar we are already in the Millenium. As of 1999 our calendar is four years behind which puts us already in the year 2004. Now that is something to really think about. That's why so many things are happening around us. That's why tension is building up over in Jerusalem and everything around us is happening so fast. Days seem to be shorter. You wake up at sunrise and before you know it the sun is setting. The weather patterns is strange.

In 1999 I heard churches that were stocking up for the supposedly year two thousand calamity say they would use that time to evangelize. Why should we wait until a calamity hit, whether it is an economical disaster or a global catastrophe, to win souls into the kingdom? Go out and win them now. Some souls may not make it through the disasters that are coming. The Bible tells us that men heart shall fail them for fear because of the things that are coming upon the earth.

Why put off for tomorrow what can be done today? Why should you wait until a comet hit to win souls into the kingdom? We need to warn them and win them over to Christ before the comet hit because some will not make it through this type of disaster. The comet that God revealed unto me is going to do very heavy damage. The impact will be felt worldwide. The world will not be the same from the impact it will cause. God said that it's going to pop up out of nowhere and man will not know what to do. It is going to put the world in a state of chaos.

As I view the movie, Deep Impact, the Spirit of the Lord said to me *"prepare."* Something is getting ready to happen and people need to repent. Even Hollywood is preparing us, but nobody is talking about repentance. There were actual scenes where the Antichrist could have actually stepped in. Just take a moment and think, when a disaster such as this happens, what will get America up and running again? We are looking at problems here, problems there, problems everywhere. America will be at her weakest state. They will be desperate for help, seeking peace and a solution. You know how the devil shows up in your weakest state. He shows up in a disguise.

Who knows what will usher the Antichrist in? But, know that the Antichrist time is near. He is already in the world and has not yet identified himself. The signs are yet around us, the scanner, the microchip, satellites, monitors, computers, the Euro, and unification. These are things they have been working on for years and are getting ready to go into play real soon for the real thing. It's just a matter of time.

Technology has increased tremendously at a rapid speed. If Hollywood in the movie, Enemy of the State, can portray *"losing your rights to privacy"*, showing technology in its farthest state of advancement, it leaves me asking the question how far are we actually from this really occurring? After viewing this movie, God spoke to me and said, *"this is a thing of the near future. He went on to say fear not for I am with you."*

Even before I had viewed the movie, God had given me dreams of about two years ago in which I knew had something to do with the Antichrist but only I didn't grasp a hold of the technology being portrayed in one dream in particular. I recall as nightfall came you could walk outside of your house and see a screen projection in the sky with a figure of a person talking. Satellites were being used to project one's image up in the sky for all to see. And we should know by now who is going to want to be seen by the world. Leaves me to wonder why are these Christian organization trying so hard to raise money for these communications equipment when in all reality they will not have control of them. They are setting themselves up for an end of their own privacy and are setting themselves up for their own persecution. They better go ahead and preach the gospel like crazy and use them to their advantage because they will lose access to them one day. The Antichrist and his government are going to use all of this technology to keep tabs on everybody in the world especially Christians. You are the enemy to his New World government. Remember you got something that he wants to rid this world of and that is the witness of Jesus Christ.

To continue with the dream, I recall when this person is finished talking; there would be a display that would pop up on the screen. And this display was a skeleton skull with two cross bones. Even from this I believe we better keep our eyes on a certain country and a certain group of people. Other dreams I recall seeing monitors up everywhere even in houses. I remember seeing helicopters patrolling above and men in uniform patrolling the grounds.

All of these devices man created has set the stage for the New World Order. When this order takes place it will put an end to personal privacy. The more technology used the more they can keep tabs on you. In this movie, they had over a hundred satellites up in space tracking your every move. They had 18 acres of mainframe computers underground. They could break into your computer files, email and monitor your phone calls. The calls you make on your phone could bounce off satellites and they could pick them up out of the air.

Even with your clothes on they had devices that could go beyond your clothes with the capability to read what brand of underwear you have on to whether or not you have hair on your legs. They could pull up everything about you. They even had control of your bank accounts and credit cards with the ability to shut down your money. In the New World Order there will be no such thing as calling in to report or resolve this type of issue. Once this thing is up and running "cashless society" is in affect. As you can see we are moving more and more towards that today.

Can you imagine going to the ATM and they tell you your card has been declined? Not the decline as we know it today, where you can call in and report or resolve a matter. I am talking about the "decline" that means your money is gone forever. Why did they recently as of early year 2000 go up and take a snapshot of the whole world? What does the government have cooking in the pot?

Let's get rooted and grounded in God. Let us begin to hearken unto the voice of God. The Antichrist time is near upon us. My fellow sisters and brothers in the Lord, the Antichrist is going to hate you with a passion, but you must know that God loves you and He is by your side as He promised, even in the hour of temptation.

Let us remember to watch and pray. Let us wear out the Garden of Gethsemane.

In Revelation 13:18 it reads, **Here is wisdom. Let him that hath understanding count the number of the beast; for it is the number of a man; and his number is six hundred threescore and six.** Please remember as for the number 666, Don't Take It!!!

WHO HATH EARS TO HEAR, LET HIM HEAR.
Let him who hath ears to hear be listening, and let him consider and perceive and understand by hearing.

At this point I know by now you need to take a break
This pause I grant unto you a good time to take
As I look back on the awesome power of God to reveal
The unknowable, unrevealed deep secrets of His
The visions, dreams and interpretations all belong to God
The wisdom and understanding from heaven they did fall
Some of them left me pondering
Some of them left me amazed
Some of them left me troubled in my spirit for many days
For God is very awesome
When it comes to visions and revelations
He used poems, scriptures and even people
As back up confirmation
For the things of God is powerful
There is only so much the flesh can take
Thank God He didn't reveal to me like
He did Daniel and Ezekiel
The way He showed them will give you the shakes
Many visions John in the book of Revelations did surely see
To forewarn us of how the future will definitely be
I can relate to Paul who suffered many afflictions
But in the midst of his sufferings
Received revelations and visions
Some days I was given a thorn in the flesh
But knew exactly what was going on
God is about to pour down more revelations and visions
From His heavenly throne
There were times I would awaken out of my sleep saying,
Lord I can't take it!
Only to be comforted by His Holy Spirit saying,
Child you can make it
The things of God are deep and heavy for the mind to attain
He commanded me to write them on the tablets plain
The knowledge I am passing on to you is for your benefit
So you won't be caught off guard when these things hit
The visions shall surely come to pass, for they are at hand
They have been written plain on tablets for all to understand.

6

A Message To the Ungodly

Woe! Unto those who refuse to take heed, for the kingdom of God is at hand. For the wages of sin is death, but the gift of God is eternal life through Jesus Christ our Lord. How you choose to live your life on earth will determine your eternal destiny. Why choose death over life eternity?

You may say, well, I am a good person. But, I must tell you, being a good person does not get you into heaven. I recall telling my mother, who was trying to preach me back into church, "I'm not a bad sinner; I'm a good sinner." The nerve of me to think that way. I actually thought I was on my way to heaven. But little did I know I was being blinded by the devil just like many are today.

True enough mother raised me well and I gave her no problems but the question still stands, have you made amends with God? You may be a good person, but have you repented of your sins? That was the question I should have been asking myself. Just because you are a good person does not mean you are saved. Good people go to hell too. No matter how many charities you give to or no matter how many good deeds you have done, the question still stands, have you repented of your sins? Do you have a personal relationship with Jesus Christ? You may ask, what sin? Or you may say I've never sinned before.

Well, according to the Bible in Romans 3:23, *For all have sinned, and come short of the glory of God.* And according to Ecclesiastes 7:20, *For there is not a just man upon earth that doeth good and sinneth not.* We were all born into sin. The only person that was on earth without sin was Jesus.

I John 1:8 says, *If we say that we have no sin, we deceive ourselves, and the truth is not in us.*

9th *If we confess our sins, he is faithful and just to forgive us our sins, and to cleanse us from all unrighteousness.*

10th *If we say that we have not sinned, we make him a liar, and his word is not in us.*

The Bible says that every knee shall bow and every tongue shall confess to God. Each and every one will have to give an account of himself before God on Judgment Day. God says that the soul that sinneth shall surely die. But Jesus has made a way of escape for us in that He died on the cross for our sins that we might have the right to the tree of life through repentance.

Because of Jesus' death on the cross we now have access to the Father. We are no longer hidden from His presence. When Jesus gave up His spirit and the vail tore from top to bottom, it signified that the new and living way through Jesus was now open into the presence of God. Sin keeps you out of the presence of God but because of the death of Christ that can be rectified through repentance. Had it not been for the shedding of blood on the cross, we would all be doomed for hell.

Just take a moment and picture Jesus carrying that heavy cross up Calvary's hill and then being nailed to the cross with nails going through both of His hands and blood dripping. Now that's a lot of pain and suffering He went through for you and me.

Even today being resurrected and seated on the right hand of God the scars from the nails being driven through His hands are still there. If you don't believe it ask doubting Thomas in John 20.

No matter what suffering and pain Jesus went through you still continue to hold on to your sin. After all He's done for you; you still continue to persecute Him. He loved us enough to leave His heavenly home and give himself as a sacrificial lamb, so that we may have eternal life. You now have the free will to choose life or death. If you continue to reject God by continuing to live in your sin, then hell is awaiting with outstretched arms to engulf you up in flames eternally.

REALITY OF HELL

Yes, hell is real. And there are friends and relatives there who wish to come back here on earth to tell you to take heed to the warnings of repentance from God's people. You see it is already too late for them. They already had their chance. When you die, that's not the end. Your soul lives on eternally. Isaiah 5:14 reads, ***Hell enlarges herself daily and opens her mouth without measure, for the disobedient and rebellious ones.***

In this scripture alone, we've already learned that hell is a "she". And it has a mouth. Therefore, hell has a body and so does Christ in reference to the body of Christ with many members. But, whatever part of hell you end up in, it looks like you'll be entering the mouth first and end up somewhere either in the left or right arm, the belly, the left or

125

right leg. There is plenty of room in hell. Hell stretches and stretches and never runs out of room.

While you are burning in the coals of fire, you will have all five of your senses in hell. They will be even stronger than ever now. Let's take a look at Luke 16:22 concerning Lazarus the beggar and the rich man who would not feed Lazarus the bread that fell from his table. It's a dangerous thing to be rich and stingy. It can land you a front row seat in hell. Some of you have relatives who won't even give you a dollar if you asked for it. Some people are so stingy they see a person in need and won't even spare them five dollars. Now that's bad. And it's also sad because they don't even realize that God honors giving. Take a look at II Corinthians 9:6-15.

God has already expressed in Psalm 41:1, **Blessed is he that considereth the poor.** God's heart is in winning souls and seeing about the poor. When you go out of your way to help others in need, God honors that and will reward you in due time. The angels in heaven are recording those good deeds that you do and don't do.

However, your good deeds without repentance will do you no good anyway. The rich man will tell you the consequences you will have to pay for your sins and for not having mercy on the poor. Both Lazarus and the rich man died. Lazarus went to paradise and the rich man lifted up his eyes in hell.

The verses in this chapter let you know that you will have all your senses while in hell. Take a look at the words in parenthesis as you read.

While in hell, the rich man looked up (sight) and saw Lazarus lying peacefully in the bosom of Abraham, which is Paradise. He cried out, Father Abraham have mercy on me and send Lazarus that he may dip the tip of his finger to cool my tongue.

For I am tormented in this flame. (feel) Torment meaning torture. He could feel the torture of hell. He had the sense of (taste). A taste of hell. He was quite aware of his surroundings.

Then in verse 25, Abraham spoke to the rich man (this indicates that the rich man could hear). And took him back to his rich days on earth when he refused to help the poor man Lazarus. Then the rich man told Abraham to send Lazarus to his father's house to warn his (rich man's) relatives that hell is real.

This is what the messengers of God are trying to get you to see today, that hell is real. And people make jokes, saying they are going to party when they go to hell. But, I'll tell you that the only ones that are going to have the party are the demons. They are going to party all over your foolish soul and that will not be a party to brag about.

So, Abraham told the rich man, "For they have Moses and the prophets to listen to, why should I send Lazarus?" The rich man then said his relatives would be more persuaded if a dead man came back and preached to them. Abraham told him, "if they don't listen to Moses and the prophets, neither will they be persuaded through a dead man."

We learn quite a few things from Lazarus and the rich man. One is that you are in a conscious state after death, secondly is the reality and torment of hell, and thirdly, there is no second chance after death and last, it is impossible for the dead to communicate with the living. And I will say it again; *it is impossible for the dead to communicate with the living.*

In other words, when Uncle Randy and your favorite Auntie Beverly dies, you cannot in no way possible communicate with their spirit. When you engage in a seance and strange things began to happen, it is because you are tapping into the spirit world. You are tapping into the kingdom of darkness where evil forces abide. They are real and don't play. Yes they will play on the mind. Once you have tried to make contact with your dead relative you have opened the door for these spirits to come in and disguise themselves as your dead relative.

You are opening the door for them to come in. Even the secular world has invited them to come into the toy stores and sit on the shelves in the toy and game sections for you to purchase. You look on the shelves and you will see magic games, ouija boards, eight balls, magic wands, etc. and even in the cartoons the characters are talking about magic and spirits. Then there are your horror movies and video and computer games. The devil is everywhere.

All these things you open yourself and your family up to and you wonder why strange things are happening in your house. You need to take out everything that is not of God out of your house and burn it. And again, as for seances, once you have tried to make contact with your dead loved one, you have opened the door for a spirit to come in and disguise itself as your dead loved one.

II Corinthians 11:14 reads, **And no marvel; for satan himself is transformed into an angel of light.** Now, if satan can disguise himself as an angel of light, what make you think he can't disguise himself as cousin Willie. Communicating with spirits in high places and powers of darkness from another spirit realm goes against the principles of God.

All of these sightings of the Virgin Mary are nothing but deception from the pits of hell to distract people's attention away from who the real Savior of the world is. A lady once said we should worship

Mary instead of Jesus. Her view was that if it had not been for Mary, Jesus would not have been born. But little did she and others realize that God is in control. If Mary had not been obedient to God, God would have found some kind of way for Jesus to get here.

God has already given us in the Ten Commandments not to worship any graven image or any likeness thereof. So, whatever statue you kneel down before everyday is your god. God says *thou shalt have no other gods before Him.* He is the one and only God.

I truly thank God for Mary. Mary was highly favored in the sight of God. Evidently she was a woman of a quiet and meek spirit in which I Peter 3:4 says that a quiet and meek spirit is of great price in the sight of the Lord. A personality trait we all need, so that God can do great and mighty things through us. God did a great and mighty thing through Mary.

According to Philippians 2:10-11, that at the name of Jesus every knee shall bow and every tongue shall confess that Jesus is Lord to the glory of God the Father. Even Mary shall bow. Hail, Mary cannot save you. Mary did not die on the cross for your sins. Jesus did. No one can come to the Father except by Jesus Christ.

In reference to the sightings of Mary, if you are weak in the spirit the devil can make you hear things and see things that are not even there. Satan is an actor and the master of deception. Let us remember that he can disguise himself as an angel of light. He even disguised himself at Mecca. Making people think God came in the person of another man other than Jesus Christ and spoke. The devil can go to Mecca too and disguise himself as anything pertaining to the things of God. He too, travels faster than a speeding bullet. I didn't say he was superman, but he's an imitator. He speaks also and the Bible says he's the father of lies and the truth is not in him. But God says, "*my sheep know me, they know my voice and a stranger they will not follow.*"

DESCRIPTION OF HELL

Now back to the subject of hell, you already know that you will have all five of your senses in hell with biblical proof behind it. You will be able to feel the torture of heat. You will be able to hear the sounds of terror, the screams and groans of others, the sounds of weeping and gnashing of teeth.

Lets not forget the worms mentioned in Isaiah 66:24, ***And they shall go forth, and look upon the carcasses of the men that have transgressed against me: for their worm shall not die, neither shall their fire be quenched; and they shall be an abhorring unto all flesh.*** Also read Mark 9:42-50

As you can see, this is a place where the worms never die, just eating at your flesh day and night. Even through the darkness you will be able to see others in torment, you will see demons and satan too, nothing but fire and brimstones.

There are preachers in hell. The ones that sugarcoated the gospel and led God's people astray. They didn't preach that sin is wrong, hell is real and time is drawing near. If they don't preach according to the principles of God, they get the worst form of torment. The demons have a field day on preachers in hell.

You will be able to feel the agony, pain and torture of satan's angels as they harass you day and night nonstop. You will have your speech saying let me out of here, it's hot, and I need some cold water and fresh air. Also crying out to God, I'll repent, I'll live right. But, you had your chance while on earth. And it's most definitely too late to repent now. It's too late.

One last thing, let's not forget the sense of smell. There's plenty to smell in hell. The smell of burning flesh and the bad odor that demons carry. You think garbage smells bad or a dead skunk or a sewer smell bad, wait until you get a sniff of a demon, it's horrible!

Revelation 21:8 reads, **But the fearful, and unbelieving and abominable, and murderers, and whoremongers, and sorcerers, and idolaters, and all liars, shall have their part in the lake which burneth with fire and brimstone: which is the second death.**

PERVERSED GENERATION

As you take a look at the world today, so sad, so sad to see how it is being so contaminated with sin. *The world is in trouble with God. They must repent. God has extended His mercy long enough,* these are the words, the Lord spoke unto me. *Sin is tearing this world apart. No longer do they try to hide.* Everything is coming out of the closet. They flaunt their abominable sin publicly and on national TV for all to see. Daily headlines and TV show a high rise of mockers of God walking after their own ungodly lust in society today.

The Bible says in Isaiah 59:5 that the wicked hatch cockatrice's eggs, and weave the spider's web: he who eats of their eggs dies, and from an egg which is crushed a viper breaks out for their nature is ruinous, deadly, evil. Their webs shall not become their garments, neither shall they cover themselves with their work: their works are the works of iniquity,

131

and the act of violence is in their hands. Their feet run to evil and their thoughts are the thoughts of iniquity; desolation and destruction are in their paths and highways. They don't know peace and there is no justice or right in their goings. They have made unto them crooked paths and whoever goes in them does not know peace.

America is putting the stamp of approval on things that God has forbidden in His Word. They call evil good and good evil. In their perversion they are adding light to their darkness and darkness to light. They no longer add light to their darkness in a secret place. They no longer add light to their darkness and keep it under a bushel. They have lit it up and set their abominable sin on a pedestal for all to see the filth they partake in.

God has sent a special woe unto you who pervert moral distinctions. By your actions, America you are mocking God to act if He can. Isaiah 5:18 says **Woe unto them that draw iniquity with cords of vanity, and sin as it were with a cart rope.** You are pulling your idol of sin along. Thinking and not believing that God is going to rain down His judgment upon the unjust. Your perverseness is ridiculing God and telling Him to come on and speed up your prophetic vengeance so that we may see it. Where is your comet, O Mighty God? We hear that it is coming. For years they've been saying Jesus is coming and He hasn't came yet, O Mighty God.

God took me to Ezekiel 12:22-28. I will put an end to their mocking. God says, *"the days are at hand, and the effect of every vision. There shall none of my words be prolonged any more, but the word which I have spoken shall be done,"* saith the Lord God.*"

132

God is going to send upon this world rude awakenings like never before seen upon mankind. You have asked for it and you will get your just reward. Every word God has spoken in the Bible shall come to pass; it shall be no more prolonged: for in your days, O rebellious generation will God say the word, and will perform it.

Isaiah 55:11 says ***So shall My word be that goeth forth out of my mouth: it shall not return unto me void, but it shall accomplish that which I please, and it shall prosper in the thing whereto I sent it.***

God says in His Word that all souls are mine: the saved and the unsaved. You have erred from His Truth. You have listened to false prophets who have prophesied lies and false dreams and have caused you to forget the name of God.

God says woe unto the false prophets who have prophesied lies in His name causing the people to err. God says He has not sent them and neither has He spoken to them. They are speaking out of their own heart and not out of the mouth of the Lord. They are giving the people false hope. Whispering sweet nothings in their ears basically for money.

God said that if He sent them He would have given them (prophets) a word for the people that would cause the people to turn from their wicked ways. Instead the false prophets are telling the people that peace is coming. As I sit here and write, God told me to tell you that peace is not coming, no, not by a long shot. The only time we will experience peace is when the church is caught up to be with Jesus.

The Bible says ***Behold, a whirlwind of the Lord is gone forth in fury, even a grievous whirlwind: it shall fall grievously upon the head of the wicked. The anger of the Lord shall not***

return, until He has executed, and till He has performed the thoughts of His heart: in the latter days ye shall consider it.

Believe me we are living in the latter days. Be leery of preachers and false prophets that make the future look good and say that God is bringing healing to the land. They are making your future look good to get you to dig deep into your purses. This type of deception will only leave you thinking that you have all the time in the world to repent, when in reality you don't.

If you could only feel the urgency as I write this book. The Bible tells us that the earth shall be destroyed with fire and knowing that these things are going to happen, you should be repenting. Take a look at II Peter 3:10 and take note that God is going to once again rid the earth of sin but only this time by fire.

But the day of the Lord will come as a thief in the night; in the which the heavens shall pass away with a great noise, and the elements shall melt with fervent heat, the earth also and the works that are therein shall be burned up.

There are prophets and preachers that are being soft on you and telling you what your itching ears want to hear and are not warning you of these things, but lo and behold God will have a bone to pick with them on Judgment Day.

The world of today is nothing but modern day Sodom and Gomorrah. It is even worst. America has multiplied her abominations more than Sodom. The world today has made the abominable to be the norm. The abnormal thing to do has become to the wicked normal. America has given a red flag to God and a green light to her indecent, obscene, immoral character. Her abominable sins are uncovered.

Yes, America is like Sodom full of pride, fullness of bread, prosperous ease and yet they dance to the tune of wickedness, being arrogant and committing unlawful acts in the sight of God. America has forgotten that it was God who has blessed them with abundance. They have become idle in their ways and idle in their thinking leaving plenty of room for the devil to set up his workshop. A workshop he so busily works in to plan his strategies to deceive, steal, kill and destroy. The more doors become open unto him the more rebellious this country gets. Unless America turn from her wicked ways and repent, God is going to do her like He did Sodom, take her out as He see fit. For once this country will know that He is God.

Jude reads, **Even as Sodom and Gomorrah and the cities about them in like manner giving themselves over to fornication, and going after strange flesh, are set forth for an example, suffering the vengeance of eternal fire.**

Likewise also these filthy dreamers defile the flesh, despise dominion, and speak evil of dignities (church leaders, etc.)

You see, in the beginning, God made man in His image and He made woman to be his helpmate. Read Genesis 1:27. **And God blessed them, and told them to be fruitful and multiply and replenish the earth.**

In other words, God made Thomas and Gail; and God made Michael and Barbara to be together. He did not make Sally and Sue to be together or Bob and Jim to lie together. That was never in God's plan.

To say that you were born some other kind of way, other than the way the scriptures confirms unto you is like saying God is imperfect. God is a perfect God and He doesn't make mistakes.

Leviticus 18:22 reads ***Thou shalt not lie with mankind, as with womankind: it is abomination.*** Here you have it in scripture and there are many more in the Bible pertaining to homosexuality.

Leviticus 20:13 tells us, ***If a man also lie with mankind, as he lieth with a woman, both of them have committed an abomination: they shall surely be put to death; their blood shall be upon them.***

They will tell you in a minute homosexuality is not in the Bible. Of course the word *"homosexuality"* is not in the Bible because they did not have that vocabulary in their speech back then. Even a six-year-old child can look at these scriptures and understand what God is saying.

As you read more of the chapter, God speaks against incest in the family, women having sexual relations with animals, the wizard who just may be your neighbor.

People who commit such heinous sin shall be consumed with fire. The same sins they committed in the Bible days are the same sins they are committing today except man has given a different name for them.

Roman 1:26 reads, ***Even their women did change the natural use into that which is against nature.***

*27*th ***And likewise also the men, leaving the natural use of the woman, burned in their lust one toward another, men with men working that which is unseemly and receiving in themselves that recompense of their error which was meet.***

*28*th ***And even as they did not like to retain God in their knowledge, God gave them over to a reprobate mind, to do those things which are not convenient.***

29th**Being filled with all unrighteousness, fornication, wickedness, covetousness, maliciousness; full of envy, murder, debate, deceit, malignity; whispers,**

30th **Backbiters, haters of God, despiteful, proud, boasters, inventors of evil things, disobedient to parents.**

31st **Without understanding, covenant breakers, without natural affection, implacable, unmerciful.**

32nd **Who knowing the judgment of God, that they which commit such things are worthy of death, not only do the same, but have pleasure in them that do them.**

Again the Bible says woe unto them that call evil good and good evil. Some of you defend the wicked in their sin and you cheer them on to do their thing. You respect the person of the wicked (show partiality to) and deprive the righteous of justice and according to Proverbs 18:5 that is not good. You punish the just for their stand on the Truth. You are just as much of a partaker in the sins of the wicked as they are, no matter what it is. He that justifieth the wicked, and he that condemneth the just, even they both are an abomination to the Lord.

There are times when God will lead me to go on the Internet and speak a word. And the subject may be a particular sin or just sin in general. God will give me a response to share, which turns out to be a scripture most of the time. God wants you to have backup to show the people their transgression.

No matter how many scriptures you show these people concerning the matter, it goes in one ear and out the other. It is almost like they are saying I don't care what God has to say. We will do what we want to do. We'll handle our sin how we see fit. You show people what God has to say about it in scriptures and they overlook it in disbelief. They act like it's not even there and will come up with their own philosophy. How can you overlook the scriptures? Disobedience to the scriptures is showing your unbelief in the Word of God.

People nowadays don't want to hear the truth. You try to show them what the Word of God has to say about their sin issue and they want to accuse you of nick picking and being too hard. *They will say you can attract more flies with honey than vinegar. Or they will say you are scaring off more people with your message than you are attracting them.* Time is of the essence and it is no time to be helping people put their sin on a silver platter. You showing the people in scripture how God expects them to live will only leave them accusing you of condemning.

Know that showing people how to live according to the Word of God is not condemning. They will call you judgmental and self-righteous and holier than thou in a minute. Their minds are not focused on the fact that the Holy scriptures is actually God speaking His purpose and will for our lives. The Holy Bible is a guide for everyday living. But it seems to be too strict for some. For some it is too hard to abide by.

To those of you who have been called names for preaching against sin, remember; blessed are ye when men say all manner of evil against you. Know that the Word of God says in Isaiah 54:17 that for every tongue that shall rise up against thee in judgment (discernment) thou shalt condemn. This is the heritage of the servants of the Lord, and their righteousness is of me, saith the Lord. They accused Jesus of a lot of things. Do you think He let name-calling, critical remarks, etc., stop Him? No, He kept on preaching and teaching.

God warns against sin and it is the duty of the Christians to show the people their transgression in a godly manner. I will not overlook the fact that there are some people that will use the Bible to get at people; they are the ones that are not being lead by the Spirit of God. It is important to be led by the Spirit of God in approaching saved and unsaved people concerning sin issues.

When you run across a person whose spirit rises and chew you out for speaking truth into their life; it is the truth that you speak and the Word of God that has found that person and is convicting them of their sin. The Word of God has found them guilty of sin. The Word of God you speak is cutting at their flesh. It is piercing them in the heart and they can't take it. The Bible says that the Word of God is quick, powerful and sharper than any two-edged sword, piercing at the divine asunder of soul and spirit.

The scriptures being rightfully applied, will convict, condemn, step on some toes, and hurt some feelings. It will get the job done. The Word of God itself says in John 8:32, and ye shall know the truth and the truth shall make you free.

In Jeremiah 23:29 God has questioned, *Is not my word like as a fire? saith the Lord; and like a hammer that breaketh the rock in pieces?* Now that is powerful.

As I began to address these things to God about how people get touchy when you give them the Truth, He responded to me. And by the way it is a blessing to serve a God who will talk. He responded to me in a poem entitled, *They Want Sin On A Silver Platter*. This poem in its entirety may be found in my book, *Hidden Treasures of Wisdom and Knowledge*.

> *They want sin on a silver platter*
> *With you Lord I know its not so*
> *They want sin on a silver platter*
> *When you have said in your word, "NO"*
> *They want sin on a silver platter*
> *They want you to give them a pat on the back*
> *They want sin on a silver platter*
> *They want you to say it's okay to do this and that*

I have also added this poem in its entirety toward the back of this book. People want their sin more than they want God. There's more compromising going on than conviction.

If you find yourself engaging in any type of lifestyles that are an abomination in the sight of God, don't let the enemy cheat you out of life eternity. If you are engaging in a gay lifestyle, don't let the devil continue to deceive you into thinking you were born that way. God doesn't make mistakes.

Homosexuality and other acts pertaining to it is nothing but a disease and an evil spirit straight from the pits of hell dominating ones' personality and lifestyle. It is an abomination in the sight of God. What you need to do is go to Jesus for help with any type of sin. He is the only one that can deliver you. He had nails driven through His flesh for you. The prints are still there. He has already taken care of your problem on the cross and all you got to do is make the first step and watch Him change you.

You can go to all the help groups you want, but the only help group that can bring total deliverance is the Father, the Son, and the Holy Ghost. When they get finished with you, you'll have a new walk and a new talk. They will get the job done. No matter what sin you were struggling with, when the Holy Ghost gets finished with you it should no longer be a struggle. That sin or lifestyle should become a thing of your past and should not linger on.

The world is condoning same sex marriages and adoption to take place in this type of lifestyle that God has forbidden. The preachers that are officiating these ceremonies and allowing this type of lifestyle to hold positions behind the pulpit stand an even worst punishment of damnation. The blind can't lead the blind. They will both fall into a ditch. Woe be unto you! saith the Lord.

I hold nothing against gays, prostitutes, drunks, drug addicts, etc. I love everybody. This is not to pick on you; it is to show you your wrong and to steer you into the right direction. It does not take a former gay to understand homosexuality and so forth for any type of lifestyle. As a child of God, God will not have me ignorant to the things of the devil. I know very well what's going on. The saints of God should have enough power behind their belts to command these entities that are dominating people to flee. But here is the key. They go not out but by fasting and prayer.

God led me into your direction because He loves you and hates your sin. And that is with any sin. God wants you to be saved and delivered. The devil just wants your soul; he doesn't care about you at all. You can go to all the secular help groups and counselors you want and waste all your time and energy but the bottom line is, they can't do you like Jesus can. There is nothing too hard for Jesus. You have to want to be delivered from that which has you in bondage. Some people don't want to be delivered. People will find all kinds of excuses for being delivered because they don't want to give it up. There is no such thing as big sin and little sin. Sin in whatever form carries a penalty. It carries an eternal punishment. The eyes of the Lord are in every place,

beholding the evil and the good. He says in Jeremiah 23:23, ***Am I a God at hand, saith the Lord, and not a God afar off?***
24th Can any hide himself in secret places that I shall not see him? saith the Lord. Do not I fill heaven and earth? saith the Lord.

VIOLENCE TODAY

The world has shown in so many ways, God we don't want to have anything to do with you. America allowed someone to take prayer out of the schoolhouses and look what happens, demonic spirits take over the minds of kids. Violence is on the rampage amongst our kids. Some schools have to use security systems to screen for weapons, drugs, etc. No amount of metal detectors, safety classes, etc., can stop the devil from doing his work. What these kids need is salvation.

When kids go on shooting sprees, they not only kill the person who has ticked them off (parents, girlfriend, etc.), but they go over to the school yards, jobs, etc., and shoot up innocent people. And now parents are wondering, what are we going to do with our children. Well, the answer is blowing in the wind. You took God out of the plan and now you've got to put Him back in the plan to see a change.

The Bible says in Proverbs 22:6, ***Train up a child in the way he should go; and when he is old, he will not depart from it.***
Blame it on society all you want, but it start at the home first. And then we can look at a society that promotes violence on TV, in our cartoons, video games, music, books, clothing, and etc. You name it.

All of this junk is getting fed into the brain and when that happens the devil goes to work on the mind. He goes to work on a mind that hasn't been taught that they need a relationship with God. He goes to work on a mind that hasn't been taught about salvation, heaven and hell and that Jesus is the answer.

That's why the Bible tells us to train them up while they are young so when they think to do bad, that seed (the Word of God) you planted in them will come to life at the very moment of temptation. The voice of the Lord will speak to their heart and they will remember when they were taught, thou shalt not kill. Thou shalt not steal. Love thy neighbor. Thou shalt have no other god before me. And honor thy father and mother that thy days may be long upon the earth. The Ten Commandments can be found in Exodus 20:1-17.

Parents need to instill the commandments and laws of God into the minds of the children. According to Proverbs 3:1-4, writing them upon the table of their hearts and binding them about their neck will not only deliver them from evil but it promises certain awards: longevity and peace. The favor of God and man will be with them, and so will guidance, health, prosperity and a proper response to discipline. Children today have lost respect for their parents and elders. Proverbs 6:20 tells us, **My son, keep thy father's commandment, and forsake not the law of thy mother:**
21st **Bind them continually upon thine heart, and tie them about thy neck.**
22nd **When thou goest, it shall lead thee: when thou sleepest, it shall keep thee; and when thou awakest, it shall talk with thee.**
23rd **For the commandment is a lamp; and the law is light; and reproofs of instruction are the way of life:**

If we do things God way the country wouldn't have as much problems as they are having with the children of today. You ask the question why this and why that? The answer is blowing in the wind. The parents are not raising these kids up on the principles of the Bible and therefore they turn into murderers, thieves, gangbangers, devil worshippers, etc., and you're wondering why my child? Well, that's what happens when you reject God and His ways.

According to Deuteronomy 11:26-28 you are either blessed or cursed. If this is not enough information for you, go to Deuteronomy 28:1, it not only tells you if you follow God's ways you are blessed but it also show the benefits. If you choose not to follow God's ways you fall under the curse. Deuteronomy 28:15 shows the curses that will befall you. You took prayer out of the schoolhouse; not realizing it is prayer that changes the course of events in the first place. Prayer is power to keep evil out. Prayer is your means of communication with God. You don't want to hear mention of the name of God or anything that pertains to God in the schools. You can't exclude God away from something and expect good to befall thee. You have put the curse on yourselves.

In schools during Halloween you have these kids promoting the devil faithfully every year. You go to the extremes to celebrate this pagan festival. You dress up like ghosts and goblins talking about trick or treat smell my feet and give me something good to eat. Society have the kids more pumped up for the devil at Halloween time than they do for Christ during Christmas. The school system doesn't mention Christ at that time because of other people's religious beliefs. They send the kids home with a picture of Santa going down a chimney and reindeers flying magically through the sky. People prefer myths over prayer and commandments in the schools. You have replaced Christ who is, with a Santa who isn't. Filling these kids heads up with a bunch of garbage talking about Santa Claus is coming to town. He isn't coming to town JESUS is. You don't want to acknowledge God for who He is and Christ for who He is and then you have the audacity to ask the question why this and why that is happening.

LITTLE MIKEY

I take this moment to introduce you to little seven-year-old Mikey. Little Mikey is bringing weapons to school and reciting chants over his classmates. He's been watching too much TV. His shelf is full of video movies that depict magic and violence. We need to be aware of what our children are watching. Cartoons have more violence in it than regular TV. They are contributing factors in your child's change of behavior, especially the ones where the characters are reciting chants calling down gods and spirits. Your child will begin to pick up on these chants and start saying them and you wonder why is he acting strange and why strange things are going on in your house. These things are real!

TROUBLE MAKER ANTNEY

And then there's Antney. You're wondering why Little Antney is causing so much trouble in school and they want to kick him out. He's beating up on other kids and being sassy to the staff. He's rebellious and don't want to obey and he embarrasses you out in public. You better get a hold of Antney while he's young. Society blames Antney's behavior on the fact that a single parent is raising him. That's no excuse.

No parent is alone raising a child. Jesus can help you raise your children. God has already given instructions on raising our children. And His way is the right way, but the world we live in think that God's ways are too strict.

DISCIPLINE BY DEED OR WORD

Proverbs 29:15 says **The rod and reproof give wisdom: but a child left to himself bringeth his mother to shame.** Your kids are about to drive you crazy. The 17th verse tells us to correct thy son and he shall give thee rest; yea, he shall give delight unto thy soul. There are two ways you can discipline your child and that is by word or by deed. Society has told us that if we use the rod it is considered child abuse.

I recall my older siblings telling me, "you better be glad you wasn't around when granddaddy was living because granddaddy didn't take no smack." Yes, back in those days nobody took any smack. When you disrespected your elders back in the days you would either get it coming with a paddle, a tree limb, a belt, a cord or even a pop on the mouth. But it would be such a discipline that you would never forget that would cause you to get your act together and never do it again. The schools can't even discipline kids by deed anymore. Nowadays any type of discipline by deed is called child abuse.

Proverbs 23:13 tells us to **Withhold not correction from the child: for if thou beatest him with the rod, he shall not die. Thou shalt beat him with the rod, and shalt deliver his soul from hell.**

God says the rod is not going to hurt your child, it will save them from an untimely death. The ugliest thing to see is a teenager being sassy to their parent. That teen is not too old for the rod by deed. Yeah, they can use it right on the mouth and I guarantee you they won't give you any more lip service. The respect level amongst our young people has gone down hill. But they are never too old to get zapped. You better get them straight while there is hope.

Some of them that are left undisciplined go off into their own thing. Before you know it they become involved in gangs, occults, etc. You can tell when they are involved in something they shouldn't be in. Their attitude change. They change their looks according to whatever group they hang out with.

Some of them dye their hair every color in the rainbow. Some got tattoos every where on their body while others adorns themselves with body art to go on certain parts of the body that are pierced. Then there is the saggy group. Their faces look harder than a rock. They wear certain colors etc., that distinguish what they belong to. There is another group that wear death-look makeup, black attire, and their hair spiked jet-black. Everything about them is just black. Their appearance is a constant reminder of something out of Tales from the Darkside.

TOMMY THE DEVIL WORSHIPPER

And then the parents wonder why Tommy committed suicide. That's because those occult demons told him to sacrifice his soul to the devil. They probably lied to him by promising him a position of power in hell. But he was never taught that the Bible says the devil is a deceiver and a liar. He is a deceiver of the world and was a liar from the beginning and the Father of lies. The devil is always speaking to people's minds and he figure if he can get to your mind, then he can get your soul. That's all he wants is your soul and the chance to say hot steaming words of torment to you when you get there. What people fail to realize is the devil talks. He talks to the mind. He even talks to a Christian's mind, but they recognize him and immediately use their spiritual weapon against him. But Tommy had no spiritual weapons. Tommy didn't even have the power that the devil lied to him and told him he had.

Tommy was hanging out with devil worshippers. He listened to rock music forward and backward. And when he listened to it backwards strange things begin to take place in his mind. His wall was adorned with pictures of demonic looking people and as he listened to his music and smoked they would actually come to life in his mind.

One night while his parents were asleep, Tommy got a hold of some bad stuff and the demons began to speak suicide to his mind. Before he took his self out, he thought about taking his parents with him. But, it didn't happen. I guess it wasn't their time yet. Tommy didn't know enough about hell to know that it was a place of everlasting torment. He thought it was a place to go party and have fun. Tommy didn't know that Jesus was the way to eternal life and that he should have no other gods before him. He wasn't raise on the Bible. Had it been instilled in him, it could have saved him from hell.

BIG MONEY JOHNNY

And then there's Johnny. Let's not forget Johnny. Johnny is living a lifestyle of drugs and crime putting his family lives in jeopardy. He leaves the house wearing brand name saggy attire. Braids in his hair and a bandana hanging out of his back pocket or tied to his head. He carried a gun in his coat pocket. Riding around in a stretch limousine like he's the president of the United States.

But little did he know he was just a little ant getting ready to be stepped on. He keeps more greenbacks in his pocket than his parents. He hang out with the boys throwing up signs thinking he's all that. He even has a new walk. Street life has him looking twice his age. He's not even cute any more. He stole, he murdered and never got caught but it all caught up with him one day. Johnny got stepped on. Bang, bang, bang. A bullet went to his head, one to the heart and the other in the leg.

Yeah, the devil wanted Johnny real bad. Johnny wasn't taught the Ten Commandments. Thou shalt not kill. Thou shalt not steal. He didn't know he would one day have to pay the consequences for all the wrongs he did. He was left unrestrained by his parents. They didn't raise him up on the teachings of the Bible. If he had been taught, it would have saved him from an untimely death.

Violence does not discriminate at all. It can happen in an upper class community as well as a low class community. God will allow it to happen in an upper class community to take you off of your high. You try to move away from violence thinking it won't follow you. Violence can follow you to the mountains, to the country, or to a nice quiet community.

You better wake up! Your family is never safe without the blood of Jesus Christ, which provides divine protection for those who obey God's precepts. The devil is busy and he doesn't care about your hail, Marys and other ceremonial practices. He doesn't care if Larry has a 4.0 grade point average or that

Altheria is the secretary for the President of the United States. He doesn't care if you are rich or poor. He will use anyone that he can to carry out his plan. It is the upbringing on the principles of God and the blood of Jesus that the devil himself cannot override. When you've got Jesus you've got power.

The devil doesn't come in the image of a character with a pitchfork, horns and a long tail wearing red. His kingdom exists just like the world we live in exist. He comes in various forms. He is a for real spirit. A spirit that preys on the minds of people whom he can use to carry out his missions to kill, steal and destroy. He has a demonic host who sees to it that evil get her dirty work done. This demonic host is very busy and faithful to him in these last days. They know that time is of the essence and they have but a short time left to cause as much chaos as possible.

SPIRITUAL WARFARE

Ephesians 6:12 describes them as principalities, powers, rulers of the darkness of this world and spiritual wickedness in high places who are assembled for mortal combat. The trash society feeds to your kids depict these things. These principalities, powers, mentioned in this scripture are whom kids are wrestling with. And because the kids have no relationship with Jesus Christ they have no spiritual weapons to fight back. All they have is tangible weapons, which are guns, bombs, knives, etc. Tangible weapons cannot destroy the works of the devil. Spiritual weapons include the sword of the spirit, which is the Word of God that you can use to bruise the enemy's head when he comes your way. Let's not forget prayer. Prayer is your only means of communication with God. Through prayer you obtain power from God to command the enemy to keep his hands off of your family, etc.

This all may sound crazy to you but the Bible says that people perish because of the lack of knowledge. Some of these pastors need to get a revelation and let people know there is a spiritual warfare going on out there and these powers are trying to take out all they can to hell with them. It is time for people to get a relationship with Jesus Christ and put on the whole armour of God.

The whole armour of God is mentioned in Ephesians 6:13-18. There is too many people perishing and there are too many that are blinded by the truth. Time is of the essence. And it is time for you to know who God is and who the devil is. It is time for you to get out of those dead churches where there is no manifestation of God's power demonstrated to heal your problems, to deliver you from the bondages of satan and to mend your broken and trodden down hearts. Everybody wants to run to a family psychologist and psychiatrist when the answer is in GOD.

What kind of society do we live in today that when our children throw hints at us saying they are going to commit a violent act, only to get ignored? We are so busy we can't pay attention. You try to say there were no warning signs. But yes there are warning signs. You were just too busy and blind to discern them. We better listen and know that warning comes before destruction. The devil is putting these thoughts into people's heads and is causing them to act out what they are thinking and saying. God is not to blame for anything that goes wrong in our society. God will allow things to happen to get your undivided attention. God is a God of love, peace and joy. You pushed God away leaving room for the devil to have nothing but a field day in the school, homes, etc.

Its amazing to see that as soon as tragedy hits home, here come the what, how, why and when questions. What will we do with our kids? The answer being very simple is to start raising them on the principles of God as they are laid out in the Holy Bible only. How did something like this happen? I explained it from Ephesians 6:12. We are wrestling against the demonic hosts of the air. What the devil mean for bad, God will turn it around for good. Sometimes something will happen to get people's attention toward God. Why did it happen? God is trying to get the world's attention. And last but not least, when is it going to stop? And I will answer a question with a question, when are you going to put prayer back into the schoolhouses? Remember that you took God out, now you got to put Him back in and put the devil on the back burner. That's your solution. It's too late to tell Hollywood to cut back on violence in movies because the seed has already been planted. You are looking for solutions in all the wrong places when your solution is in GOD.

If you are one of those thinking that the children of today are the future leaders of tomorrow, if that is the case then we are in for a dead future. Unless we grab a hold of the principles of God and abide by them there is no future. What will God have to allow to happen to get the world's undivided attention towards Him? Will it take Him speaking to that comet, asteroid or meteor saying, "Go unto the inhabitants of the earth for they yet remain to be a rebellious people?" Will it take something that bad to happen even though it is already prophesied to happen? If you take a look at what's going on with the violence amongst our children today it is just

God's way of letting you see what will happen when you exclude Him out. It is Bible prophecy fulfilling itself. If you take a look at Matthew 24 and you see these things happening, know that the end is not yet. However, you asked for it! And it will only get worst. You haven't seen anything yet. And what you're really telling God is, time has changed, O, Great and Mighty One, you really don't expect us to live by the Ten Commandments, do you?

But, God says in Malachi 3:6, *I am the Lord, I change not.* God is the same today as He was back then and His Word will forever stand. He will not change His Word to suit your lifestyle. People think just because we are in a new day and age that the Ten Commandments no longer apply to us. Matthew 5:18 says that *till heaven and earth pass, one jot or one tittle shall in no wise pass from the law, till all be fulfilled.*

19th *Whosoever therefore shall break one of these least commandments, and shall teach men so, he shall be called the least in the kingdom of heaven: but whosoever shall do and teach them, the same shall be called great in the kingdom of heaven.* As you can see by those two scriptures that every letter and every scripture in the Old Testament is very important in the Bible and shall be fulfilled.

No matter how controversial the Ten Commandments may be to some, there is only one God. God is the only Supreme Being, no matter what your religion has lied to you and told you. God's Word is God's Word and God's command is God's command. Everything that He created that breathe the breath of life must obey His command up to the littlest jot and tittle. The Ten Commandments is not just another document that should be posted along with other historical documents just for decorations

153

in school entryways. It should be posted in every classroom and it must be imparted to the children in order to see change. We must take God's commandments seriously and do as it says. If your religion has a problem with obeying God then your religion is vain and useless. It's a waste of your time. They found every excuse in the world to keep those Ten Commandments out of the schools. If they opposed to having the watered down version of the commandments posted then you know the real version didn't stand a chance. They want no parts of God to begin with. Keeping the church separate from the state equals to more hell being let loose in our society especially in the schools. It's only Bible prophecy fulfilling itself. As we know, things must take place to lead up to the wrath of God being poured down.

It really does make a difference in a child's life when they have a god-fearing parent or parents who lives by the principles of God. My mother told me that when I was born my granddaddy brought me home from the hospital and he died a week later. I was the last grandchild. The question never dawned on me until now, what did granddaddy pray over me as he held me in his arms? I hear the word *"obedience."* The Lord is bringing to me how the patriarchs of old pronounced benefits upon their children <u>often near their own death</u>. Even if spoken by mistake, once a blessing was given it could not be taken back. Read Genesis 27.

I am reminded of the scripture that says if you obey the commandments and laws of God your seed will be blessed and their seed will be blessed. It's like a chain effect from generation to generation. I never expected God to reveal something like this unto me that my grandfather spoke a blessing over me near his own death. I knew grandmomma to be a saved woman of God. And dear mom is forever before God travailing for her children even to this day and those prayers paid off. Yes, I remember those days of being home and walking through the hallway eavesdropping on momma praying to God as she called out the names of each one of her children in prayer. And right now today all six are living and in good health. It is by the mercy and grace of God that I turned out to be who I am and what I am today and I am forever thankful for momma's prayers and for God's faithfulness to grant them.

As tears began to form this very moment, the Lord is bringing to my remembrance a poem I wrote titled, *Looking Over The Years*. Here is an excerpt that fit this very moment:

I didn't turn out to be a crackhead as you can see
Nor a prostitute out on the streets
A gangbanger I didn't turn out to be
Neither a pickpocketer, a murderer or a thief
There are a lot of things I didn't turn out to be
Thank God for His love, grace and mercy.
It was momma's prayers that helped me
It was God Almighty who didn't let me turn out to be
Those things that displeased Him.

When you come from a background with a generation of saved grandparents and a saved parent you can't help but come out a blessed child. I highly recommend parents and grandparents to start blessing their children and grandchildren especially at birth. Blessing is the act of declaring, or wishing favor and goodness upon others. The blessing is not only the good effect of words; it also has the power to bring them to pass.

155

I find that to be true that whatever you speak on your child will certainly come to pass. Mother prayed to God for one more child who turned out to be me even though she asked for a boy. But God had other plans. You know how in the Bible days when the women asked God for a child and He granted them their prayer and put a special touch on the child to do a work for Him. Mom would always tell me, "you're special" I prayed to God for you. God is going to use you, she would say. I could not understand what she was talking about and I use to ask myself, what is she talking about and why do she keep saying that?

The understanding did not become clear to me until I rededicated my life back to God and maintained an intimate relationship with God. He too told me I am special more than once as I am on my knees praying and all I can do is smile and remember that mother said it too. Mother knew exactly what she was talking about.

So between my mother, grandmother and grandfather, I could not have gotten away from God if I tried. Prayer kept His eyes and hands on me from since the day I was born. So, we need to start saying positive things over our kids and grandkids especially when they are born and rededicate them back into the hands of God. Pray the blessing of *obedience* over them and see don't they lead blessed lives. Blessing them will make a lot of difference in their lives.

OTHER GODS

The "In God We Trust" on the currency has become to the world "In Man We Trust." The Ten Commandments continues to be ignored. And speaking of commandments, I feel the Lord leading me to one in particular because there are too many people worshipping everything else but God.

Exodus 20:3 reads, ***Thou shalt have no other gods before me.***

4th ***Thou shalt not make any graven image, or any likeness of anything that is in heaven above, or that is in the earth beneath, or that is in the water under the earth.***

5th ***Thou shalt not bow down thyself to them, nor serve them, for I the Lord thy God am a jealous God.***

People are serving all kinds of gods: Buddha, Shiva, Ganesha, moon gods, sun gods, etc. They serve gods that can't even speak. People worship nature gods that are associated with rocks, trees, lakes, etc. God himself created those things and has commanded us not to worship anything beneath the heavens. I Chronicles 16:32 tells us that the sea roars, the field rejoice, and the trees of the wood sing out at the presence of the Lord. Even nature worship God.

DECORATIVE STATUES

The saved as well as the unsaved need to be careful concerning the statutes, etc., that we buy to adorn our homes. We must be careful about what we have in our beautifully decorated collections. They can be the reason why strange things are happening in your house. Some of these things have a background in idolatry worship.

Some people have in their homes for instance, a statue of Buddha. They worship this thing and it's only wood or ceramic. You worship a god that cannot save you. This figure can't even give you direction; it can't even warn you that the enemy is coming. He can't even heal you and yet you have him sitting in your living room, probably in an expensive glass case or a cherry oak stand. He can't do anything but sit where you placed him.

Isaiah 46:7 says, **They bear him upon the shoulder, they carry him, and set him in his place, and he standeth; from his place shall he not remove: yea, one shall cry unto him, yet can he not answer, nor save him out of his trouble.** He has no life. God is life. God is everything His people need him to be. God says in Isaiah 45:22, **Look unto me, and be ye saved, all the ends of the earth: for I am God; there is none else.** When God says to have no other gods before Him He means it. It is a commandment.

I Timothy 4:1 warns us, **Now the Spirit speaketh expressly, that in the latter times some shall depart from the faith, giving heed to seducing spirits, and doctrines of devils; speaking lies in hypocrisy; having their conscience seared with a hot iron.** Once again, what people fail to realize is that God is not changing His Word to suit the mess that they engage in. It's either God's way or no way at all. Before its all over with as it is said in Philippians 2:10, **That at the name of Jesus Christ every knee shall bow, of things in heaven, and things in the earth and things under the earth;**

11th **And that every tongue shall confess that Jesus Christ is Lord, to the glory of God the Father.** I couldn't imagine serving a God that couldn't speak. I couldn't imagine serving a God who couldn't deliver me in time of trouble. I couldn't imagine worshipping a God who can't protect me and warn me of things to come. I can't imagine serving a God that when I call upon him in the time of need he does not answer. But these things are not so, with

God Almighty, Creator of the universe and every living thing in it. The God of Abraham, Isaac and Jacob is very much alive today. The same God that walked and talked with Moses is the same God yet present in my life today.

Who is your god, today? Your god can be a statue, your leader, it can be a material possession such as money, your luxury car, your house, drugs, TV, or even your husband or wife. Anything you give more attention to and is more important to you than God is considered your god, or your idol.

Isaiah 46:9 reads, **Remember the former things of old: for I am God, and there is none else; I am God, and there is none like me.**

What the world fail to realize is God is God and He holds the world in the palm of His hands, everything in this world belongs to God, even money. God has power beyond your imagination. He holds the keys to life and death. You can continue to run, but you can't hide. God is awesome; He has eyes everywhere. He's watching you as you read this book, waiting to get your response today.

THE WRATH OF GOD

You hear talk about the wrath of God, but do we really know how serious it is? Talking about it is one thing but actually feeling it is another. I recalled awakening out of my sleep from a dream that left me praying to God, *"Lord please don't let me dream something like that again."* It was basically a nice day outside and I and about four other sisters in the Lord were all socializing in a room that had a big glass window where you can view the outside.

All of a sudden as we were sitting and talking it started snowing. It had to have been somewhere in the summer because we all got excited over it. It came at a time least expected. It started snowing heavily and then all of a sudden strong wind gusts started blowing at a high speed. And then it started thundering and lightning. I've never heard such loud thundering before in my life. It came down so hard that the world could split into pieces. It was horrible. You could hear and feel God's anger in the thunder. You would have thought the big glass window would have splattered all over the place by now, but it didn't. We saw all kinds of weather formation take place one after the other. It felt like what the scripture described as the powers of heaven being shaken. Only God has the power to do something like that!

The room started to tilt a little to the point where you couldn't keep your balance. I remember hearing someone say we need to get on our knees and pray. We knew by then that God was doing something out there and it wasn't pretty. It was so bad out there I could feel a rush going to my head. It was like a tightness or pressure in my forehead. I had to actually hold my head. You could actually feel the fury of God and that is not a good feeling at all.

As I think on the dream it brings back to my remembrance Luke 21:26, the scripture that says men's heart will be failing them for fear and for looking after those things that are coming on the earth. Sounds like its going to cause some physical distress to the point where people will go into cardiac arrest and high blood pressure will be rising, you name it. That's how bad it will be. Now is the time to get covered under the blood of Jesus Christ.

Joel 2 describes the Day of the Lord during the time when God pours His wrath down as being a day of darkness, a day of clouds and of thick darkness. It is a day as has not been ever the like, neither shall be any more after it, even to the years of many generations. He says let all of the people of the land tremble for it is nigh at hand. Some physical disturbances had taken place wherein the earth quaked, the sun and moon darkened, the heavens trembled and the stars withdrew their light. For the day of the Lord is great and very terrible and who can abide it? I'm telling you in the dream and in another dream the Lord gave unto me concerning His wrath I thought my head was going to explode. You had to have been mighty strong to withstand something like that. Verses 2 and 11 mention "the strong." This is a reference to God's people. The only people that I know that will be strong and who executes (carry out) God's word is God's people. The righteous has supernatural protection from God's wrath. The "seal" is their escape from the wrath of God.

If you are not on God's side you better get there. You better get there as quick as you can. Like I said above, the snow came at an unexpected time of the year. We can say the same for God's wrath. It will come when least expected. It shall come and serve justice on the wicked, disobedient, unbelieving and rebellious ones. The reason why that big glass window didn't break was because we were seal-proofed. You hear of glass being weather proofed but I tell you even a weather proof glass could not have stood what was going on outside. If you would have been a sinner in that room the glass window would have broken and you would have been too through because you did not repented of your sins and lived according to God's Word. We had the seal of God upon us and He therefore recognized us as His own. Only the righteous will be able to escape the wrath of God. God actually protected us in that room because He recognized us as His own.

Now I see why the scripture says that people will be hiding in the cleft of the rocks. Revelation 6:15 tells us that people hid themselves in the dens and in the rocks of the mountains. And said to the mountains and rocks, fall on us, and hide us from the face of Him that sitteth on the throne, and from the wrath of the Lamb;

For the great day of His wrath is come, and who shall be able to stand? The pressure from His wrath will cause a person to go into cardiac arrest. It will cause your high blood pressure to rise. You think you got perfect health now, if you're still not saved by the time His wrath comes I guarantee you about six different health conditions will have come upon you by the time you experience something like that.

In the other dream, even as I felt myself coming out of it I had the worst feeling in my head and as I proceeded to arise out of my bed it subsided. You see God's wrath is for real people and is no joke. It is time to repent. I tell you like the voice of one crying in the wilderness to repent for the kingdom of heaven is at hand. I am preparing you in this book for you to get your house in order so that when He comes back He can receive you unto Himself.

Romans 1:18 reads, **For the wrath of God is revealed from heaven against all ungodliness and unrighteousness of men, who hold the truth in unrighteousness.** Here, man is yet condemned because truth is given unto him and he by his actions rejected the truth. I have done my part by speaking nothing but the truth to you throughout this book with scriptures to back me up. You've heard the Word, now what will you do with it? Will you receive it or reject it?

For God so loved the world that He gave His only begotten Son, that whosoever believe on Him shall not perish, but have everlasting life. God doesn't want you to perish. But, if you continue to reject God, in hell will you lift up your eyes and your master satan will laugh in your face and perhaps say to you, you should of taken heed to God's servant when you read the book, *Visions of God's Coming Judgments.*

Yeah, I gave her a hard time as she wrote it, putting every obstacles and hindrances in her way to keep it from going forth. She stayed on the wall because she knows who God is. I used whatever weakling I could find in the midst to try to cease her work. But she knew she had victory over me. She was obedient and faithful to her God and kept on writing. God gave her the revelation and she passed it on to you and you didn't want to believe. You listened to me instead and your heart I did deceive.

So, don't get taken in by the spirit of deception. Take the people in the cult for example. When Hale (hell) Bopp made its grand entrance; even they sensed something about the comet. But the devil tricked them. They were receiving information from another spirit realm and got tricked out of life eternity. They got the wrong revelation from the kingdom of darkness. Deception is what you call it. What a waste!

There is no way possible you can commit suicide and get a one way ride to Heaven's Gate in a spaceship. One of the Ten Commandments tells us, Thou shalt not kill. According to Revelations 21:8 murderers cannot enter into the kingdom of God. Suicide is murder and once you commit this sin, you have no time to repent; however it will land you a one way ticket to Hell's Gate. And God does not deal in zoom me up scottie spaceships to bring you to Heaven's Gate. When the righteous die, his or her spirit ascends into the bosom of Abraham which is paradise and there they rest. Only the righteous shall enter in. Only the righteous.

WAKE UP CALL

It's time for America to wake up and see the signs around them. God is speaking to you in so many ways. He sees you in your sin. The devil has you so blinded about your soul, salvation and hell. He knows he only has but a short time left before God sentences him to the lake of fire. Right now, he is busy trying to steal, kill and destroy all he can to take with him. He's blinding the minds of people, making sin look good, making you think you got plenty of time to repent. Revelation speaks of satan having only but a short time left, so if his time is short, what make you think you've got plenty?

Jesus is standing with outstretched arms to receive you into His fold today. Ask Him into your heart today before it's too late. In that great and terrible day of the Lord, men shall be running to and fro, there will be no where to hide and certainly no place to go. Who will be able to escape the wrath of God? Only the righteous, you see.

LEFT BEHIND?

The world has been ignoring God for generations. I hear different debates on who will be *"left behind"* after the church is caught up. If you knew the God that I know you would know that He is a loving God.

164

He would that no man should perish but have everlasting life, therefore He uses others to get His message across to warn people. Some will take heed while others will remain in their sin. God is going to give everyone a chance to repent even until the end. So we can stop going around prophe-lying saying that the lukewarm and sinners will be left behind. That is not true. The only ones that will be left behind are those who after seeing the power of God being demonstrated by Him sending down the plagues of locust, grievous sores, scorching heat, darkness and yet they repented not. Instead of repenting while they had the chance, they remained rebellious, blasphemed God even the more and refused to reverence Him. Rebellion is as the sin of witchcraft, and stubbornness as iniquity and idolatry.

Just like the people in the movie, Titanic. They were out in the middle of nowhere, they knew they were doomed. Even as the boat tilted, they partied and drank until they sank. Nobody was thinking about God. They wanted to get their last party in. It's no different today; some people see the signs around them and still won't repent. They know that the end is near and Jesus is coming. They keep holding on to sin.

Some of you reading this book, if you could see into the spirit realm you would be able to see yourself hanging off the edge of a cliff by a thread. You are hanging by a thread not a rope. Some of you who are getting this message, it might be your last chance; there may not be a tomorrow for you. God is giving all a chance but there will be some that will harden their hearts until the end and not take heed. The Bible says that these are the ones that will be cast over into the lake of fire with the devil, the antichrist, and the false prophet. These will be the ones that will be *"left behind."*

Revelation 21:8. ***But the fearful, and unbelieving, and the abominable, and murderers, and whoremongers, and sorcerers, and idolaters, and all liars, shall have their part in the lake, which burneth with fire and brimstone: which is the second death.***

And then Revelation 21:27 tells us that there shall in no wise enter into the kingdom of heaven anything that defileth, neither whatsoever worketh abomination, or maketh a lie: but they, which are written in the Lamb's book of life.

If you are one of those who say, well, the scripture says all I have to do is believe and that will make me saved. I can believe and still hold on to sin. I must tell you that *believing* carries a deeper meaning. It means "to adhere to, to accept and to trust. You have to believe on Jesus and the Father who sent Him. John 5:24. Believing means you got to adhere to and abide by the Word.

I John 5:10 says ***He that believeth on the Son of God hath the witness in himself; he that believeth not God hath made him a liar; because he believeth not the record that God gave of His Son.*** You got to believe the Bible and every account that was given of the Son from the beginning to the end and obey the commandments. If you don't abide by His Word then that makes you an unbeliever. Whosoever believes that Jesus is the Christ is a born-again child of God. And everyone who loves the Father also loves the one born of Him. By this we come to know that we love the children of God: when we love God and obey His commandments. The true love of God is that we do His commands and these commands are not burdensome or oppressive. Living for God is not boring like some may think.

According to I John 2:3, if you don't keep (practice, observe) His commandments, you don't even know Him. You just know of Him. He that says he knows God and keepeth not His commandments is a liar and the truth (of the Gospel) is not in him. He who keeps His word, in him truly is the love of God perfected: by this we know that we are in Him. The 6th verse tells us that whoever says he abides in Him should walk and conduct himself in the same way in which Christ walked and conducted Himself. There are too many out there talking that talk and ain't walking it. Yes, they will talk that Jesus talk but their walk is all crooked and they ain't fooling nobody but themselves. Luke 6:46 says why call ye me Lord, Lord and do not the things that I say.

SIGNS OF THE TIMES

Now is the time to get your soul right with God. The Book of Revelation is unfolding before your eyes. The signs of the end-times are more intense than ever now. And the Bible speaks of some of these signs being such as:

> ➤ technology increasing in Daniel 12:4,
> ➤ falling away from Bible truth in II Timothy 4:1-4
> ➤ denial of creation in II Peter 3:3-6
> ➤ increasing crime and evil in II Timothy 3:1-5
> ➤ children being disobedient to parents in II Timothy 3:1-5
> ➤ men will have power to destroy the earth in Revelation 11:18
> ➤ heresy, apostasy in II Thessalonians 2:3, II Peter 2:1,2 and I Timothy 4:1-2

➤ false christs and false prophets in Matthew 24:24
➤ deceptive miracles in II Corinthians 11:13-15
➤ change in weather pattern in Matthew 24:7
➤ moral deterioration in II Timothy 3:1-5
➤ and many more.....

The amazing thing about all of this is when you see these things come to pass the end is not yet! There are rumors that Jesus is back on earth in human form. He is here, but not the way the world expresses it. The next time Jesus appears on earth, the Bible expressly tells us that He is coming on the clouds with power and great glory and He shall send His angels with a great sound of a trumpet. Matthew 24:30. Beware not to let any man teach you different. If someone approaches you and say he is Jesus Christ you better run as fast as you can. If they say He is downtown don't believe it; if they say He is at the local mall in your city don't believe it. If they say He is at the convention center don't believe it. But rather believe and know that He is in your heart.

Another sign of the end-time is fear, distress of nations and there shall be signs in the sun and in the moons, and the stars; and upon the earth distress of nations, with perplexity; the sea and the waves roaring. Men's heart failing for fear, and for looking at those things, which are coming on the earth: for the powers of heaven shall be shaken.

These are just a few signs to let you know time is drawing near. ***These are the end-times.***
Matthew 16:2,3 tells us, ***When it is evening, ye say, It will be fair weather: for the sky is red. And in the morning, It will be foul weather to day: for the sky is red and lowring. O ye hypocrites, ye can discern the face of the sky; but can ye not discern the signs of the times?***

168

chapter

7 *A Message To The Godly*

As I finished my spirit led research concerning stars; the Spirit of the Lord was upon me as He ministered to me on my knees. He told me to tell His people, those who are faithful and have lived by His commandments and laws, *"When you see these things come upon this world, do not be afraid. It is Bible prophecy and it must come to pass. As I have said in My Word, I will never forsake thee, I will keep thee, hold on, it won't be long."* He went on to say, *"Be ye ready, for ye know not the hour the Son of Man cometh."* He's coming in an hour you least expect.

In other words, get your house in order. He says, he's pouring out His blessings and opening doors for those who have been obedient and who have sought Him diligently. This is the time of rejoicing, the time of Jubilee! What they've been saying will happen for years is finally about to happen. Jesus is coming very soon. Watch, pray, and be sober. See the signs around you. Now is the time to get excited for the Lord. Get excited for the Lord, I say!

God's eyes is on the church as a whole and individually. The church is plagued with a lot of division, different beliefs and sin. The church is not on one accord. Jesus is not coming back for a divided and unfaithful church.

ADULTEROUS CHURCH

Spiritual adultery has plagued the church. The church has committed spiritual adultery breaking off the marriage covenant with God by going back into sin, doing those things God has forbidden. The church has become unfaithful to God.

The church so comfortably sleeps around with the enemy to the point that she has fallen into a spiritual deep sleep and needs to be shaken out of it. Just about anything goes in the church now and they say it's okay to do this and it's okay to do that. You compromise the Truth. When you hear the Truth it goes in one ear and out the other. You've forgotten God in so many ways and have fallen into your own beliefs and following after the doctrines of men.

Living by God's precepts is too strict and boring for you, so you do just about whatever you want to do and call yourself a child of God. You look at the sinner man and in your blinded eyes he seems to be having fun. You then follow suit in doing the things that the sinner man does. Just like Judah saw her sister Israel sinning, so they sinned also knowing the consequences they would have to pay for being disobedient to God. Like they say what monkey see monkey do. You see your sister or brother sinning knowing that God forbids it, and yet you do it also being fully aware that it carries punishment.

It's time to come back to God, O, backslidden church for your harlot days are numbered. Have you forgotten that judgment shall first begin at the house of God? Who can stand a bill of divorcement from God in troubled times like these? The church needs to get "REAL" with God. You have the audacity to talk down on the children of Israel. The church world today is just as stubborn and disobedient and is in no better shape. You are full of complaints. You act as if God does not exist. Where is your faith and trust in God?

Spiritual adultery carries a punishment. If you disobey God, you will have to pay the consequences. When you get in trouble who can you call on? Will you call on the god of your sins? I would think not because he has no power. Or will you call on God Almighty that you disobey knowing that He alone is the only One that can deliver you? The answer to the question is you will go straight to God Almighty.

GET YOUR HOUSE IN ORDER

When God expresses the fact that He wants His people to get their house in order, He is saying to re-examine yourself. Are you really living by God's every precepts? And if you're not, God wants to know, why call ye me, Lord, Lord, and do not the things that I say? Why are you committing all kinds of sin when He has instructed you not to in His Word? And then call yourself a child of God!

If you say you're saved, then God wants you to act like it. He wants you to come to the realization that you can't do what you want to do and live how you want to live and call yourself a child of God. You have one foot in the church house and the other foot out in the world.

And God told me to tell you **IT WON'T WORK!**

Just because you are a Christian don't mean you are saved. Just about anything fits under the category of the word "Christian" today. God says, Be not conformed to the things of this world; but be ye transformed by the renewing of your mind, that ye may prove what is that good, and acceptable, and perfect, will of God.

171

COMPROMISING CHURCH

Nowadays there are so called saved people that try to justify their sin because they don't want to give it up. A good example is drinking wine. You try to find all kinds of excuses to drink wine because you don't want to give it up. You say, oh they drank it in the Bible days and another excuse you use is, well, the Bible says that it's okay as long as you don't get drunk. Proverbs 20:1 reads, **Wine is a mocker, strong drink is raging: and whosoever is deceived thereby is not wise.** Hosea 4:11 says, **Whoredom and wine and new wine take away the heart.** Wine will cause you to err. It will cause you to turn your back and not consider any of God's ways and to neither consider the operation of His hands in mercy and judgment. Yes, the devil got people fooled thinking it's okay to take a little sip. Even when you do a little sip, you have already erred. Point blank and simple, the Bible instructs us to put off the old things that our old man use to do!

I must say with time being as short as it is why take a chance? It would be wise for you to get a Bible dictionary or other Bible helps and do some in depth historical research on the wine used back then, and stop listening to Sister Know-It-All and Brother Compromiser and get the revelation for yourself. I will leave with you Isaiah 5:22 which says, **Woe unto them that are mighty to drink wine, and men of strength to mingle strong drink.**

SHACKING UP

Another issue we need to look at is "shacking up" and we all know what that is. It is a couple's way of testing each other out before they consider marriage or it can simply be one mate's way of saying this is as close to marriage as our relationship will get; I really don't plan on being tied to you forever. God does not condone shacking up. He has already laid down principles concerning marriage and everyday living. And God does not condone common law marriages. It is a man made fix up and is not scriptural. If you would seek God and wait on Him to send you the right mate, then you wouldn't have to worry about if he or she will turn out to be a fatal attraction or a hand that rocks the cradle. You won't have to worry about whether your marriage will turn out to be a nightmare on whatever street you live on. If you wait on God, He will send you the right mate.

In today's world there are saved people sleeping with their boyfriend or girlfriend and will get mad if you tell them it is wrong. It is wise to be led by the Spirit of God when you confront anybody with his or her sin. Speak the truth in love. In all reality you are trying to help them out because time is too short and that sin issue is causing them to miss Jesus.

Now, if a saint has a scripture to back them up against a person's wrong; then God has already mentioned in the Bible that the scriptures is for reproof and correction, for instruction in righteousness. With that said in the scriptures, a saint has permission from on High to correct and to reprove. Remember that you must be led by the Spirit. The church needs to wake up because time is too short. For the Lord himself will descend from heaven with a great shout and with the trump of God. Instead of you getting caught up to meet Jesus in the air, you'll be getting caught between your dirty sheets. And believe me there will be no dirty laundry in heaven. Don't even think about sneaking through the gates or climbing over the walls. That's a no, no.

173

The Bible says in I Corinthians 7:9 to the unmarried, *if you cannot contain* (self-control) *yourself then by all means get married. It is better to marry than to burn.* People will try to use all kinds of excuses to hold on to their sin. They will say, well, nobody is perfect and the Bible says that we were all born into sin or we all have sinned and come short of the glory of God. What it all boils down to is you need to know when to use the scriptures and how to rightfully apply them. The closer we get to the end of the age, people from the pulpit down to the laymen have become immune to saying the phrase, nobody's perfect. It's the biggest excuse in the church today. Some of you know better. Try telling it to God on Judgment Day and see what happens. I must say unto you that Galatians 5:16 says *to walk in the spirit and ye shall not fulfill the lust of the flesh.*

The works of the flesh are as follows: adultery, fornication, uncleanness, lasciviousness, idolatry, witchcraft, hatred, variance, emulation, wrath, strife, seditions, heresies, envyings, murders, drunkenness, revellings, and such like: of the which has been told to us before, that they which do such things shall not inherit the kingdom of God.

In order to keep your flesh under subjection, you must fast, pray and stay in the Word. Pray in the spirit on a daily basis so you will have power to resist temptation. As it is said, no prayer, no power. Much prayer, much power. Crucify the flesh through fasting and prayer. Learn how to say "no" to the flesh. There is too much compromising amongst God's people. If you compromise you jeopardize.

A *saint* who is described as a person living an upright life, being rooted and grounded in Christ, can look temptation in the face and say nothing shall separate me from the love of God. They can shout the

174

victory. When the devil says boo to a saint, the saint says boo back and some more; but when the devil says boo to a weakling, he is easily driven like the wind and goes back into his old ways. He is not rooted and grounded in Christ.

Right now is the time to get rooted and grounded in Christ and established in the faith. What some of God's people need is that something deep down on the inside of them that will make them do right when they want to do wrong. That is the Holy Ghost. Yes, temptation will come our way, but we are not to give in to it. We have the power to overcome temptation.

And a lot of it is not temptation, it's just willful sinning and being disobedient to God. Yes, God forgives sin, but people have taken God's grace and mercy for granted far too long. Here you are dipping and dabbing in and out of your sin and you keep saying to yourself, God will forgive me. One day God is going to cut you off and you won't have a chance to repent. God is no one to be playing around with.

Hebrews 10:26 says, ***For if we sin willfully after that we have received the knowledge of the truth, there remaineth no more sacrifice for sins.*** When you willfully sin, you are telling God: God I hear what you are saying, but times have changed and I don't see anything wrong with what I'm doing.

The excuse very commonly used is, it is hard to get rid of my sin. I must say unto you that you have been taught that nothing is too hard for God. You know that if you take your situation to God that He will help you. You don't want God's help. No excuse whatsoever will get you pass the judgment seat and into the kingdom of Heaven. When you sin persistently and you know the Truth, you are putting yourself in opposition to God, setting yourself up for the judgment.

UNEQUALLY YOKED

The Bible tells us in II Corinthians 6:14 to be ye not unequally yoked together with unbelievers: for what fellowship hath righteousness with unrighteousness? What communion hath light with darkness? There are saved people who are all out in left field with their own meaning of this scripture because they just got to have Joe or Bonnie.

When two people are equally yoked in God's eyes they are in one accord. When you are on one accord you can see eye to eye on things and therefore you can come to an agreement on issues that arise.

If you are saved you have no business marrying or courting someone unsaved. By all means please be a light unto that person and let him or her know where you stand in Christ and what God requires of you as a single person. Don't bank on that person getting saved after you marry them. It is a trick of the enemy. Please take a cold shower and wait on God.

If you are an entrepreneur you have no business having an unsaved partner. What kind of agreement can you ever come to without the two of you bumping heads? God may be guiding you in one direction concerning the business that the other can't comprehend and therefore conflicts evolve. You are operating in faith and the other one isn't. And that does not mix very well.

Here you are: the cash flow is low, leaving the open to buy tight and God tells you to order, so you order, but the other partner thinks you are crazy. Crazy isn't the word for you. He or she doesn't know that the just (saved) live by faith. Know that the Bible tells us that whatever we set our hands to do is already blessed. But these promises as well as others only refer to those who are obedient to God's Word.

176

It all goes back to the blessings and the curses. The saved person falls under the blessings and the unsaved person falls under the curses. You try to put the two together as one and it will never work because they have disobeyed God already by being unequally yoked. God will not bless in the mist of disobedience. A repentance has to take place.

When you are unequally yoked, the one that falls under the curse is cursing the other person causing his or her blessings to be hindered. You wonder why things aren't working right, that's because you have disobeyed God. You know the scripture. You know it's not the will of God. You put yourself out of God's will and therefore find yourself in a predicament all because of the choice you made. You went outside of God's will. You asked for your troubles and now you have to pay for what you knew and did.

SEX BEFORE MARRIAGE

There is premarital sex and sexual immorality going on in the church house from the pulpit down to the members taking form in many ways. The preacher is sleeping with the missionary or molesting young boys. The deacon is going from sister to sister. As soon as a pregnancy pops up among the singles then comes the quickie marriage. It's cover-up time. Sometimes it's one partner's way of tricking or entrapping the other. Why marry someone who didn't think enough about you to marry you before you got pregnant? Desperation and lust will cause you to miss Jesus because you disobeyed the Word of God concerning these issues. People nowadays don't wait on God to make things happen. They go out and make things happen themselves. This is not the way God structured relationship and marriage.

He has laid down principles for the unmarried and married. Do you not know that your body is the temple of God? You are no longer your own. You have been bought with a price. Where is the fear of God? Do you not realize that God is a consuming fire? (Deuteronomy 4:24)

According to I Peter 4:17, **For the time is come that judgment must begin at the house of God: and if it first begin at us, what shall the end be of them that obey not the gospel of God?**

Jesus did not go around sleeping with Jairus' daughter and neither did Peter take unto himself Aquillas' wife named Priscilla. The Bible says that Jesus went around doing good. He went about preaching, teaching and healing all manners of sicknesses and disease. Jesus was doing the work of the Father. He was taking care of kingdom work. He demonstrated the divine nature of God by showing forth God's power to heal, deliver and set free. Jesus' number one priority was doing the will of His Father. We are to follow in His footsteps as He commanded in Mark 16:15, **Go ye out into the world and preach to every creature**. Set the captives free and open the eyes of the blind. The church has their priorities all mixed up. Winning souls seems to be the last thing on the list. The church is caught up in everything else other than the vision that God has set forth.

The Holy Ghost was prevalent in Peter's life. He preached the gospel of repentance and healed the sick in Jesus' name. Paul said in I Corinthians 2:4 that he did not speak with persuasive words of wisdom, but he demonstrated the power of God, so that the people's faith rested in the power of God. They and others were set forth as an example of what God is expecting out of the church. And that is to demonstrate His divine nature by putting on God-like qualities so that sinners may be drawn unto Him and by demonstrating His power to heal, deliver and set free.

The church is sleep and doesn't want to abide by God's Word. They are so caught up in other things that don't even have anything to do with winning souls. Hell enlarges itself daily and I wonder how many people that have gone to hell were actually pulled to the side and taught the message of salvation? God is going to hold the church responsible if we don't wake up and tell somebody about Jesus. If we take care of God's business, He'll take care of ours and give us the desires of our heart, but first we must obey.

SMOKING

Since we're talking about the temple and getting your house in order. Let's go into the area of smoking. Church service is over and people are outside smoking on church premises. You are saved and you smoke and don't see anything wrong with it. It is a saved person's responsibility out of love and as a child of God to show you in Romans 12:1 that you must present your bodies a living sacrifice, holy, acceptable unto God, which is your reasonable service. You may get mad or puffed up, but it is only because the truth has found your sin no matter what it is and the Holy Spirit himself is convicting you. You shall know the truth, and the truth shall make you free. After hearing the truth you are responsible.

Your leader should have enough revelation knowledge to let you know that your body is the temple of God. Every cigarette puff you take into your body is defiling the temple. You are abusing the temple of God.

179

The following scripture lets you know the consequence you have to pay for defiling the temple.

I Corinthians 3:16 says, **Know ye not that ye are the temple of God; and that the Spirit of God dwelleth in you? If any man defile the temple of God, him shall God destroy; for the temple of God is holy,** which temple ye are.

If your leader isn't teaching you this, God will use little bitty me to let you know smoking and anything else that is not of God that comes in contact with your body is wrong. You can be delivered from your addiction, no matter what it is. The question is do you want to be delivered?

What it all boils down to is some people don't want to be delivered from that which they are holding on to. They will find an excuse to hold on to their sin. Is hanging on to your sin, no matter what it is, really worth you losing out on the things that God has in stored for you?

Let us remember the scripture tells us that our body is the temple of God and we should not defile the temple. Our body is where the Spirit of God takes up residence. God is a holy God and He cannot and will not dwell where sin is. It is best now to seek the Lord while He may be found and call upon Him while He is near. One day you are going to call on God and He will not hear you. It's best to let Him deliver you now while He can be found.

Again, we must follow in Jesus' footsteps. And believe you me Jesus did not walk around smoking Benson and Hedges and neither is God sitting on His throne drinking white Zinfandel. Jesus set the example for us, in that He went around doing the will of the Father. Let the same mind be in you that is in Christ Jesus. A lot of things you are holding on to are causing you to miss out on God. You are jeopardizing those things that God has in stored for you.

The Bible says that if any man be in Christ Jesus, he is a new creature, old things have passed away and behold all things become new. The old nature is gone. You now have a new nature. Those things that you used to do before you got saved should be a thing of the past. You should not even desire to do those things anymore.

Again, Romans 12:1 reads, **I beseech you therefore brethren, by the mercies of God, that ye present your bodies a living sacrifice, holy, acceptable unto God, which is your reasonable service.** In I Peter 1:16 God tells us to *be ye holy: for I am holy.*

CUSSING

Some of you are letting your mouths do more than pleasant talk. God says in Ephesians 4:29 to let no corrupt communication proceed out of your mouth. There are people who say they are saved and have filthy communication coming out of their mouth. They curse. They talk that Jesus talk. They curse. They talk that Jesus talk. The scripture goes a little further down to say whatever comes out of your mouth should be that which is good to the use of edifying, that it may minister grace unto the hearers.

A lot of you are ministering a lot more than grace. You are ministering cuss words and a lot of you are ministering gossip. God says in Colossians 3:8-10 *to put off filthy communication out of your mouth and lie not one to another, seeing that ye have put off the old man with his deeds;*

10th *And have put on the new man (nature), which is renewed in knowledge after the image of him that created him:*

You can be delivered from cussing. All you have to do is ask Jesus to deliver you from it. When you become saved you are a representative of God and you must represent Him right. Have you ever in your lifetime been out in public with someone and they started doing something unseemingly?   And you repeatedly tell them to stop, but they keep doing it. All of a sudden you kind of let them go ahead of you because you don't want anyone to know they are with you. Well, can you imagine God doing that to you because you won't put off the old man? Your refusal to do so puts Him in the position to disown you because you are misrepresenting Him? He has instructed in the Bible to put off these old things and you refuse to, therefore you place yourself in the category with the children of disobedience. There is no place in the kingdom of God for disobedience.

PARTYING (REVELLING)
Galatians 5:21

There are saved people hanging out at the nightclubs, the comedy clubs and the jazz clubs. Instead of running to Jesus when problems hit home, there are saved people who will run to the jazz club to so call soothe their minds. When they have the blues and feel depressed they go to the comedy club to uplift their spirit. Your mind may get soothed or razzle dazzled for an hour or two, but when you leave that club, the problem is still there. You have a whole night left to toss and turn with worry and no sleep.
Jesus says to cast all your cares upon Him: for He careth for you. And He also says come unto me all ye that labour and are heavy laden and I will give you rest. He will give you peace in the midst of your problems. Not only peace, but a solution also.

We as saved children of God are to involve ourselves in those things that are healthy for our spiritual growth. We are to lend our ears unto those things that will edify our spirit man. Getting off into worldly entertainment does not edify the spirit man.

You hang out with the old crowd and then you wonder why you're having such a hard time and why God won't answer your prayers. You're compromising, that's why. The Bible says that if my people which are called by my name, shall humble themselves, and pray, and seek my face, and turn from their wicked ways; then will I hear from heaven, and will forgive their sin, and will heal their land. When you exercise the above then God's eyes and ears will be attentive to your prayers. God has told us over and over again that we as children of God are chosen and set apart for holy use and you don't want to hear that because you want to hang on to the old nature.

The devil has put into your mind that it's okay to do this and that. You make your own road rocky by being disobedient to God's ways. You are making life harder for you and it will continue to be that way until you sell out.

II Corinthians 6:17 tells us, **Come out from among them and be ye separate saith the Lord, and touch not the unclean thing; and I will receive you.** He also tells us in I John 2:15, **Love not the world, neither the things that are in the world. If any man love the world, the love of the Father is not in him.** When you become saved you can't hang out with your old buddies like you use to. You are suppose to let your light shine and show them the way to salvation. What fellowship does righteousness have with unrighteousness? What communion does light have with darkness?

183

Those places you use to hang out should be a thing of the past. If God tells you to go to your old hangout because He has a word for you to speak to someone there: by all means go and give what thus saith the Lord and get out of there. God could be testing you at the same time.

GAMBLING

Saved people are frequenting the gambling casino halls and playing the lotto and bingo. Some of them have the audacity to handle the financial affairs in the church. Some of them have the nerve to be on the Mother's Board. Some of them have the nerve to be leaders in the church. Some of them are singing in the choir and on the usher board. You name it! They want to try their luck; however, there is no luck in Christ. You are either blessed or cursed. Saved people have given a deaf ear to what God has spoken in His Word. God made promises concerning prosperity and finances.

He first of all says in Deuteronomy 8:18, *I give thee power to get wealth.* God will put moneymaking ideas in our heads and its up to us to act on them in order for Him to move. He also says in John 14:13, *"And whatsoever you ask in my name that will I do that the Father may be glorified in the Son."* In Philippians 4:19 He says, *He'll supply your every need according to His riches and glory.*

Now, what part of His promises did you not understand? Or where is your faith today? Is it in Vegas, Saturday night Bingo or the state lottery? Remember that according to Romans 1:21, the just shall live by faith.

PSYCHIC SAINTS

There are some saved people letting their fingers do the dialing to the 1-900-Psychic Hotline. Throwing away money that they could be sowing into God's kingdom. They desperately want a word from God. They want someone to prophesy over their life. They don't want to humble themselves before God in fasting and prayer for an answer. God takes too long for them. So they go to the psychics. They put their trust in the psychics instead of God. Horoscopes too.

The psychic phenomenon is spreading rapidly. The psychics hold conferences where they give seminars. You can even get a reading online. They get away on spiritual retreats. They have travel agencies where you can book mystical journeys. Witches have websites and online chat groups. They even lease out booths at area malls. They have swung into the marketplace promoting their products and services. Advertising enchanted jewelry, potions, games, etc. You name it. Mood rings, power beads, lucky charms, occult signets, magnetic bracelets, enchanted this and that. They advertise their jewelry by saying they release certain powers and energy.

When you see jewelry advertised as enchanted please know that "enchant" means to put a magic spell on. Saved people better watch what jewelry they are wearing around their neck, ankle and wrist. The same goes for some of these new teas, sodas and juices being introduced in the market. God releases His power from heaven and does not have to use worldly goods to show forth His power. If you need healing or relief from something, you don't have to look to jewelry for those things. Look to God. He is power. He is your source of energy. God is everything you need Him to be. He says, ***I Am that I Am.***

Psychic ability is an imitation of the gifts of the Spirit mimicking the things of God. The gifts of the Spirit that comes from God are the gift of discernment, healing, prophecy, word of knowledge, word of wisdom, tongues and miracles. These are gifts that the Holy Spirit imparts to individuals for the edification of the body of Christ. The devil imparts also and he has his own network of people deceiving people. They are using their talents out of their own natural human ability and God is not in it.

These psychics and other groups affiliated with them are being driven by powers of darkness and are getting their information from the kingdom of darkness. They are tapping into a spirit world of evil. Their gift is being used to the service of the devil to deceive others. Many people are being deceived.

Psychics studying the New Testament look to Jesus as the paradigm of a psychic. In other words they look to Jesus as one to whom they can pattern their own lives. Yes, Jesus did miracles and healings. The works that He did came by the divine supernatural power of God. God anointed Him with the divine supernatural ability to carry out His mission upon the earth.

The psychic group interprets Jesus' miracles in psychic classifications. For instance they see Jesus as a medium because of His communication with Moses and Elijah in Matthew 17:3. They view the transformation as a materialization and Mark 7:31 as a psychic healing and Matthew 12:22 as an exorcism.

The Bible gives us examples of sorcerers, etc., who tried to do their works in the name of Jesus and this misuse backfired on them. It backfired on them simply because doing it in the name of Jesus was contrary to the ways in which they practiced. They used spells, chants, and potions.

They saw Paul working miracles and people were being healed and the evil spirits departed from them. Read Acts 19. They took note of the fact that what Paul did in the name of Jesus brought about results much better than what they practiced to get results. Little did they know you got to have a relationship with Jesus Christ to get those types of results. The devil himself can heal and perform miracles, but they don't last. They are counterfeit works. Revelation speaks of him giving power to the Antichrist and the false prophet to perform lying wonders in the tribulation period. They deceived a lot of people during that time. The devil mimics the things of God. Just because you read about sorcery, magic and divination in the Bible does not mean it is of God. I believe God's purpose was to expose the works of satan and to let you know that these things are real and were forbidden and outlawed.

Upon viewing a commercial promoting a psychic hotline number. A woman was interviewing people who were praising the psychics for their psychic abilities. When the interviewer got to this one lady who was in tears, she asked her, Why are you in tears? She responded and said she was in tears because the psychic she spoke to gave her hope for the future. I couldn't believe my ears because only Jesus can give you hope for the future. *Deception, Deception, Deception.* They set these commercials up to be so convincing that a weak minded Christian is tempted to dial it up.

Man cannot predict your future. Only God knows you inside out. It was God that made you in the first place. Only God can see into your future because He is omnipotent and omniscience. He is all-powerful and all-knowing. If you need to know something He has invited you in Hebrews 4:16 to come boldly to

187

the throne of grace. And in James 4:8 He says to **draw nigh unto me and I'll draw nigh unto thee**. He's only a phone call away, 1-800-Heaven. The best thing about this call is, it's FREE!

Jeremiah 33:3 says, **Call to me and I will answer thee, and I will tell you great and mighty things which thou knowest not.**

Don't seek after other spirits from another spirit realm. You are opening doors for the enemy to come into areas of your life. It is not the will of God for you to seek after psychics, charmers, diviners, consulters of familiar spirits (mediums), wizards (spiritist) (witch), observers of times (astrologers). They all fall under the category of witchcraft. They have ties to the New Age Religion, which is nothing but a cult, a group of people that have strayed away from God and don't want to abide by the principles of God. They try to mimic the Bible and yet they are far from living it.

There are people right in the church who operate under these titles. Unless you are in tuned with God, you will not be able to discern these spirits. They are sitting right in the midst. In these last and evil days we need to be in tuned to God because satan is busy. He has his workers busy right in the midst.

I will leave you with an encounter I experienced in June of '99. I'll start from the beginning because I know God orchestrated the whole thing. About an hour before closing up at work, I developed a craving for hot wings. I began to debate on which store I wanted to get them from because my plan was to get three items and get out and take a straight shot home. The only store that would give me a straight shot home was the one I hated going to the most. I went anyway and picked up the last package of wings. I thought to myself, umm Lord you left the last package just for me.

I walked pass the checkouts examining which ones was the shortest and before I was down to two, a woman was standing in a line motioning to me to get my attention. I stopped to see what she wanted and she said, "Come here for a moment because I am picking up some strong vibes from you. Come here and let me talk to you." And once again she said she was picking up very strong vibes from me. She began to dig in her purse for something. She went on to say, I am a spiritualist, and I want to give you my card. I am a medium and I do readings. I then responded to her and told her I don't believe in that stuff because I am a child of God. When I said that, she said oh and began to back off.

You got to let the devil know who you are. When you say you are a child of God you have said a *whole lot* and nothing else has to be said. Those vibes she was picking up on was the Spirit of God inside of me. In all reality only God can tell my future. The best thing about Him is He isn't going to lie about it. As I went to stand in a line she then got out of hers and stood behind me, but she wasn't behind me for too long. Those holy vibes was too powerful for her.

In a matter of seconds she told me three things about her which all boils down to holding the title of a witch. All I had to say to her was I am a child of God. All she had to say was I am a witch. But no, they try to dress it up nowadays by using the words spiritualist, medium, palm reader, psychic, etc. They are all the same. Yes, God can deliver them just like He can anybody else. But they also got to know what the Bible has to say about them. According to Deuteronomy 18:10-14, **For all that do these things is an abomination unto God.** For the Lord thy God did not suffer the children of Israel to do so and neither does He suffer you to do so today.

GOSPEL MUSIC

Let's talk about gospel music. Ask me has gospel music gone too radical or off the deep end and I'll tell you, not all but some. All you need is the anointing of God in your life and millions will get saved. The anointing is what breaks the yoke.

We are now living in a day and time that when you turn the radio on during gospel hour you have to sit a minute and try to figure out if it's church music or R & B. In this day and time we are living in they both sound alike. Gospel music should be such as when you hear it; you will get that spiritual sound and that spiritual message that will bring about results in one's life.

How do you get that spiritual sound and that spiritual message that will bring about results in a person's life? That is through the anointing of the Holy Spirit. The anointing does not act worldly or unseemly. The anointing does not result in debates and disputes. The anointing is on a mission to heal, deliver and set free. Singing is a ministry. It is God using you to minister to individual needs through songs. When it is endowed by the anointing of God you will see people getting saved, burdens being lifted, chains being broken, people getting healed. You will see changes take place.

I recall hearing this song on a gospel station and the song stopped me dead in my tracks. The tune to this song was the tune from an old R & B song I had long forgotten about until I heard the tune of it in gospel form. As I stood there and listened to this song it did not usher me into the presence of God. Instead, it ushered me way back into my past when I was in high school. I actually had flash backs of my past. Now that's taking me backwards.

The Bible says to *enter into His gates with thanksgiving, and into His courts with praise.* But, how could I? I couldn't reach God in that song, I couldn't get that spiritual uplifting I needed listening to that song. Nowadays there are gospel songs out there that are doing a lot more than supposedly glorifying and edifying. And there are many more out there that sound worldly, making you want to do more than just meditate on God. Slow songs make you want to slow dance and the fast ones make you want to throw down like the world do. Psalm 100 tells us to **make a joyful noise unto the Lord.** Be in the spirit as you do it. If you're not in the spirit then your praising and dancing will appear to be just a wild performance.

According to Ephesians 5:19, we should be speaking to ourselves in psalms and hymns, and *spiritual songs,* singing and making melody in our heart to the Lord. I will share with you a portion of my poem titled, *Gospel Singers* that can be found in its entirety in my book, *Let the Holy Spirit Embrace You With Poems of Inspiration:*

> *Your music is sounding like the world*
> *You can hardly tell it apart*
> *Before you know it, you've hit the billboard*
> *Being numero uno on the chart*
> *Your song is on the airwaves*
> *And has hit every nightclub in town*
> *They're not listening to the message*
> *They're listening to the sound*
> *They're not getting the message at all*
> *And that is a crime shame*
> *All you're doing is pumping them up*
> *To do nothing but shake their thang*

The church world today has chosen to act like the world do, whoop and holler like the world do, rap and dance like the world do, when God has set before us principles to live by and has said, Be not conformed to the things of the world. There's more humping and bumping and sliding and gliding going on in the church world today than there is in the nightclub. The problem is when you pattern yourselves after the world when scripture tells you not to. And then there is the excuse that this is a new generation. My response to you is God is not going to change His Word to suit this new generation. Neither do you have to come down to their level to win them over to Christ. You don't have to change the way you look, talk, walk, or sing to get someone's attention toward God. You don't have to dress like a particular crowd to win them over to Christ. The anointing that you carry will win them over.

Yes, they danced in the Bible days. II Samuel 6:14 says that David danced before God with all his might. I guarantee you it was a *holy* dance. He wasn't in the presence of God doing the footwork and the rocking chair. These are just the names of a couple of the devil's familiar moves I received from the young folks. In Exodus 15:20 Miriam and a chorus of women did a deliverance dance with tambourines. I guarantee you it was a *holy* dance. The term *dance* in the Old Testament was a whirling motion. Nowadays, dancing is more than just a whirling motion. We mess up when we pattern our rhythmic moves after the world. Dancing can be portrayed as a sensual art form or an act of worship. Being children of God, it is portrayed as an act of worship unto the Lord. It's okay to do your victory and deliverance dance. It's okay to do your praise dance with the musical instruments, but is it holy unto God? Once again the

Bible tells us to make a joyful noise unto the Lord. But who are you patterning after when you bring into the church the phrases similar to, *"the roof, the roof, the roof is on fire"*, or *"wave your hands in the air and wave them like you just don't care?"*

We better wave them like we care because you don't just come into the presence of the Lord waving no any kind of way. In the midst of your waving, your hands could be throwing signs up to God without you even realizing it. You don't have to adopt worldly gestures. We must be reminded that there is nothing worldly about God. So we must be careful about how we go into the presence of God because God is a King in all of His majesty and is to be highly referenced in a holy manner as He sits high upon His throne.

The church has gone too radical
With their music and their songs
What an awful shame to think this is the only way
To reach the lost young ones
You make up all kinds of excuses
Saying this is a new generation
You better wake up and smell the spirit of deceit
And ask God for a revelation
The anointing, the anointing is what it takes
To cut through those rebellious minds
Not rapping, singing and dancing like the world do
Acting like a bunch of clowns
You see God is not in all that
He has His eyes on you
John 4:24 says God is a Spirit and
You must worship Him in spirit and in truth.

People have a misconception of what the anointing is. They think everything they hear is the anointing! Just because a person can hit a high note they think it is the anointing. The anointing has nothing to do with how long you can carry a note or how high you can go. The anointing is on a mission to deliver, heal and set free. There is a big difference in singing under the anointing and being born with the talent to sing. You can be a non-talented singer and the anointing can hit your vocal cords and God will accomplish that in which He set out to do through you. Whereas, a person with the natural talent to sing can sing and nothing happens.

Nowadays you have to be careful of who you listen to because some of these people singing gospel songs don't have a relationship with God. It's one thing to sing the gospel and live it and it's another thing to sing the gospel and don't live it. We must live what we sing and preach. There's no need in you trying to talk that talk if you aren't going to walk it. Make up your mind. Some do have a relationship with God, but at some point they have taken a wrong turn down Compromise Street. Conforming a certain way for popularity and money. Compromising to get ahead. All of a sudden their ministry is not about reaching people it's about fame and money. People can't wait on God to make them a success so they turn to man who will change things a bit and pull them away from God's standards.

As for this book or any other books I have written, I cannot let a publisher, etc come in and change anything about it, from the front cover to the words in print to the back cover just to make it sell or become a bestseller. God has ordained everything I write and you can't change what God has ordained to suit anything. If they don't think it's saleable then I being a child of God must press on because I know what the Word of God says concerning His promise of success. And He also says that whatsoever I put my hands to do, it is already blessed. Knowing that God is a God that cannot lie, I must stand on His word and wait on Him. That waiting process is what kills some of us. In our mind God takes too long. We must know that with God there is a time and season for all things.

The closer we come to the end, Compromise Street seem to be one of the most popular Christian hangouts. Their taking a wrong turn down Compromise Street does not give other Christians the right to single them out by name and look down on them. It does not give the Christian the right to go put on their robes and go into the judge's corner and condemn them to damnation. It does not give Christians the right to slander their names, to badger them and hang them on the cross and bury them six feet deep and sentence them to damnation. All because in your eyes they are wrong and in your eyes they are unfit. You seem to forget that there is hope. There is hope for everyone and God has the final say so on everyone. God is not through with any of us just yet. When you see people take a wrong turn pray for them. Don't slander their name. The Bible says pray ye one for another. Prayer changes things.

There are some singers who grew up singing in the church and singing for God did not bring in enough green backs, so some of them turned God a loose and are now singing for the devil. Using their God given talent to glorify the devil. Those who get nominated for awards on national TV have the nerves to let the word *"God"* form out of their mouth. Here they are living like the devil, with filthy lyrics and cussing in their songs and the first thing they say is I give thanks to God. What god is they talking about I ask myself? Because God Almighty does not endorse a work you carry out for the devil. It is not God who has rewarded you? Satan rewards you. You are working for him not God. There are some that are not living what they are singing. There are some that are confused. One minute they're singing gospel thinking they are doing God a service, but deceiving themselves and the next minute they're singing R&B. Some are singing both at the same time. You can't serve both God and the devil at the same time.

Why is gospel music under severe attack? We must remember who the master of music was in his days in heaven. Satan (Lucifer) at the time had built in instruments in him. In Ezekiel 28:13 it tells us that every precious stone in the Garden of Eden was satan's covering; the workmanship of his tabrets wast created. Can you imagine what a beautiful sight he was? He was the minister of music in heaven. Now he has crept his way into gospel music, oh yes he has and the church world is not being spiritually discerning at all. The devil had special privileges in heaven; he had wisdom and beauty. He lost all of those things and therefore attacks the church by attacking the minds of people because he once had wisdom. Creeping into gospel music because he was once anointed to sing. Deception is what you call it. And the church world is buying right into it.

I once heard a preacher say that the devil hasn't crept into gospel music. Well, it looks like the devil has given that preacher a pair of top of the line blindfolds. The devil has told the church to put rap in the church, put rock in the church, put jazz in the church, etc., but pattern it after the worldly sound.

God is a versatile God but He does not need worldly help. The Holy Spirit can give you whatever sound you need; however it will be unique and it will have that power to accomplish the work that God need to get done.

A Message To The Godly

We need to start letting the Holy Ghost take full reign in orchestrating, giving us the right beat, the right tune, the right notes, the right moves, etc. I guarantee you when we let the Holy Ghost take over we will see the anointing of God bring about a change in people with a New Kingdom sound.

Singers you don't have to conform
to how the world sings
For attention and for money
God will open doors for your music career
He will bless those he's anointed
The anointing is what brakes the yoke,
deliver and set free
The anointing is power to get results
And see miracles happen through thee
For God will make you rise to the top
Above all the rest
Put Him first in your singing and music career
And watch Him make you a success.

Gospel music is one of the most highly debated subjects in the Christian arena. Who's causing the uproar? The church folks. Who's behind it? The devil. God is going to birth a new sound into this earth that will cut out all of the debates, disputes, etc., concerning gospel music. God's sound is called a heaven sound or a kingdom sound. It is a sound that the devil can't touch. It is a unique and peculiar sound and has no worldliness about it whatsoever. There is nothing worldly about God or the things of God. Gospel music today has people disputing more over the issue of music than being focused on winning souls into the kingdom of God. And that's the trick of the devil. God is not in the midst of debates and disputes. He says to shun them.

197

GODLY DRESS

Not only do the church act worldly, but they look worldly too. I Thessalonians 5:22 tells us to **abstain from all appearance of evil.** Nowadays, you can't tell a saved person from an unsaved person. I Timothy 2:9 and 10 tells us to **dress in modest (decent) apparel, but which becometh women professing godliness.** God wants His people to wear the best and as you wear your best you must remember you are to set an example for the rest. Don't dress in a way that will draw negative attention to you, for it is very difficult to see the Jesus in you that you proclaim.

When we look at the scripture that says come unto me all ye that labour and are heavy laden and also the scripture that says if any man thirst let him come these two are invitations to the sinner man to receive salvation and eternal life. This is a heart issue not a dress issue. When we hear the popular phrase or cliché "come as you are", it takes the wrong meaning of inviting Christians to come to church wearing mini's, high splits, shorts, tank tops, tight attire, etc. It should be addressed to the sinner meaning to come no matter what condition your heart is in. If you are a drunkard, prostitute, drug addict and so on, come unto Christ and He will receive you as His own. Only they should be able to come and wear what they got and once they've receive salvation then comes the learning process which very well includes I Timothy 2:9.

Saved folks come into the house of God wearing anything. We are to set the example of modest dress for the newcomers. You are to dress in a manner that set you apart from the world. When you have been saved for some time you should know better. You should know by now that when you come into the house of the Lord you are entering into the presence of a King to offer up the sacrifices of praise and worship. You shouldn't come into His presence looking any kind of way because God is a King who sits on a throne surrounded by all of His glory and majesty and He deserves our best.

A godly man should not adorn himself with an earring in his ear. A godly man should not walk around with an open shirt with his chest all hanging out and pants about to fall off. He should not dye his hair every other color but the color he was born with. He should not over adorn himself with three and four gold chains around his neck weighing him down and ten rings on his fingers with his fingers about to fall off. Now, if the Holy Spirit is prevalent in your life, He will convict you and show you how to dress as godly men and women. He'll pull you to the side and say, daughter your dress is too low or son two rings are sufficient for you.

Some preachers try to be soft on I Timothy 2:9. I have a poem titled, Godly Women of Dress. It might convict you. But it has God's stamp of approval on it. If it's offensive to you then the Holy Spirit is trying to tell you something. Those of you who have a personal relationship with God know that the Holy Spirit does not cut any corners. He doesn't play and He tells it like it is. I'm just the obedient messenger.

If you are a child of God it is not modest apparel when the split in your dress or skirt is going in the direction toward heaven above your knee and your cleavage is going into the direction of hell for all to see. In otherwords, one is too high and the other is too low. If you have on an outfit that you have to keep adjusting as you wear it then you don't need to wear that particular outfit.

Ministers of the gospel and others who hold positions in the church such as altar workers, intercessors, ushers, etc., need to be extremely mindful of modest dress. In all reality you are representing God.

We godly women of dress need to lighten up on some things in the household of faith. You are dying your hair every color under the sun but the color that God gave you at birth. Your hair is red as the sunrise, gold as the sunset and blonde as the driven white snow. God has already given you an identity. Be happy with it. You are beautiful in His sight. A precious jewel. You are the apple of His eye. And that's all that matters.

Some of you have on red lipstick trying to preach the gospel and black nail polish trying to lay hands. You need to tone it down a bit. If the people out on the streets see you dressed like them, then your message will not be convincing. You wonder why people don't get saved in your church. That's because they look at you and see that you look and act no different from them. You are distracting their attention away from the Word of God that is going forth; therefore they leave the same way they came in. As you look around today, you can tell we are near the end of time because things are reversing back, especially with fashion and people are almost dressing the same way they came in. And that is naked. Even saved folks are wearing hot pants dressing like the world. You should have enough Holy Spirit in your life to come out of them.

God is calling for an order in dress among His people. You see time is whining up and God is getting ready to send some workers out on the field, but first if you are out there representing Him, you got to be presentable as holy women and holy men of God.

THE SYBILIZED CHURCH

Let us take a walk inside the church and this is what you'll see. There are some saved people committing carnal sins like backbiting, sowing discord, strife, envy, jealousy, hatred, holding grudges, unforgiveness, lying, etc. They are committing fornication and adultery. If Hollywood could come and take a back seat in the church they could cut a movie and make billions. The title of the movie would be *The Sybilized Church* because the Sybil syndrome has plagued the church.

There are all kinds of personality types and groups that can't seem to come together and agree on nothing. You have jealousy over here and party strife over there. You're disputing over issues concerning such things as the relations of men and women in the church, spiritual gifts, food laws, speaking in tongues, salvation, baptism, the fall of man, marriage, tithing, the resurrection of the dead, the Lord's Supper, etc. Just to name a few.

Instead of standing firm on what the Bible teaches about certain issues; one group is actually following the Bible, another group is believing their own way, and another group is going 50-50. And there are some that just don't believe a word in the Bible. We as the church are supposed to be perfectly joined together in the same mind. Is Christ divided? NO. We should be able to come together as one in agreement. Romans 16:17 says, ***Now I beseech you brethren, mark them which cause divisions and offences contrary to the doctrine which ye have learned; avoid them. For they that are such serve not the Lord Jesus Christ; but their own belly by good works, and fair speeches deceive the hearts of the simple.***

201

SPECTATORS

As we go a little further in the church, there you will find spectators on the bench. They watch everything that goes on in the church. They have a calling on their life, but God can't quite use them just yet because they are just sitting back watching; judging others and criticizing their ability to carry out God's work. *Judge not, that ye be not judged.* The spectator can't quite figure out why Sister or Brother So and So is praying for others, working the altar or prophesying. In the spectators eyes something is not right about Sister or Brother So and So. The spectator has this person all on the examining room table when they should be examining themselves.

The spectator sees too much and complains about anything they see that goes on in the church. The spectator whispers back and forth in church talking about people while service is going on and then have the nerve to pass notes while the preacher is preaching. Some things are just better kept said to yourself. You need a spiritual muzzle on your mouth.

The spectator seems to forget we all have three fingers pointing back at us. And back to the sister or brother that you have in questioning of his or her ability to perform God's work, my question to the spectator is have you not forgotten that God is a forgiving God? Your sister or brother can make amends with God at any moment and yes, God will turn around and use them for the perfecting of the body. If you have any type of relationship with God you would be able to sense the ways of God. You would know that God will use whomsoever will let Him. And secondly, God does not think like man and neither are His ways like man. If they were we'd be in a lot of trouble.

Time is short and God is on a mission to save, deliver, and set free. He uses willing vessels to get His work done. If you want to sit back and be a spectator in the midst, not fulfilling what God has given unto you to do, then He'll use someone else in your place. They will reap your blessings.

KNOW-IT-ALL

The spectator has a first cousin named "know-it-all. It must be something that runs in the family because the spectator is guilty of it too. They come in the church and sit back and read folks. It's not like they are operating in the gifts of the Spirit, but they are operating in the f-l-e-s-h. Instead of coming into the house of the Lord focusing in on God and tending to themselves, they come in focusing in on others. They try to figure people out and they try to read them by the expression on their face. Discerning folks in the flesh. They got what you call that know-it-all spirit and if they don't be careful it won't be long before they will have their own psychic network. They are going to find themselves using a crystal ball, reading palms, using tarot cards, giving seminars, handing out business cards and leasing out some space, perhaps at the mall.

The know-it-all spirit is one who knows everything there is to know about God. At least they think they do. But little do they know there are higher heights and deeper depths in God. And no man on this earth knows all there is to know about God. God is never-ending. Brother or Sister know-it-all has the things of God all down packed, so they think. You can't tell them anything because they already know. You will find yourself getting cut off, etc., trying to explain something to them.

203

SIDELINERS

The spectator is very much related to Sister and Brother Sideliner. Sister or Brother Sideliner is useless and fruitless in the midst. They sit idle, eat the Word and leave. Sister or Brother Sideliner goes around bragging about their calling but when the opportune time comes for them to operate in their calling they switch careers in a matter of seconds. There's a major league team of them in the church.

They will tell you in a minute God called me to be a prayer warrior, but when it comes time for altar call they just sit. They will tell you in a minute God called me to be an armor bearer, but whose arms do they bear but their own. They will say I'm called to preach or teach but as soon as they are asked to exhort they run. They have passed up many opportunities to the point where they are not asked anymore and then they have the nerve to get mad saying, "they never ask me to speak." They say God called them to do this and that but no where in the Bible has God set some in the church to be side liners.

TATTLETELLERS

Then there are the tattlers in the midst. Better known as tattletalers or tattletellers. They tell tales on their sister or brother. They run and tell everything. They are saying things they ought not concerning their sister or brother. They run to leadership telling on others in the church to the point where sometimes it turns into a lie in hopes to either get their sister or brother in trouble or make them look bad. Your motive can be a number of things, even as low as trying to get them kicked out of church. You need to be disciplined. If somebody say boo to you or hurt your feelings, instead of taking it to God you go crying to leadership. When will you grow up?

The Bible says your mouth must be put to a stop. You are corrupting the church with your lies and gossip and bickering. You're causing havoc and you need to be rebuked. Depending on whether it's a lie or the truth, you think you are doing both God and your leader a service, but God is watching and listening. He knows your motive. You too Sister or Brother Tattler needs a spiritual muzzle.

Know also that while you are tattling, backbiting, gossiping, and whispering on your brother or sister, be aware that God do reveal things by His Spirit. He reveals to His anointed ones. He has already spoken in His Word, Touch not mine anointed and do my prophets no harm. He means just that.

I want to say saints of God don't be so evil, but you can't even be called a saint because a saint knows better. A person that does evil does not even know God.

Third John 11 says, **Beloved, follow not that which is evil, but that which is good. He that doeth good is of God, but he that doeth evil hath not seen God.**

There are things that you tattle to your leader about that you can take straight to God yourself. Your sister may have an attitude problem with you. Well, all you have to do is rebuke that spirit that is on her and watch the Holy Spirit do a 360-degree turn around on her attitude. You'll be amazed.

Your brother may have offended you. The Bible tells you to go to that brother or sister. But you choose to go to the pastor, etc., instead. Your brother may have said some truth to you that convicted you in your spirit. Instead of you looking at it as a helping tool, you get all sensitive and run and tell.

The truth hurts, you know. There are some things you don't have to run to your leader about. He or she has enough responsibility on them already. Just get on your knees and pray and watch God move. The Bible tells us to pray ye one for another and also to love one another.

WHIPPING UP THE LEAVES

There is so much going on in the church world today and God is inspiring me to write these things so that we can be ready to meet Jesus when He comes. Jesus is not coming with the church world in the mess it is in today. There are too many spots and too many blemishes in the midst. He's coming for a church without a spot or blemish. A lot of mess going on in the church world today cannot enter into the kingdom of God. The sheep are scattered. Envy, strife and jealousy is in the mist. People are leaving churches on bad terms. They are not leaving with the right spirit. No amends are being made. Something is wrong. And you think Jesus is coming back with the church like it is? Where is unity? Where is love? Who is responsible for going after these sheep that have left the flock?

I am reminded of a dream that God gave to me one night. In this dream there was writing in the sky and I could not understand the language. I asked someone in my dream did they see the writing in the sky and they said, yes, and they interpreted what God had written in the sky.

He was saying, He's whipping up the leaves. The following day it came back to me, "He's whipping up the leaves." Then God began to give me a poem concerning preachers that are leading His people astray. The poem started out saying:

Woe! Be unto the preachers
that are leading God's people astray
Don't you know you will be held accountable
for that soul one day?
You're caught up in getting money
And you're caught up in politics
You're caught up in being in the spotlight for popularity
Do you not know that God's work
is not about you at all?
It's about winning souls into His kingdom,
so that they don't fall.

The poem in its entirety is long and can be found in my book, *Let the Holy Spirit Embrace You with Poems of Inspiration.*

As I wrote this poem, He brought back to me, *He's whipping up the leaves* meaning all foolishness and mess going on in God's house and in the church world today must come to a cease. In other words, He's cleaning house. He's sending a whirlwind of destruction through the church. God let me know that what grieves Him is what He sees going on in the church. He says that the Holy Spirit is going to expose some, if it means calling you out by name and exposing your sin. He'll do it! Don't think that He won't.

The Holy Spirit is getting ready to expose. If you're sinning and sitting in the pulpit, God is going to allow something to happen to you to get your attention, to steer you back in the right direction or to get you out of that pulpit. At the same time to expose you to the people and put somebody in charge that will let the people know that sin is wrong, hell is real and time is drawing near.

Even as I am near the end of this book, the Holy Spirit has already started taking the covers off of preachers. Preachers are already making the headlines in the local newspapers. They are being exposed nationwide for all to see. God's way of letting us know that what's hidden in the dark will surely be brought out in the light. Preachers are getting busted for picking up prostitutes, swindling God's money, videotaping beneath women skirts, vandalism of church property out of anger. Just to name a few.

The more background investigation they do on the preacher the more dirt they find. You'll find out he had a mistress on the side, too much sugar in the bloodstream, a history of criminal acts, et cetera. The most popular one today is priest committing sexual acts with young boys in the church. Leaves me wondering, where is the gift of discernment in the church? Well you say, nobody's perfect. True enough nobody is perfect, but why let Jesus come back and catch you in your shortcomings. Your shortcomings will certainly not make it into the kingdom of heaven.

When I read about these things all I can see is the hand of God getting ready to do some serious work upon the children of disobedience. And then as I read about these things it only leaves me wondering what kind of relationship do these people have with God? Because the God that I know, warns me beforehand that the enemy is coming to try to trip me up. The God that I serve warns me that temptation is coming and I got to handle this thing exactly the way He instructs me to in order to come out victorious. If you got an intimate relationship with God, He will prepare you ahead of time for the weapon that the enemy is getting ready to strike you with to try to bring you down.

SHEPHERDS AND THE FLOCK

God is heavy on the preachers more than anything else in this book. Why? It is because they are responsible for His sheep. You see when the head isn't right the body can't function right. It becomes dysfunctional. God's eyes are glued on the preachers. You know what you're doing is not right and God sees what you are doing. You are like unto the scripture that says, ***Woe unto them that seek deep to hide their counsel from the Lord, and their works are in the dark, and they say, who seeth us? Who knoweth us?*** And God's question to you preachers, prophets, teachers, evangelists, apostles in Jeremiah 23:23 is, ***Am I a God at hand, saith the Lord, and not a God afar off?*** 24th ***Can any hide himself in secret places that I shall not see him? saith the Lord. Do not I fill heaven and earth? saith the Lord.*** God sees everything. The eyes of the Lord are in every place, beholding the good and the evil.

Some of you are not teaching the people the truth and therefore their blood will be required upon your hands. The reason why some of you can't preach to the people about sin is because you're just as guilty of sin as they are. So how can the blind lead the blind? They all will fall into the ditch. Under false pretense you manage to run a church some kind of way.

Romans 10:15 says ***how shall they preach except they be sent. You have not all obeyed the gospel.*** Some of you fall up under disobedience because you have not been the shepherd God has called you to be. Some of you are not even called to preach you're standing in a dangerous position. You are not lining up with the Word of God in any of your teachings.

You are in that position because man set you there. You need to get a revelation from God as to where you are supposed to be in ministry. Just because your father is the pastor of the church does not mean you are suppose to take over when he dies or retire. That is tradition in the church. And speaking of retiring, there is no such thing as retiring in the ministry. Jesus said to occupy until He comes; however, some of you do need to step down anyway and let the real leader of the church step forward and fulfill his calling.

It is not man's place to set apostles, prophets, evangelists, pastors, teachers, etc., in the church. Who does? I Corinthians 12:28 says that **God has set some in the church first apostles, secondarily prophets, thirdly teachers, after that miracles, then gifts of healings, helps, governments, diversities of tongues.**

God put people in their proper places. God does the calling. God qualifies and equips. Some people call themselves into the ministry. They will hook a title to their name trying to be something they are not and go their merry way frequenting churches prophe-lying, testi-lying, teaching things that have no scriptural bearing and teaching doctrines of devil. They are far from the Truth.

Speaking of prophe-lying, God says that some of you are not even called to prophesy you're hearing voices from another spirit realm. You're saying, thus saith the Lord, when the word did not come from Him. God says sword and famine shall consume you because you're deceiving His people with a false vision. Many have gone astray and fallen in the way of Balaam hiring themselves to do religious work for personal gain being a perfect example of deceit and covetousness. The New Testament condemns the greed of all who are well paid to tempt God's people to compromise their moral standards.

PASTOR WANTA-BEES

Oftentimes you hear people say they want to start their own church. Sometimes I wonder do they know what they are saying? Its not like God has called them to be pastors but they want to do it anyway. There can be a number of reasons why they want to start their own church. Some look at it as a money making venture because they don't want to take on a job. Some just want that position of authority. Some people just have a problem being under leadership. They don't want to listen and they don't want to learn. They think they know it all and therefore feel like they are ready to take on this big responsibility. When in all reality God has called them to sit and be taught and nurtured for a long spell.

I must ask anyway, why put such a burden on yourself that God didn't give to you to begin with? I guarantee you if you took a survey of area pastors and first ladies they'd tell you that overseeing a church is not easy. God places those whom He knows are capable of taking on this type of responsibility. He places a special anointing upon them. This calling is not for everybody.

Yes, God qualifies and equips. But some people can't even manage their own personal lives let alone trying to oversee others. You better wait for the audible voice of God before you make a big step like that. As you can see from this chapter, God is on the preachers very heavy and He doesn't play when it comes to His flock. So think twice.

WOMEN PREACHERS

We know that with God all things are possible. However, there are churches that don't believe in women preachers. This has been a controversial issue for centuries probably because of what Paul said in reference to women keeping quiet in the church. Common sense will let us see that it carries a different meaning when you can look throughout the Bible and find women holding positions in the church. Instead of taking the time out to do historical research on a given chapter, people will take one scripture out of a chapter and run away with it, misinterpreting its true meaning.

The main controversy is women pastoring a church. God ordained man to be the head. In some cases when the head isn't man enough to respond to the calling then his better half steps forward and lead the flock. In some cases the suppose-to-be head hides behind the title, but does not fulfil it and the other half holds the same title and fulfils it. Question mark! The head will have to answer to God one day.

Now back to women preachers, throughout the Bible women held offices in the church. Miriam, Deborah and Anna were prophetesses. In Acts 18:26 God used Priscilla and Aquilla to explain "the way of God more accurately" to Apóllos the preacher. In Romans 16:1 Phoebe was a servant of the church, a deaconess alongside with Paul. We are all servants of God called to deliver the message of salvation. He has already instructed us to go ye into the world and preach the gospel. You don't have to have a title to deliver a message from God. Just make sure it is coming from God. Regardless of whether you are a woman or man, God will use whomsoever will let Him to deliver His Word.

God used a donkey to speak to Balaam. Do you think the donkey had a title other than the fact that it was a donkey? What amazed me with that event is that Numbers 22:33 clearly states that the donkey was a "*she*". If God opened up a donkey's mouth what make you think He won't open up a woman's mouth or even your own pet to speak a word. We must be reminded of who God is and what God can do. Anytime you are out on the streets witnessing, what do you call that? You are simply preaching the gospel of repentance. At least I hope.

The Book of Joel clearly tells us that God is going to pour out His spirit upon all flesh. We haven't even witnessed the great move of God yet. But when it comes, look out! Whether you are a man, woman, boy or girl, God is going to use you in a great and mighty way. God has used me to deliver several messages in this book to give unto you. And it has to get out before I explode. I know by now you have found sermons you can preach from this book. Tell me God won't use a woman to preach the gospel. As one preacher so plainly put it, in the natural, Mary carried the Word (Jesus) in her womb for nine months and may I add that she delivered a good message (Jesus).

MASQUERADE SECT

The Lord led me to II Corinthians 11:13-15. We must be aware that some are not who they say they are. There is a masquerade sect in the church world today. There are false teachers, false prophets and prophetesses, evangelists, televangelists, preachers, apostles, etc., disguising themselves as ministers of righteousness. Just because someone says he is an apostle does not mean he is a true messenger of God

213

or is sent of God.

Some are like the toy called the transformers. Just like the master of disguise himself, satan who can transform himself as an angel of light. How would you be able to discern these spiritual masks unless you are in constant communion with God? In times like these we need to be able to discern that which serveth God from that which do not. We need to know spiritually what is sitting in the congregation and in the pulpit.

At masquerade parties they have on their masks and nobody knows who's who unless you're just good with voices. Unless people get in their rightful places within the body of Christ, the Holy Spirit is going to host an unveiling party and everybody that needs unveiling will be there by divine appointment.

There are masquerade sects up in the Christian TV ministries being viewed all over the country. Some of these Christian empires get on TV and sponsor telethons begging for money. They beg for money longer than they preach the Gospel. As a matter of a fact you hear more begging and singing coming out of their mouths more than you hear the Gospel being preached. Even the faith preacher is begging. My Bible tells me I never seen the righteous forsaken nor his seed begging bread.

As for a child of God individually, he or she has no business going around begging folks for money. Especially going around to your fellow sisters and brothers in the Lord with your hands out all the time. Why don't you bless them sometimes? If you find yourself in the position of always begging then something is wrong! You always have your hand out but don't want to give. You are always on the receiving end. Instead of you allowing God to move upon somebody's heart to help meet your need, you go ahead of God trying to make the need get met. God doesn't need your help!

Luke 6:38 says, ***Give, and it shall be given unto you; good measure, pressed down, and shaken together, and running over, shall men give into your bosom. For with the same measure that ye mete withal it shall be measured to you again.*** Evidently your measure level is mighty low because you remain broke all the time. If you are applying the principle of giving in your life then this scripture leaves no room for begging. You've singled out certain people who you think got money and they have caught on to your bad habit and try to stay out of your path. Even your kinsfolk dodge you because you have a bad habit of begging. The scripture that says ask and ye shall receive does not mean for you to go around asking, it means for you to go directly to the Father, believe that He will do it and receive.

The Bible instructs us to sow seeds. Sow seeds in your time of need. It doesn't necessarily have to be money either. Give away something that you want and not something that you don't want. Possess a spirit of giving and not a spirit of stinginess. Stinginess will cause you to miss out on the blessings of God. God knows who is able and who is not and the ones you think got money usually don't. The only reason why they seem like they got so much is because God has given them peace in their situation; therefore, they lead a worry-free environment. Instead of going around speaking negative in their situation by saying, I'm broke" all the time, etc., they speak positive and stand on the Word of God concerning their finances, etc. They tithe and practice the principle of giving. They know God as Jehovah Jireh, their provider and when a need arise they go to Him because that's what He has

215

instructed His children to do. Ask and then watch Him move. Make the request known unto Him and He'll open up the doors.

If you find yourself struggling, then you need to re-examine yourselves. You need to ask God why and what do I need to do to get beyond this point? Some of you got so much sin in you; God won't even answer you directly, so He has to use someone else to deliver a message to you. You are your biggest hindrance. Your struggles can be there for many reasons. It can be due to disobedience to God. Your compromising and not being submissive to God can cause you to miss out on the promises of God. He promised provision for His people but the key is obedience. Some of you don't even tithe or give as the Word of God has instructed us to and you expect God to give unto you and to beckon to your every call. You think He owe you something. It doesn't work like that. Refer to II Corinthians 9.

We as children of God are supposed to display God's divine nature. Begging is not a part of God's character. God is rich in houses and land and according to Psalm 50, the cattle on a thousand hills belongs to Him and the world and the fullness thereof. Romans 8:17 tells me that we as children of God are heirs of God and joint heirs with Christ. Leaves me wondering why would I have to walk around with my hands out all the time? Unless I have been bad and disobedient liken unto the child who approaches mommy or daddy asking in a sweet tone, Please daddy please can I have this, I promise I won't be bad anymore, only to get a response of NO, not right now. So we as children of God, being rightful heirs to His kingdom, have no business going around without. We must go to Him in prayer. The key is obedience. The key is definitely obedience.

I will share with you concerning some of these Christian programs that sponsors what you may well call beg-ga-thons on television. You see God will reveal to you who's real and who's not. I recall one day turning on the television to a Christian program. But before I turned it on, I had fellowship with God in prayer. As I was praying I heard the Spirit of the Lord say, *"Sow,"* just as loud and clear. *Sow to the homeless, those in need and hungry.* I did it promptly that same day. But, the amazing thing is how God knows what steps we will take next before we even know.

After praying I then turned the television on and in my view there was a person standing in front of a podium hosting a telethon trying to convince people to commit a certain amount of money by a certain time. They made it sound so convincing you'll fall for it. I asked, Lord, I wonder how much they are paying this person to do this because they were really giving their all in all into this thing to the point where they looked stupid begging. It looked more like a performance than anything else. It just did not look becoming as a saint of God begging.

When you spend quality time in the presence of God you will see things for what they really are. The best actors and actresses come out of the church. This is not the way God structured for His people to function. If you need help for the up building of the kingdom, go to God and He'll open the doors. If you are a child of God you don't have to beg. Even when you are working on a project for God you still don't have to beg. When you are working on a project for man you will have to beg.

God says we better be leery of some of these so call Christian organizations who always have their hands out. Some are hiding behind the message of salvation pretending like they are raising money for a good cause. They are using the message of Jesus Christ as a front. And here you are saint of God sending in pledges you can be giving to a local church that is struggling or to the poor. God is concerned about the lost and the poor.

The Bible says, he who winneth souls is wise and blessed is he that considereth the poor. You better focus your attention where God's heart is at. *God's heart is on lost souls and the poor.*
If you go where God's heart is, I guarantee you will see a lot more blessings flowing your way.

The Bible says in Matthew 7:22, **Many shall say to me in that day, Lord, Lord, have we not prophesied in thy name? And in thy name cast out devils? And in thy name done many wonderful works?**

23rd **And then I will profess unto them, I never knew you: depart from me ye that work iniquity.**
Yes, you did these things, but what was your motive for doing them? Was it for filthy lucre gain? Were you trying to impress others? Or were you trying to get recognition?

These religious empires or sects, perpetrators, et cetera are praising God with their lips but their hearts are far from Him. They are deceiving even some of the very elect. Unless you are tuned in to God in fasting and prayer you will not be able to recognize these perpetrators because they appear to be godly on the outside and on the inside they are something else. They are wolves in sheep clothing giving God's people a false vision concerning the future, prophesying lies in Jesus' name, doing counterfeit healings in Jesus' name and casting out demons in Jesus' name. They are wearing their mask and wearing it well. They are like the *lion* that looks

218

and sounds so imposing; however, God has given spiritual eyes to some to discern real and fake.

Who will benefit from some of the things they say they are raising money for? For example, who will benefit from all of these satellites and stations going up all over the world? Who wants to be in a position to be seen by the whole world? The answer to these two questions is the Antichrist. And you Christians are steady dishing out of your pocket to these people not realizing what's going on.

Just because Bishop So and So said a word to suit your needs, you want to send him fifty dollars. Just because Pastor So and So was on TV working up a sweat screaming and hollering, you feel like God is leading you to send him a love offering. Be careful because there are a lot of voices out there. You even go so far as to claiming some of these preachers calling them your pastor. You don't know anything about him and he doesn't even know you period. You don't even know what kind of life these big timers are living outside the pulpit, but you want to claim them as your own and send them all your money.

When you find yourself in a time of need, who is going to be there for you? It won't be Bishop Bigtimer from TV. I guarantee you that your local pastor will be right by your side. I don't care how much sweat is dripping off a person's body while he or she preaches or how many tongues he or she can speak, you better know that the devil is clever; he can preach, speak in tongues, prophe-lie, and do counterfeit healings too. He got wolves in sheep clothing behind the pulpit. He got a lot of people fooled already. We better begin praying in the spirit and asking God where to sow our seeds. And believe you me He will tell you. The answer that He will give you may very well be geared towards helping the poor and your local church.

What they are raising money for will end up benefiting the Antichrist anyway. We must remember that he is going to take over the world and that includes every piece of equipment for communication purposes. Christian organizations that bears the symbols of or of the like that John saw in Revelation 13:2 and what Daniel saw in Daniel 7:5 you better be leery of them. These symbols resemble the one John and Daniel saw. We need to study symbols adopted by any Christian organization and keep a close watch on the preachers that are in these empires.

Saved people today will come out better anointing themselves and going on a fast and switching the TV channel over to a garbage talk show and stretching forth their hands in prayer interceding for those lost souls who are caught up in all kinds of heinous sin. It's a lot better than watching a bunch of people putting on a show having a form of godliness and denying God's power. The Spirit of God can reach these lost souls a lot quicker through your prayers. All will hear the gospel of Jesus before He comes back. How will they hear?

As I have said in Chapter 2, God is raising up a new breed of prophets, evangelists, teachers, etc., whom He is going to send out there to reach these people. God has His own set of plans. He has already provided the way to reach these lost souls. Knowing that God is rich in houses and land, I know that we as His children can go to Him and ask for anything according to His will. And watch Him open up the windows of heaven and pour us out resources that will provide whatever we need to spread the gospel of Jesus Christ without us having to pay one red cent.

We must remember that God is all-powerful. When God is in whatever you set your mind to do for His Kingdom He can touch the minds of people and overshadow them with the spirit of giving to supply you with whatever you need without you having to come out of your pocket. God has connections and He is an orchestrator. He has His own set of plans for His message coming across to the whole world. Let us not forget who God is and what God can do!

To those masquerade parties that are hiding behind the gospel pretending for whatever gain: know that God has already said He's whipping up the leaves. Sounds like a whirlwind of destruction is about to take place if you don't get right. God is very very serious about His sheep. You are either going to do things God's way or He is going to unveil your mask openly. If the preachers don't lead the people according to God's precepts, they are going to cause a lot of souls to miss out because of their ignorance. Jesus is not coming back until the church is ready. Some changes got to be made within the church body.

THE POWERLESS CHURCH

God says that the preachers are not allowing Him to be God in His own church. Yes, that church house that you call yours does not belong to you. It belongs to God. You have not allowed God's Holy Spirit to take up residence in the sanctuary. It's dead and dry. People are nodding off to sleep. Some churches do not know about the Holy Spirit. They are being taught that the Holy Spirit is not of God and that it is of the devil. Your blasphemous tongue will have to answer to God on Judgment Day. You are causing the people to miss out on the blessings of God. If the Holy Spirit is not present then you will not see the manifestation of God's power to perform miracles and healings.

There are people in your congregation walking on crutches, wearing hearing aids, sitting in wheelchairs, and claiming all kinds of sicknesses. Where is the message of the cross and healing? Where is the message of faith? Where are the gifts of healing? Some of you preach that healing is not for today it was for the early church. That's a lie. I'm a witness to the fact that miracles still happen today.

God wants to manifest Himself in these last days. How can you go against the truth according to God's Word and mislead people? That's a very dangerous thing to do. You have shut God out of the church for years. You have no fear for God at all! Your walls of tradition and teaching after the doctrine of men are causing the people to miss out on the blessings of God. God has given twelve gifts to the church for the edification of the body of Christ. They are no where to be found in your church because you have locked God out. You limit God. You have no power. You have no power to cast out demons, you have no power to heal the sick, and you have no power to get from point A to point C.

Speaking of power and gifts, some of you preachers say God is your shield. He is your protector. But yet you have a bodyguard by your side and a security guard at the door. You say you have guardian angels on both sides of you with a legion above you and goodness and mercy following behind. But what's up with the bodyguards? Where is your faith and trust in God? Where is your spiritual radar that allows you to detect the enemy? Where is your power to destroy his works? You leave no room for the gifts of discernment to operate. You make the word of God of none effect. If you get some of that sin out of the congregation you won't have to worry about the devil acting up. You don't suppose to run from him. He is supposed to run from you. According to the word of God you have power. Then too how can you have power when you lock God out?

Here satan is, causing havoc in the church, speaking to people's minds, manipulating, seducing people and has his own workers in the midst and the church doesn't have any power to run him out. He is performing a three-ring circus act inside the church and the church can't even bury him. It's almost like satan is staring you back in the face saying, Paul I know, Jesus I know but who are you? Who are you to command me to flee? He knows you're not right and he isn't going nowhere unless you go do your first works over and repent to God. He's looking at you and shaking his head asking, How can satan cast out satan? How can satan rebuke satan? He is asking how is it that I have to adhere to any of your commands when I am the one who is behind all the garbage that is going on in your life and all the garbage that is going on in the church. You see, satan knows who got power and who don't. When you shut God out and don't let Him be God amongst His people then you have no power. The Spirit of God is power.

SANCTUARY

You defile God's sanctuary by allowing ungodly things and activities to go on inside of it. There are souls dying on the streets and here you are hosting Halloween parties and bingo up in the church. And God knows what else is going on inside. Whether you are hosting them in the basement, etc., you should be aware that every room inside as well as the perimeters outside the church is God's and should be respected as so. You want to call your Halloween

223

party a Harvest celebration, well go out and bring in the harvest and let's have some church. Instead of bringing souls in, some of you are celebrating and bringing the Druid customs into the church.

The sanctuary is supposed to be holy and respected as God's sanctuary. The pulpit is supposed to be sacred. You allow anything up in the pulpit. And you have the audacity to wonder why miracles and healings are not taking place in the church. I previously gave one reason to be because you have locked God out. Now the other reason is because there is sin and unbelief in the camp. II Chronicles 7:14 says *If my people, which are called by my name, shall humble themselves, and pray, and seek my face, and turn from their wicked ways; then will I hear from heaven, and will forgive their sin, and will heal their land.*

Why should God waste His time manifesting His glory to a bunch of disobedient, stiff-necked, hardheaded rebellious people?

God cannot dwell where sin is. The atmosphere has to be right for miracles and healings to take place. It has to be an atmosphere of faith and one accord.

The only thing God is going to manifest to a rebellious church is His wrath. He's going to send a whirlwind of destruction. Like He told me in the dream, *"I'm whipping up the leaves. I'm whipping up the leaves. All foolishness and mess going on in the church world today must come to a cease."* The church world need to go back and do the first works over.

Revelation 2:4 *says, Remember therefore from whence thou art fallen and repent, and do the first works; or else I will come unto thee quickly, and will remove thy candlestick out of his place, except thou repent.*

You're preaching everything but the gospel of Jesus Christ. Some of you preach against other preachers of the gospel like you are God's one and only gift to the church. One of the worst things that can come out of a preacher' mouth is when he stands behind the pulpit and talk negative about another preacher. Out of jealousy you preach against God's anointed, being ignorant to I Chronicles 16:22 which tells you, **Touch not mine anointed and do my prophets no harm.** If you have nothing good to say about anyone whether they be saved or unsaved then don't say anything at all.

Crowds and crowds of people including some of your members whose faces show that they are in dire need of something from God are drawn by the thousands to conferences held by these hand full of anointed preachers. Yes, you can count the anointed ones on your fingers. Remember that everybody isn't who he or she says they are.

Some preachers throw a jealous fit because their members go hear these other speakers. Not discerning the fact that there might be a message there for that person. True enough a revelation message that God does not intend on giving to you to preach no time soon.

Some preachers just look at the crowds of people that these speakers draw and their carnal mind is thinking money. Feeling somewhat resentful you say, Look at all that money Bishop or Evangelist So and So is collecting. Deep down inside you is just flat straight out jealous. These handful of anointed ones have enough God fearing sense to allow the Holy Spirit to inspire them to invest back into the kingdom of God by maintaining an ongoing ministry to God's people by producing their own videos, music tapes, sermon tapes and publishing their own books. They give back. Like the scripture says, I give thee power to get wealth. They know that the God of Abraham, Isaac, and Jacob is serious when it comes to feeding His sheep. They know who God is.

Yes, God is pouring out His blessings upon these well known anointed evangelists with exceeding wealth because he or she is obedient in giving the people what God wants them to have and that is the unadulterated Truth. The Bible tells us to speak wholesome words. And when you stand behind the pulpit and speak negative about another, it is not edifying the body of Christ. You're corrupting God's people with unwholesome words.

You can be blessed just like them if you grab a hold of God's principle of giving and apply it. If you desire a big flourishing ministry or a big church sow a seed into a big ministry so that some of that grace they have can rub off on you. You may say, well, they don't need my money. I must say that you are right, they don't need your money; however, you do need some of their grace. It is time to put away jealousy. Do yourself a favor and do some research to find out how Bishop So and So's ministry got from point A to point C without him having to go through all the other letters of the alphabet. It all goes back to following the principles that God has given us in His word. You are either going to grab a hold of the principles of giving or get left behind.

God is getting ready to raise up some millionaires in this new Millenium. Everybody will not be able to get in on this type of blessing because God knows some of you are not going to act right with that kind of money. In other words He can't trust you. God says there are future millionaires sitting in the congregation. It has manifested itself in the spirit. It has manifested itself in His glorious light and it is only a matter of time before it is manifested in the natural for all to see. It's all in God's timing. The Holy Spirit says that some of you preachers don't even know what you have sitting in the midst of the congregation and some of you do and still haven't caught on to what He is trying to get you to see. That's why it is so important to be ye kind and loving one toward another because you never know. The ones that you view as less important are the ones God is going to bring to the TOP.

Okay, you've got Sister Singer who is going to become a well-known gospel recording artist by the grace of God and then you have Brother Writer who will become a well-known author with books that will become bestsellers by the grace of God. And let's not forget Young Jr., who didn't look like he would amount up to anything, yet needed a couple of hundreds for books in his first term of college. You see, in the spirit, God has already blessed him with a multimillion-dollar business. You can't see it in the natural but you know in your spirit that it will happen. You need to use wisdom behind what God is allowing you to see and start reacting. Some of you don't even know what you have sitting in your mist period. You can't even discern a saint from an ain't.

To those of you who do see the blessing in the spirit, don't wait until you can see the manifestation of the blessing take place in the natural before you decide to help, be there for these vision-minded people at the beginning. They won't even need your help after the manifestation; instead you are going to need them. As a matter of a fact they really don't need your help period; God is just trying to give you an opportunity to be in on their blessing. With or without your help, God will supply them with whatever they need to get them going with His work.

Some people got that I won't believe it until I see it happen syndrome. Like I said before, either grab a hold of the principle of giving or get left behind.

The Holy Spirit will let you know what's in the midst for a reason. Since you know that these things are going to happen by the grace of God, you should be the first one to invest in these people. When the manifestation of their blessing come into effect you will get blessed with some of that grace also. You can never get enough of God's blessings. These people are what you call investment opportunities and God has placed them in your mist to give you an opportunity to be blessed by them. When they come to you for help to get them started it is not a wise thing to brush them off or keep them hanging. God has given them a vision and the church needs to back them up with support to go forward with what God has placed in their hearts to do. Its time out for having picks and chooses on whom you will and will not support. Member or non-member of your congregation we are all part of the body of Christ and we must be there for one another.

You say there is limited amount of funds to help, well what a better time to sow when the funds are low. You can by pass all of that church red tape and reach into your own pocket for a fifty or a hundred-dollar bill. Your fifty can very well come back to you five thousand or fifty thousand and your hundred can come back to you ten thousand or a hundred thousand. Once you extend your help especially to something that you know is of God, then your support will not go unforgotten. God will make sure of that. If we can grab a hold of the spirit of giving and guard our heart from the spirit of stinginess we will come into the fullness of the blessings of God.

FORGIVENESS

God is also bringing to my attention a sin issue gone public involving a prominent figure in the political capitol. He brought to my attention that the leaders in the church as well as the secular world needs to be reminded of David. David was a righteous king and a man after God's own heart. He committed sin with Bathesheba. He tried to cover it up and had her husband killed in battle. Remember that God's eyes are forever on the righteous.

Nathan the prophet exposed David's wrongdoing. Whatever is done in the dark will surely come out into the light. And when you get exposed, like the Holy Spirit is getting ready to do with the church, you can't help but fall on your face and repent. David repented and God forgave him.

The Bible says that David was a man after God's own heart and a righteous king who fell into sin. If you consider yourself a righteous preacher and a righteous man or woman of God, what make you think you can't fall into sin?

Now when someone you know has committed a sin whether they are in the political spotlight or they happen to be your next door neighbor, etc., that issue is between him and God because nobody else can forgive sin. If he has confessed, apologized to others, and repented to God please know that God has forgiven that person. It is not right for you to stand behind the pulpit and call that person by name preaching a sermon on him or her, talking negative about them and sentencing them to hell. I can't help but wonder who gave you the keys to life and death or heaven and hell? God has the final say. You are shoving the sin he or she has committed back into their face when God has already forgiven them. You are not being mindful that God says to forgive one another so that your Father in heaven may forgive you also. Be ye merciful, as your Father also is merciful. We must speak wholesome words that edify the body.

The Bible says in John 8:7, he who is without sin let him cast the first stone. We as man have no heaven or hell to put anyone in. There is only one throne and God sits there. There is only one Judge whom we all will have to give an account to for ourselves one day.

RELIGIOUS BONDAGE

There are leaders who are yoking God's people back up with their man made religion. God has given only Ten Commandments for man to live by and yet you have acquired unto yourselves your own rules for the people to live by. Do you not know that God does not need your help? He has already laid the foundation. He has given us the Bible. You deceive God's people and have therefore caused them to err from the Truth. They are under spiritual bondage with your set of off the wall nonsense rules. Christ has set them free and yet you enslave them with your practices and teachings. Galatians 5:1 tells us to *Stand fast therefore in the liberty wherewith Christ hath made us free, and be not entangled again with the yoke of bondage.*

Hear this: Pure religion and undefiled before God and the Father is this, To visit the fatherless and widows in their affliction, and to keep himself unspotted from the world. James 1:27
Pure religion is expressed by acts which includes visiting the sick, feeding the hungry, giving to the needy, ministering the gospel of Jesus Christ to the

lost and keeping yourself uncontaminated from the world. Pure religion is not a matter of rules and regulations.

SUGARCOATED PREACHING

There are people that flock to certain churches by the hundreds because they know the preacher won't expose their sin. They join the big congregation because they know the preacher can't monitor them. The sermons are dry, dead, boring and are far from being anointed. They are putting people to sleep, but the people don't mind. You're preaching to a bunch of Amaziah spirits that don't want to hear the truth, so they come to you. They search out churches that don't preach on sin. They stay away from churches where the Holy Spirit is present to search them out. They don't want deliverance. So they come to you.

II Timothy 4:3 says, **For the time will come when they will not endure sound doctrine; but after their own lusts shall they heap to themselves teachers, having itching ears.**
4th **And they shall turn away their ears from the truth, and shall be turned unto fables.**

Yes, you tickle their ears. You preach just what their itching ears want to hear. You are a people pleaser. Paul wrote a letter to the Galatians in chapter 1:10 and he said, **For do I persuade men, or God? Or do I seek to please men? For if I yet pleased men, I should not be the servant of Christ.**

You tone down the message a bit putting all kinds of sweet toppings on the gospel Truth. You don't preach that hell, fire, and brimstone message because you got to pay that church mortgage, utility bills and even a few of your personal possessions. No, you can't risk losing members. And then you have the nerves to preach about faith and trusting God.

TITHING

Some of you preach against paying tithes. You come up with your own doctrine concerning money and the church. Simply because you don't want to give God what's due unto Him. You teach that paying tithes was for the Old Testament people. Well, what's in the Old Testament still applies to us today, except the Mosaic Law. We no longer have to sacrifice animals. Jesus was the sacrifice for us. He was the mediator of a better covenant. At the rate the world is sinning today, we'd run into an animal shortage trying to sacrifice sin offerings up to God.

People think we can just do away with the Old Testament teachings, but not so. Matthew 5:18 tells us **till heaven and earth pass, one jot or one tittle shall in no wise pass from the law, till all be fulfilled.** Just because The Ten Commandments are in the Old Testament does not mean we don't have to abide by them. Every letter of every word in the Old Testament is essential and will not fail at coming to pass. The Ten Commandments are carried over into the New Testament. Read further down to verses 21-48. I don't care how much the world has change, God has not changed, He is still the same.

There are preachers and teachers frequenting the airwaves telling people they don't have to tithe. That is very sickening to hear. When you hear things like that, know that it is a false doctrine. They are doing what I Timothy 1:6 describes as vain jangling. Desiring to be teachers of the law: understanding neither what they say, nor whereof they affirm. In other words they don't know what they are talking about. But, they are causing people to err from the truth. And they are causing people to miss out on the fullness of the blessings of God.

It's amazing nowadays how everybody has a revelation, everybody has a prophecy, everybody has an interpretation and everybody has a vision. But we must know that every revelation, every interpretation, every prophecy and every vision is not coming from God. You can't believe every spirit out there, but try the spirits whether they are of God. Nowadays you can't listen to everything out there. We need to read the Word of God for ourselves. We need to get on our knees and pray and get closer to God so that we may be able to discern false things.

Tithing is also carried over into the New Testament in Luke 18:12 and Hebrews 7:5. Some teachers and preachers will lie through their teeth and say people didn't tithe in the New Testament. In Matthew 23:23 the Pharisees paid their tithes, but the only problem was they were not tithing the normal way. They took it upon themselves to add on to the items required to be tithed. God has already laid down the rules or requirements for tithing. He has given us examples of those who paid them in the Bible days and they all paid a tenth. You wonder why God is always blessing Sister So and So. That's because she is obeying and exercising the principle of tithing and giving according to the Word of God.

Man, today, has either taken away by saying we don't have to pay tithes or they have added on top of what God has already instructed. You cannot alter requirements that God has already set forth. You can't say, let's do it this way or that way. If you are not obedient in giving God the tithes which is a tenth of your gross plus an offering then you are robbing God in His own house.

According to Malachi 3, you are considered a thief and disobedient. You limit the blessings of God upon your life. God could have asked for ninety percent and yet you have a problem paying ten. The money you make is God's money to begin with and it is by His grace that you have a job to make it. Even if you come up short on your check and paying your tithes will make you short on something, God still requires you to pay ten percent. This is where your faith and trust in God is tested. Believe me He will provide for what is lacking. I see it like this, as long as I faithfully pay my tithes and give my offerings, I will not go lacking for anything and man can't take away something that God has already given unto me and has said is mine anyway.

Have you ever been in a situation where you were paying your tithes on a regular basis and all of a sudden you quit paying them? In the midst of your not paying them everything started going wrong in your life. Well, that should be a sign sure enough that God does require us to pay tithes.

God says that when you pay your tithes and offerings He will rebuke the devour for your sakes. The devour being the devil himself cursing your finances, health, etc. He will keep the devil from sucking you dry. Your barns will be full, your finances will flourish, you'll be in good health, and anything you touch will be blessed.

If you find yourself not reaping these blessings, then you need to find you a church that teaches paying tithes God's way. God says, put Him to the test and see won't He open the windows of heaven and pour you out a blessing that you won't have room enough to receive. Read II Corinthians 8 and 9.

MONEY-HUNGRY PREACHERS

Some preachers are abusing money that is coming into the church. You need to stop playing monopoly with God's money. The money in the offering basket is not yours, it belongs to God. It is not there for you to splurge on luxuries. You can't take your luxuries to hell with you. Oh, yea, preachers go to hell too. Just because you are a preacher does not exempt you from hell. You brought nothing into this world and you sure won't take God's money and luxuries with you. You're going to leave out of here the same way you came in.

According to Psalm 24:1, the earth is the Lord's and the fullness thereof. Everything in this world belongs to God. The money in the offering basket and the luxuries you store up is God's. You need to take notes and know that the offering is for the up building of the kingdom of God. It is not for the up building of your personal bank account. God sees what you are doing with it. There is nothing hid that God doesn't see.

Some of you know the name of every purse that enters your church. Some of you have already calculated the offering up in your head before offering time by the number of chairs being occupied in the service. Some of you have other ways of calculating. You spend more time taking up offering than you do preaching. You are not preaching the unadulterated Word of God for fear of losing members. You don't want to lose those that pay for that $300,000 home and that gold trimmed Cadillac. There's nothing wrong with it if you're preaching the unadulterated Word of God and your members want to bless you. The problem is when you are the crook in the pulpit and is in this for filthy lucre gain.

Proverbs 23:4 says, **Labor not to be rich: cease from thine own wisdom.** Don't be in the ministry just for the money. Your coveting after riches taking the front seat over feeding God's sheep will land you a platinum gold card into hell. The demons in hell are going to give you a special treatment of torment. They love preachers.

Some of you are so obsessed with money to the point where you call around to churches to ask if you can hold a revival. The Bible says that your gift will make room for you, so why are you on the phone? You're not letting God open doors for you; you're opening doors for yourself. You can't wait on God because in your world it's not about God it's about money. It all goes back to being called and not being called to preach. When you are called of God, He is the door opener, the orchestrator and appointment maker. All you have to do is follow His lead. You see, you've been playing too much monopoly. Rolling that dice looks good for a moment until you land in jail. You're exposed now. What's hidden in the dark will surely come out in the opening.

It's best to be led by God when it comes to His money because He's watching everything, especially you, preacher. There are some spirit-led preachers of the gospel who don't mix personal lives and church money together and yet God provides for them. They walk by faith. Faith in knowing that God is not slack concerning His promises. And knowing that if they take care of God's business, God will surely take care of theirs. However, there are some that are hooked on money for self-gain when they should be hooked on Jesus for souls. Instead of crying out for money, you should be crying out to God in fasting and prayer. And let Him be God in His own house amongst His people. You need to let the Holy Spirit take full reign over you and save your soul from punishment.

Like I said before God's eyes are heavily glued on the preachers. You know what you're doing is not right in the eyes of God. There is no way in the world you can be filled with the Holy Spirit and sin as much as you sin in the pulpit.

It won't hurt for you to pick up a Bible dictionary and look up the word "shepherd" and ask God to give you the vision for the church. The Bible says that where there is no vision, the people perish. You have no prophetic revelation. If you did the church would not be as loose as it is today. You are causing the people to fall under judgment. God is telling you to steer the people in one direction and you are steering them in another, therefore leading them wrong.

There are some of you that think you got the perfect church. But I guarantee you if you go on a thirty day fast you will not only come out with the vision but you will be able to look out in the midst and see Minister Fake, Brother Backbiter, Sister Jealousy, Missionary Jezebel, and Deacon Nightclub. You'll see the devil in the choir, in the pulpit, greeting people at the door. You'll see mess everywhere. The next section on spiritual washing mat will attest to it.

It's time for the preachers to get on the right track. You've got to preach it like God has given in His Word. You've got to lay aside this preaching after the doctrine of men and let God give you revelations. It is time for you to put down these traditions that have no biblical basis and get with God's program. Some of that off the wall stuff you practice and teach don't have anything to do with salvation. All God is requiring from people is repentance, to live by His Word and to win others into His kingdom. And here you are, teaching them things that have no bearing whatsoever on the things of God.

Paul says in Galatians 1:11, ***But I certify you, brethren, that the gospel which was preached of me is not after men. For neither was I taught it, but by the revelation of Jesus Christ.***
It is time for you to let the Holy Spirit lead you and guide you concerning the people. It is He (the Holy Spirit) that will teach you and give you what to speak unto the people. God is simply not going to allow His people to keep being mislead, it has been going on far too long. God is going to tear down your walls of tradition that you hold fast to. If it means exposure, He'll do it. Time is too short. It's time to let the people know that destruction is coming. It's time to stop telling them that peace is coming. You are giving the people a false vision. Peace is not coming.

The people need to get spiritually prepared not only for the harvest coming forth, but for the destruction and calamities ahead. Time is short even as I write this book. A lot of people souls are at stake. Pretty soon, you will witness preachers falling dead in the pulpit because they're preaching things they ought not. God has a message for those not preaching the unadulterated Word of God in Jeremiah 23:1 and 2. ***Woe be unto the pastors that destroy and scatter the sheep of my pasture! saith the Lord.*** 2nd ***Therefore thus saith the Lord God of Israel against the pastors that feed my people, Ye have scattered my flock, and driven them away, and have not visited them: behold, I will visit upon you the evil of your doings, saith the Lord.*** God is not playing when it comes to His sheep. I Corinthians 9:14 says Even so hath the Lord ordained that they which preach the gospel should live the gospel. This applies to all, whether we are teachers, evangelists, prophets, gospel singers, witnesses, etc. We must all live what we preach.

SPIRITUAL WASHING MAT

Amid the carnal sins like backbiting, sowing discord, strife, envy, jealousy, lying, adultery, fornication, etc., that has plagued the church, God gave me a dream.

On November 1, 1998 God revealed to me in a dream that His people, the church, needs to go to a spiritual washing mat. They have an evil conscience and are so full of sin and filth to the point that they need to be cleansed from the inside out.

First of all, God has given specific instructions in His Word concerning the tongue. But some of you refuse to abide, therefore some of your mouths need to be washed out with *Ivory Soap.* Your inside is so sinful you need to clean it out with some *Tide* and *Purex.* Don't forget to add some *Clorox* because what Tide or Purex can't get out Clorox will.

Remember that Jesus is coming for a church without a spot or blemish and those things must come out. When you become saved, you become a representative of God. God is holy and therefore commands His people to be ye holy for I am holy. He has been misrepresented badly amongst His people. Those ungodly ways that are trying to linger on must come out. Your conduct has to change.

Some of you have bad manners. You whisper back and forth right in church talking about people. You murmur while the Word is going forth. You're on the phone talking about everything but the Word of God. Some of your mouths are going over fifty miles per hour and then you wonder why you can't hear God. Some of you can't stand for someone else to be the center of attention so you have to jump right in and change the subject and focus the attention on you or something else.

You are a busy body in other people's personal affairs when you should focus your attention on your own business. You are envious of another because God is steady blessing them. And jealousy is your middle name. Don't you know that we all serve the same God and He gives accordingly? All you need to do is humble yourself in His presence and delight yourself in Him and He will give you the desires of your heart.

Some of you are touchy and people can't say anything to you without you getting on the defensive. Some of you will tell people off in a minute. Some are upsetting those that are trying to live right. You are letting the enemy use you to get in their path. Some of you are sometimey. One day you are showing love with handshakes and hugs and another day you are rolling your eyes. You are faker than the fur on a stuffed animal. You are not fooling any one but yourself. Some people have more mood swings than a person out on the dance floor. One day you are on the good foot and another day you are on the down swing. Some are talking about people behind their backs and smiling in their face. And God forbids if it's one of His anointed ones. I must add again that He reveals things to them by His Spirit.

You even talk about the quiet sister or brother. Just because they don't mix and mingle you slander their name too. You call them stuck-up or antisocial. You need to stop watching folks and reading them wrong. It has not come to your understanding that their quietness is attributed to the fact that they acknowledge a call on their life and they are trying to hear God and don't have time for no foolishness. They know that according to I Peter 3:4 that even the ornament of a quiet and meek spirit is of great price in the sight of God which leaves them to know God is not pleased with a motor mouth. Proverbs 25:23 says the wind driveth away rain: so doth an angry countenance a backbiting tongue.

There was once a song out that says you talk too much, you never shut up. You are just like the spectator. You see too much and talk about everything that goes on in the church. Nobody trust you enough to confide in you because they know what you are about. Their business will be out quicker than a poptart coming out of a toaster. You are the distributor of the he said she said gossip. You talk so much you can't even hear God. You consult God about something and God wants to answer you, but your ears are so clogged up with gossip. He's trying to lead you and guide you or trying to warn you about something and He can't because you are steady running your mouth, being a busy body in other people matters, etc. The only way He can get your attention is to allow some type of sickness, etc., to come upon you to slow your tongue down. Maybe a spiritual muzzle.

The Bible says that life and death is in the power of the tongue. The tongue is undisciplined and full of deadly poison. But with this same tongue you bless God and curse men. You speak negative words about folks. Some people need to take the ziplock seal off of a sandwich bag and put it on their mouth.

Proverbs 4:23 tells us to **keep thy heart with all diligence: for out of it are the issues of life.**
24th **Put away from thee a froward mouth, and perverse lips put far from thee.**
25th **Let thine eyes look right on,** right on to who? God. Stay focused on God. **And let thine eyelids look straight before thee.**
26th **Ponder the path of thy feet, and let all thy ways be established.**

27th **Turn not to the right hand nor to the left: remove thy foot from evil.**

The 23rd verse says to guard your heart. Guard your heart from all of this carnal stuff. We've got to guard our heart from bitterness, backbiting, strife, adultery, fornication, stealing, lying, pride, malice, gossip, etc. Jesus tells us in Matthew 15 that whatever comes out of your mouth is coming from your heart. Your mouth is speaking what is already in your heart. All of those evil thoughts and negative talking, envy, strife, wrath, hatred, is what defiles you. Defile means to make filthy. You become filthy in the sight of God. When you feel like you want to speak bad about your sister or brother, you need to look the devil in the eye and rebuke him. Please before you do that make sure you got some power because with some of you he knows he has to obey your command and with some of you he is just going to look at you and flat straight out laugh in your face. Even the devil knows your heart is not pure.

We need some heart transplants in the household of faith. Some of you need to trade your heart in for a pure heart. A heart is an organ that pumps blood. And some of your hearts is pumping a lot more than just blood. It's pumping garbage. Matthew 5:8 says **Blessed are the pure in heart: for they shall see God.** The word "heart" refers to the inner self that thinks, feels, and decides. The word "pure" means free from foreign matter, contamination, or corruption. What may that foreign matter be that is causing you to become contaminated? You need to be careful of whom you associate with. Sometimes you have to separate yourself because this stuff is contagious and it rubs off easily. What may that foreign matter be that has caused you to become corrupted? You have gone from good to bad. That foreign matter is everything that is coming from an evil heart. You know like backbiting, jealousy, gossiping, strife, murmuring and some.

The pure in heart are those who are bearing good fruits. Let's take a look at some. The apple is so sweet; it's full of love. The peach is so plump; it's full of joy. The orange is so juicy; it's full of peace. The plum is so soft; it's full of gentleness. The banana being long in length is full of longsuffering. The grapes are so many in numbers they vouch for the rest of the fruit of the Spirit, which are goodness, faith, meekness and temperance.

It's hard to see the fruit of mercy in you when you have unforgiveness in your heart. It's hard to see love in you when you are full of hatred. It's hard to see patience in you when you are impatient with others and you can't seem to wait on God. It's hard to see peace in you when you look disturbed and is easily provoked and stirred up in your spirit. It's hard to see gentleness in you when you are mean, rough, and harsh to others. It's hard to see meekness in you when you are wild, untamed and out of control. It's hard to see faith in you when you display mistrust and disbelief.

Scripture tells us that you shall know them by their fruits. Some of you are bringing forth some evil fruit and it shows. Your fruit is sour, bitter, spoiled, molded, discolored, disfigured and rotten. You are just a tree with bare branches whose fruit has gone bad. Matthew 7:19 says that every tree that doesn't bring forth good fruit will be chopped down and cast into the fire. Matthew 6:21 says for where your treasures is, there will your heart be also. I tell you, some of you all got some contagious, cancer spreading stuff in your treasure and God is calling for purification.

If you are living in the Spirit why are you having such a hard time walking in the Spirit? People have become self-conceited, competitive and challenging to one another, envious and jealous of one another, provoking and irritating to one another. Church folks are lashing out at one another. Some are leaving the church on a bad note. Some are walking out of line and are out of control. You got to crucify the flesh. Fast more, pray more or else you are going to find yourself in Matthew 7:19.

If you haven't been fasting and praying it will show. The flesh will show out on you. Your flesh is overriding the spirit man and is therefore doing what it wants to do. When you are walking in the Spirit your spiritual antennas will go up and will recognize the devil for who he is and what he is trying to do. He is trying to do a number of things but mostly he wants us to tear one another apart within the body of Christ and be divided. Amen.

Some of you think that God only talks to the preacher or the prophet. I have news for you, that is not so. When a fellow sister or brother says that God spoke to them concerning an issue etc., you in turn have the audacity to question their claim by asking, How do you know it was from God? Are you sure it was God? And then you'll have the boldness to say, make sure it's from God. If it isn't from God, blah blah blah. Now that brother or sister has already told you that God said...... And therefore what you need to do is give your blessings and be quiet. Your response of questioning raises doubt on your part as if you don't believe and what you really need to do is keep your doubts to yourself and ask God to help you to know the right words to say in any situation. It all goes back to disciplining the tongue. Instead of giving your blessings you become negative concerning the issue. Instead of ministering positive, you minister negative. Negativeness does not come from God. We must be careful because out of that same mouth with the tongue that is full of deadly poison proceedeth blessing and cursing. My brethren, these things ought not so to be. Doth a fountain send forth at the same place sweet water and bitter? How can people fix their mouths to say some things?

There are saved people that lie through their teeth. They are quick to tell a lie. Proverbs 12:22 tells us that a lying tongue is an abomination to the Lord. Like they say one lie leads to another. That is the flat straight out truth. Saved folks call in sick on the job knowing well there is not a sick bone in their body. They use what they call a sick day and get sick pay and they go on and lead a normal day and be the first one waiting for the mall doors to open. Saved folks tell jokes more than the comedian does. A joke is nothing but a lie. People use phrases like "just kidding", "just joking" or "psyche." In all reality they are all the same as saying, "I'm lying." We better be reminded that the Bible tells us that all liars shall have their parts in the lake of fire. Even the little things we need to be careful of.

Ephesians 5:4 list things that should not be named among us as becometh saints. One of these things is jesting (joking). Telling gospel jokes is high on the rise. Saved folks have become so bored to the point where they have dug deep into the most sacred books (Bible) in the world to make jokes for their entertainment. The unsaved are looking inside the church and making jokes. As I look up the word *"joke"* it gives the meaning to be a laugh provoking story or remark. Something not taken seriously. Look up the word *"story"* and the definition you will find is narration of a fictional tale or account: a lie.

I'm trying to figure out, where does the Bible fit in this definition? Apparently it doesn't.

The things of God are sacred and need to be respected as so. The Bible is sacred just like the Ark of the Covenant that contained the two tablets of stone (Ten Commandments), the golden pot of manna and Aaron's Rod. Only certain people were given authority by God to handle the Ark. It was something you did not want to mess with.

As with the Holy Bible, which also contains the Ten Commandments, it is to be taken seriously also. Every event, every character, every vision, every word in the Bible is to be taken seriously and not turned into a laughing stock. It is God speaking to His people and His words should not be turned around into a laughing stock for your entertainment. Where is the fear of God among the people today? If you are suffering from boredom in this Christian walk why not let God take you through the spiritual washing mat so He can clean you up. There are a lot of exciting things to do in Christ but first you got to get cleaned up to be fit for the master's use.

Some of you are users. You go around using folks. You treat your sister and brother as if they have freebietown dot com written all over them. People don't hear from you until you need or want something. In some way or another you owe people money and you really don't plan on paying up. You want everything free. The Bible says to owe no man. Don't you know by now that nothing is free in life but the gift of salvation? You need to start doing things right because you are highly misrepresenting God when you don't pay up to your sisters and brothers in the Lord. You never know when you'll need them again. If the Holy Ghost is prevalent in your life He will bring things to your remembrance.

He will let you see yourself in your wrong and He requires that you do something about it.

There is another issue that God says is a problem in the church and that is the aggressive spirit. In other words "pushy." The aggressive spirit is rough on people. It is a controlling spirit. You'll find yourself pulling on and speaking harshly to people. We should not exert force on any one to get them to do what we think they should be doing, etc. Especially in reference to those God has endowed with gifts. Some people in the church act like they are the giver of gifts. They act like they are in control of other people's gifts. If a person is not working in the capacity that they think they should be working in they got something to say.

There are some people God has not released just yet. How and when they use those gifts is between them and God. God controls the gifts anyway. What you need to do is focus on what God has given unto you to do and not on what He has given unto others to do. Focus on those hidden gifts that are dormant in your life and stop pointing fingers at others.

If you find yourself being aggressive towards others in the household of faith you need to learn how to be gentle. God is not mean, harsh and rough with His people. God does not force us to do anything, so who is man to force others to do something. God is gentle, therefore, we as children of God should be gentle with one another. Gentleness is one of the fruits of the Spirit.

The aggressive spirit in the church is very ugly and it does not discriminate. It will rest itself not only upon laymen in the church but those in the five-fold ministry as well. It attacks with unpleasant actions. It will cause a sister or brother to become offended. It will cause a weak minded person to leave the church somewhat confused. It will cause a Holy Ghost filled person to approach the aggressive spirit with the issue in forgiveness. Some of us offend people and don't even know it. Some don't even know they are plagued with this spirit until God allows something to happen to show them it is there and should be dealt with. Whether or not you were raised in an aggressive environment as a child, God said it can not be carried on into the household of faith.

To the unforgiving spirit in the church, here is what God has to say to you. The Bible tells us even as Christ forgave us, so also do we. Ephesians 4:32 says And be ye kind one to another, tenderhearted, forgiving one another, even as God for Christ's sake hath forgiven you. God has commanded us many times in the scriptures concerning forgiveness and it does not yet seem to register. How can people come to church on Sunday and shout, etc., and have unforgiveness in their heart? Somebody has asked for your forgiveness and you can't seem to forgive and forget. You can't let go of the past. Your family member or fellow sister or brother has done something wrong to you and you can't seem to forgive and let go, now, something is wrong with you. How can you be a vessel fit for the master's use with unforgiveness in your heart? Doors will remain shut unto you until you let God fix you.

In the eyes of God they have done the right thing by asking your forgiveness, but you saved, sanctified and filled with whatever ghost is out there, ain't hearing it. What good is your shout and praises on Sunday morning if you can't forgive that person and show forth some love. Love covers a multitude of sin and you need to be loving on someone as if there is no tomorrow. Here you are speaking in all kinds of tongues and talking about you're on your way to heaven. But in all reality, you are walking on a crooked path accessed by the children of disobedience and you need deliverance.

If Jesus came tonight, I feel sorry for you. When you point the finger at someone else you tend to forget that you have three more pointing back at you. You are in no better shape than the other person is. You keep holding on to the past and see what it will bring you. It will bring you absolutely nothing. Unforgiveness of the heart will hinder your blessings. If you think you are going to enter into a new dimension hanging on to the past then you might as well fix you a cot in the boat because you'll be there for a while. God is serious when it comes to love and forgiveness. You must forgive, move on and minister love, time is too short and unforgiveness has no seat in the kingdom of heaven.

God has told us in His Word to live in harmony and to love one another. He says we have to stop this suing one another in the household of faith. All of this counsel He has given in His Word and you want to go before a Gentile judge who don't have faith and trust in the Gospel of Jesus Christ to settle your private grievances, disputes and quarrels between members of the brotherhood. Immature Christians are taking one another to court. Instead of trusting wise and competent people in the body of Christ to help settle your matters you go to Judge Toody or Judge Phillip. Precept upon precept and line upon line, God has set up principles and boundaries whereby the Christian must live. We see them over and over in the Bible and we hear them time and time again being preached. The state already don't want to have anything to do with the church, so what do we look like taking counsel from them? The steps they take in handling issues don't even line up with the Word of God anyway. We have preachers taking one another to court. Members are suing the preacher and vice versa. Sisters and brothers are taking one another to court. Family members are taking one another to court. We need to get together and go to God and let Him help guide us in settling issues. He is the Wonderful Counselor, Prince of Peace and a mighty Judge. We need to start looking at our situations and asking ourselves in the midst of differences, what would Jesus do? We must get together on one accord and love on one another for love covers a multitude of sin. We need to stop being ignorant of satan's devices and stop giving him room to distract us from what time it really is.

The Bible tells us to pray ye one for another. God has put gifts in the church for the edifying of the body of Christ. But we have gone through the body of Christ like we go through the meat section of a grocery store picking out our prime choice of who *can* and who *can't* pray for us. You have set in your mind that if he or she is not a person of high rank then he or she *can't* pray for you. I'd hate to see you stuck out in the middle of the desert with one of your who cant's. You won't have any choice then. Your who *can't* will have to intercede to God to give you strength. We all know about the natural desert and the spiritual desert. God will put you in certain predicaments to get you out of your set mode of thinking. I very well understand that there are some people who are not right in the eyes of God; they need deliverance themselves and are trying to lay hands on people. That's a different story. Then too, it doesn't take God a year or two to deliver a person. He can deliver in a matter of seconds and turn around and use that person to minister prayer, etc., to you.

The Bible tells us to encourage one another and to exhort one another daily while it is called today. However, some people like to switch cars on you when they are going through their trials. They prefer to drive the Dodge Spirit cause they don't want to be bothered with you. So they dodge you. Some of them can be top picks for the national marathon because when they see you coming they race out of the door faster than a speeding bullet. Some should change their current job title to a telephone technician or a telephone operator because they either screen their calls or disconnect their phones to avoid your phone call. Sometimes some of them react this way because they know if they confide in you, you will in turn go tell their business on the mountaintop. You remember the song, Go tell it on the mountain, over the hills and everywhere. That's you to the tee. The Bible says to exhort and encourage one another: not getting into people's business and going around telling it.

On the other hand the Dodge Spirit is a distant cousin of Sister and Brother Know-it-All. They know everything already. You on the other hand know that they are going through because you can see it on their face and you can even see it behind their smile. When you are going through something, they want you to sit and listen to what they have to say to you. But when they are going through they don't want to listen to the words that you got to say that may give them the strength or the boost they need to get through. They are causing you to miss out on your blessing. All you are trying to do is what I Thessalonians 5:11 instructs us to do and that is to comfort (encourage, admonish, exhort) one another and edify (strengthen and build up) one another. Colossians 3:16 instructs us to let the word of Christ dwell in you richly in all wisdom; teaching and admonishing one another in psalms and hymns and spiritual songs, singing with grace in our hearts unto the Lord.

Some people in the church have the worst attitude. You are running people away from the church with your bad attitude and mean spirit. You try to hide it but it can be seen beyond your fake smile. You may fool some, but the true saints and God can see right through you. And then you wonder why Sister or Brother So and So doesn't want to be around you. The reason being is because your ways are crooked than a path. You are like a cancer that spread. And all of that gunk you have on the inside of you is contagious and she or he wishes not to be contaminated. When your praise goes up, it doesn't mean anything to God because you are so full of junk. Your worship to God is in vain. Your praises can't even be ushered into His presence unless you've repented. I have seen unsaved folks with better attitudes than saved folks. Some of them act more saved than saved folks.

Some people are very very disrespectful to the leaders in the church. God has put your pastor in authority over you and yet you disobey and disrespect him or her. The Bible tells us in Hebrews 13:17 to obey them that have rule over you and submit yourselves: for they watch for your souls, as they that must give account, that they may do it with joy and not with grief. Your pastor can't even chastise you or give you orders without you going off the deep end. You get angry and you talk back. Even if your leader is wrong, the Holy Spirit will deal with him or her, but in the meantime it does not give you the right to treat them any kind of way under any circumstances whatsoever. Sometimes God allows certain things to happen so you can see what it is that you need to work on about yourself. Here you have disrespected someone in authority and then you wonder why everything around you is going bad. The Bible has already said, Touch not mine anointed and do my prophets no harm. You see, you open the doors for negativity to come upon you and your family by disobeying the scriptures concerning your leader or leaders.

People with attitudes and people that find themselves candidates for the spiritual washing mat need to go listen to the Sermon on the Mount. They need to grab a hold of the Beatitudes so that their attitude may be liken unto Matthew 5. The Sermon on the Mount points out the way of righteous living for those in the family of God. Our character and lifestyle should no longer be that of the old nature. We are to let our light shine so that men may see our good works and glorify the Father who art in heaven.

Since we know that Jesus is coming like a thief in the night and the earth and the works done in it will be dissolved by fire, we in the meantime, should be in consecrated and holy behavior putting on godly qualities. We need to be more God conscious. We need to live our life being aware at all times that Gods' eyes are on us. He sees and knows everything we do. Whatever situation we face we should ask ourselves what would Jesus do? Or how would Jesus react? Jesus is the best example for us.

Some of you are holding on to the old nature and you won't let it fully die out. And that isn't going to work. Some of you need a nature change all over again. You need to start all over again as far back as being christened, baptized in water and filled with the Holy Ghost. The spiritual washing mat is going to put you in check. There is no way God is going to let you walk around saying you're saved, sanctified and filled with the Holy Ghost and act any kind of way. What's hidden in the dark must come out. You can't carry that bad attitude, mean spirit and whatever else you are holding on to into heaven. All of that crazy stuff is forbidden and is not welcomed. It's time to allow God to burn whatever is in you that is not like Him out of you and wash you white as snow. What make it so bad is there are people who hold positions in the church that is guilty of some of these things. We must realize that people on the outside coming inside are observing us, children of God. And if you are not demonstrating the divine nature of God in your life by showing forth the fruits of the spirit then the sinner man will wonder what's the use in getting saved because they act no different than the unsaved. If we are claiming to be children of God then we need to demonstrate God's divine nature so that others may be drawn to Him.

In the dream that God gave to me concerning the spiritual washing mat, God says that some of His people got loads and loads of dirty laundry representing sin. Some will be washing small loads, some medium loads and some will be washing heavy loads. Some of you are so greasy and grimy on the inside; you'll need the double washer. And know that somewhere in between those washings, a dash of Pinesol won't hurt because sin stinks in the nostrils of God.

There are others whose laundry is not even machine washable, you got to go to Purge Cleaners Unlimited. The word "unlimited" meaning there is more than one. There is a chain of them. Some of you got to go to the cleaners because it's going to take a longer process to purge some of that gunk out of you. You got to go through some fires and storms. You got to get back on the potter's wheel. He says, you're all in left field when He's telling you to stay in the right field. You are hard headed, stiff-necked and disobedient, therefore the use of *Arm and Hammer* treatment cleansing agent will be used because you refuse to let God be God in your life.

Let me forewarn you that nothing about the process will make you happy. Don't get mad with God, get *Glad.* Know that by the time you come out of Purge Cleaners Unlimited you will need some *Joy* to *Cheer* you up. When the cleansing process is over God will fill your cup overrunning with *Palmolive.* With this oil representing the anointing and the presence of God in your life, God can now use you to be effective in the kingdom.

For once in your lifetime you'll have that same power you've seen others operate in that made you a little jealous. With this anointing you'll influence the lives of others. The favor of God will rest upon you and you will have power to get results. But first, you got to go through the cleansing process. You got some things in you all the way down to the roots and only God knows how to dig deep down and take it out.

RELIGIOUS HYPOCRITES

Too many are proclaiming that Jesus is coming back for them. God says your heart is not with Him. He says, You are sitting in the midst as one of my people, you hear the Word that is going forth, but you don't do it. Being hearers of the Word only and not doers. You have a form of godliness but denying the power thereof. You are two sided. You act one way inside the church and another way outside the church. Religious hypocrite is the word for you. You are carrying what is called the *scribolic phariseetic* disease. It's not something that just broke out. It's been around for centuries. It is derived from the words "scribes and Pharisees". You need not a microscope to be able to get a view of this disease. You can see it with the naked eye. It is very noticeable and cannot in no way, shape, form or fashion be missed.

As a person carrying *scribolic phariseetic* disease you come into church shouting and carrying on, tearing up the carpet and dashing over pews. Sometimes that is the Holy Spirit chastising you for being disobedient. We know that God does not act unseemly. When the power of God hit you and knocks you down to the floor, you should come up a different person. However, when some people fall to the floor only to be pushed down by the person who is praying for them, they come up with more devil in them than they had before they got prayed for.

Some of you speak in all kinds of tongues even when the preacher is preaching and the sister or brother is giving a testimony. And that's being out of order. If everybody could interpret what you are saying in tongues, it would probably send some folks running out of the church. How can I put this other than to say that some are best suited to be nominees for the best actor and actress award in the church?

Some people go to church and give the same ole lame testimony they've been giving for years. Have not God done something different for you lately? Is not God a versatile God who takes us through trials and tests so that we may be a testimony and a witness to others letting them know how they can make it through victoriously like we did. Since God is a versatile God then your testimony should be somewhat different every time.

256

Some get up and speak with great swelling words. Every time they get up they are bragging and boasting concerning their work in the mission field. They give a good talk, but what is their motive? Who are they trying to score points with? Who are they trying to impress? Hypocrites like to be up front and seen. They like recognition and handclaps. They like attention and praise for their good deeds. The only praise and reward they will get is from man and not from God. Most of the time they testa-lie. They get up saying, "I fasted for forty days or I gave a thousand dollars to charity". So what! Does that guarantee you a seat in the kingdom of heaven? The Bible has already instructed us that when you do good deeds and when you fast and pray that only you and God should know about it, not the whole world.

Some of you get up and give honor to man longer than you do God. The Bible does say we are to give honor unto whom honor is due. Some of you go overboard giving up to ten and fifteen minutes into your testimony giving honor to man and then giving honor unto God who is first in your life and that's it. It's what you call worshipping the creature more than the Creator. Is not a testimony to be given to show forth the goodness of the Lord that He may be glorified and not man? Or is it the time for you to ravel off at the mouth talking about something totally off the wall? Matthew 15:8 says, This people draweth nigh unto me with their mouth, and honoureth me with their lips but their hearts are far from me. Some of you know not the true meaning of worship; you go to church because it's the thing to do. You've been doing it repetitiously for years. You go to church just to be going. You flatter God with your lips and you lie to Him with your tongue. You go every Sunday and then live like the devil through the rest of the week.

You've got the Bible in one hand and the rest of your body is moving to the rhythm of the worldly beat. Yes, you go to church and sing Amazing Grace, Order My Steps, and Blessed Assurance. But you're singing a lie. You haven't come into the knowledge of who God is because if you knew God you would obey Him. You know of God, but that is not the same as knowing God. Time is too short to be pretending and showing off. It's time to get real. Ole Slewfoot says there is no cure for *scribolic phariseetic* disease. But God says there is a cure and that cure is the Spiritual Washing Mat d/b/w doing business with Purge Cleaners Unlimited.

TRADITION

Mark 7:7 says that you worship God in vain: teaching for doctrines the commandments of men.
8th **For laying aside the commandments of God, ye hold the tradition of men.**
9th **Full well ye reject the commandment of God, that ye may keep your own tradition. You obey man's rules and doctrines, but you don't obey God's commandments.** God gave man the Ten Commandments to live by and that is not asking much. Man has added over two hundred off the wall rules and hold fast to them faithfully. You don't even realize you are in bondage with these repetitious acts and ceremonial practices. God is not about all that.

True religion is not a matter of rules and regulations. Your walls of tradition will come down before Jesus comes back. The blindfold will come off of you. You shall be delivered saith the Lord. God is going to do wonders in your midst. Right now there is a wall that is separating and the church world need to change their ways. Changes got to take place.

Tradition that is not Bible based does not allow God full reign amongst the people. Tradition shuts Him out. Right now you have God in a little box. God is versatile and you should expect the unexpected every time you walk in the church doors because you don't know how the Spirit of God is going to move in each service. These tic tock quickie programmed services is not letting God be God. Some people are so entangled in tradition to the point where if change came about, they'd have a hard time accepting it. They are use to following a self-made pattern that does not lead them to God. Instead of being lead by the Holy Spirit they are lead by self, wanting to run things like they have done for many years. Instead of getting with God's program they stick to their own.

God has a way of getting information to me. I read an article in which a woman wrote that she couldn't trust the new pastor just yet. The old pastor had retired and a new pastor took his place. Retirement is one of man's doing. First of all, she thought the new pastor was too young to lead. I wonder had she ever taken a moment to even read how men in the Bible were ordained at an early age. God has not set an age barrier on leading the flock.

This new pastor ran things quite differently and she didn't approve. She went so far as to express her feelings about how she didn't like how he let the kids take turns reading the Word on the first Sunday of the month and some of them giggled through the entire reading. By now I began nodding my head in disbelief because in times like these and with the things that has been going on with our kids today I think they need to be reading the Word of God twenty-four seven. The fact that the kids were giggling could be somewhat due to enlightenment they were receiving from reading the Word of God.

God's Word is powerful and it has a different affect on people. It may cause some to smile and some to cry. It will convict some and it may cause some to shout. She talked about how there was too much singing going on during the services and she couldn't believe the pastor would allow two guitars in the church. By now I'm saying to myself, this woman does not read the Bible. Psalm 149 tells us to praise God with the sound of the trumpet, psaltery, harp, and cymbals. Further down it tells us to praise Him with the timbrel and dance and praise Him with the stringed instruments and organs. Now how can you miss that unless you don't read the Bible?

The pastor made changes in the church bulletin. Using cartoon characters in the bulletin didn't fit right with her. She talked about the pastor's casual style of dress outside of his normal church attire. He wore sneakers to a banquet. She couldn't imagine how anyone could say a prayer over a meal dressed like that. He changed a certain church event that she co-organized for years which fell on the week of her birthday and replaced it for a youth trip in which she described the place they were going to be an awful waterpark. She didn't like him changing that.

Then she spoke negative about the choir director saying that the "no good" choir director was behind the change because she was in good with the pastor. She mentioned the fact that the pastor was ignoring their group meeting and instead went with the choir to that Methodist church down the street. Does any of this sound familiar to you? Can you imagine the backbiting, the whispering, jealousy, envy and gossip taking place in the church? She was the main instrument of it causing others to engage also. She later added, Lord help me to accept the things I cannot change. At least she went to God for help.

The pastor is cutting through tradition. Although he got his work cut out for him, he can do it with God's help. He knew what was important and what wasn't. He was probably related to the guy who said what does coffee and donuts have to do with God. True enough what does God have to do with some of the church functions going on today? God is about souls not raffle tickets, church dinners and fundraisers. God is about souls. We the church should be doing something that will win souls into the kingdom.

To the traditional and nontraditional church, God says that thine iniquities have separated between you and God, and your sins have hid His face from you, that He will not hear. Your sin is so great that others have to come into the presence of God for you. God says that the church need to cry out like David did when he said, ***Create in me a clean heart, O God; and renew a right spirit within me. Cast me not away from thy presence; and take not thy Holy Spirit from me.***

Even David knew God's Holy Spirit could not dwell where sin abides. He knew that sin could not enter into the presence of God. So he cried out for help. He didn't want to be separated from God. He wanted the Spirit of God to dwell inside of him. David went on to say, ***Purge me with hyssop, and I shall be clean: wash me, and I shall be whiter than snow.*** Psalm 51:7

I asked myself why hyssop? Well, hyssop was used in cleaning the house of a leper and it was used in the cleansing of a plague. Hyssop had to have been some mighty powerful stuff. It got the job done. And yet this scripture portrays how serious David was about wanting to be clean in the sight of God. We as children of God need to get right.

261

THE TEN COMMANDMENTS

As I continue to write this book, they are trying to put the Ten Commandments back in the schools. I read an article in a newspaper titled "Leaders disagree on posting the Ten Commandments." Guess who these leaders are? They are religious leaders! Religious leaders rejecting the commandments of God. These religious leaders don't think posting the commandments would make the children safer. And wouldn't have much affect on school violence. They are yet making the Word of God of non-effect so they can hold on to what they want to hold fast to.

One minister stated that the House of Representatives are trying to slip religion into school. And he worries about alienating people who are not Christians and Jews. Pastors who talk like this are those who are deceiving the people into thinking they can reach God some other kind of way. Do they even realize that before it's all over with that every knee shall bow, and every tongue shall confess that Jesus is Lord?

The Ten Commandments being posted is going to steer the alienated ones on the right path to God and the devil knows that. He has his critics at work. The devil will always raise a brow at anything that pertains to God and he doesn't care who he uses to try to stop the plan. Some of his workers are right in the pulpit. One pastor made a positive statement saying that the Ten Commandments would have a stronger effect than school rules that can be altered and then disappear into drawers. As I read that statement I can add by saying that the Ten Commandments along with the rest of the Bible has a stronger effect than the traditions and the commandments of men that some hold fast to.

Heaven and earth shall pass away but the Word of God shall not pass away. Here we have a bunch of religious leaders having a form of godliness denying the power of God to make a difference in the school system, etc. God told me to ask you, where is your faith in Him today? The sinner man has more faith than you do. Did you not know that faith without works is dead? The reason why you don't want the Ten Commandments posted is because you want to hold fast to your traditions.

The reason why others don't want to see them posted is because they are guilty of breaking the majority of the commandments. You are hiding behind a cloak, a title and a degree. You don't have one ounce of an inkling as to who God is. You don't even realize yet that the Word of God is powerful, quick and sharper than any two-edged sword. You have yet a lot to learn about God.

HOLIDAYS

Since we are on the subject of tradition in the church, let's talk about how the church celebrates and pick up on some of the customs of these holidays. It is well worth your time to do some research on these holidays so that you won't get caught up in some of the customs and lose focus on it's true meaning to you as a child of God. For instance, the Holy Spirit led me to look up the word "Easter." Easter has a pagan origin and so does some other holidays. It was originally a pagan holiday honoring Eostre, a Teutonic goddess of light and spring. The word Easter and Eostre resemble one another. Why in the world did Christians pin a pagan word to the resurrection of Jesus Christ is bewildering.

Christians have adopted Easter symbols that are not related to the resurrection of Jesus Christ. No where in the Bible did God command us to acknowledge the Easter bunny. No where in the Bible will you find where the disciples colored and hid Easter eggs and bought new clothes to wear to celebrate the Passover.

If you are going to celebrate the resurrection of Jesus Christ, why not call it Resurrection Sunday or Passover Sunday. Christians in many European countries call Easter *"Pascha."* This word comes from the Hebrew word *pesah*, which means *Passover*. But no where in the Bible will you find the word *"Easter."* We need to stick with what the Bible says concerning everything. Christians get caught up in all of these customs therefore losing focus on the true meaning of the things that pertain to God.

CHRISTMAS

Let us now deck the halls with boughs of wisdom and understanding of December 25th. Christmas was a pagan Roman festival, marking the "birthday of the unconquerable Sun, (*natalis solis invicti*); this festival celebrated the winter solstice, when the days again begin to lengthen and the sun begins to climb higher in the sky. December 25th was also regarded as the birth date of the Iranian mystery god Mithra, the Sun of Righteousness. On the Roman New Year houses were decorated with greenery and lights. When I look at the word *"greenery"* I think of the Christmas tree. And if you do some research on the Roman religion you will find that they believed that impersonal spirits or supernatural powers lived in such natural objects as trees, streams, and earth.

The Roman Saturnia (a festival dedicated to Saturn, the god of agriculture and to the renewed power of the sun) also took place at this time. Christmas customs such as merry making and giving of gifts is rooted from this festival. When we look at some of these holidays we must remember that the Roman Empire was very heavy into pagan worship and they hated Christians. They persecuted the church severely. In light of this we can celebrate our freedom and new birth in Jesus Christ. All that we need is in Jesus Christ even access to the Father. What a wonderful gift! And He deserves every bit of recognition for being Jesus Christ.

Christmas has become so commercialized now to the point where they have replaced Christ with a "x" making it Xmas. During Christmas time people are scurrying about preparing for this holiday season. House decorating has become a contest. And as I hear ministers talking negative about the Christmas tree during the season of 98, the Lord gave me a song on Christmas Eve titled *A Stream of Blessings from Heaven's Tree* that can be found in my book, *Hidden Treasures.*

There are blessings hanging
On heaven's tree for me
If I delight myself in the Lord
He'll give me the desires of my heart
My every blessing adorns heaven's tree.
Obedience is the key
To obtain what God has for me
Obedience will keep them flowing continuously
When the praises go up, the blessing flow down
From heaven's tree, down this stream
And on to me.

Even heaven has a tree adorned with all of our spiritual and earthly blessings and gifts.

I knew in '98 that God was going to deal with me concerning the "tree" come next season and sure enough He did. As we have embarked on the '99 Christmas season with my house on the market I debated on getting a tree. I began to have flashbacks of some of the preachers and teachers I heard on the airwaves finding fault in the Christmas tree. God knowing my every thought spoke to me. One morning I was lead to pray and as I was on my knees I started humming a tune aloud and singing the words within. And then the spirit of the Lord spoke and said, *"tree." It's all in how you view it. The problem is worshipping the tree.* He went on to say, *"You have the worship of God within you."* In other words I worship God and God only and He knows that. With all said and done I knew then that I must enjoy life.

Knowing that there were only limited amounts of trees left to be found, I said Lord there is only one tree lot that I know of that has a few trees left on the lot and I know they are expensive. I said, "Let me find favor with these people and get a good deal. Sure enough I got an expensive tree for the same price that I normally pay every year for a regular tree."

If you seek God with your whole heart He will speak to you. God will not lead you wrong. He waited a whole year to speak to me about the "tree" issue. You see everything but LOST SOULS seems to be an issue among Christians. Putting up a Christmas tree is no worst than or equal to the sin that goes on from the pulpit to the back of the church. The tree has nothing to do with your salvation. Unto the pure all things are pure. We must remember God made the greenery in the first place. So, how can we look at it and find fault in it just because satan had people believing impersonal spirits and supernatural spirits lived in trees.

I Chronicles 16:33 tells us that the trees of the wood sing out at the presence of the Lord. They worship God. Remember what Genesis 1:31 says, And God saw everything he had made, and, behold, it was very good. Your homes inside are beautifully decorated with plants. Sure enough you have trees out in your yard. Even they are decorated with either flowers or some kind of fruit. Who created it? It's all in how you look at it. Are you bowing down to them? Do you believe as the Romans believe? As a Christian your belief is different. You have the commandments of God in your heart and you know not to worship anything beneath the earth. When you tell people it's wrong to put up a tree, in the eyes of God, that's bondage. Just because you don't believe in it don't drag other people with you.

God tells us in Ecclesiastes to enjoy life. And when I say enjoy life, this does not mean for you to go out and run up your credit cards and spend your bill money. During this holiday season give your gifts but use wisdom in spending. We must remember that God is concerned about SOULS and not petty stuff or petty issues. He loved you enough to give someone some wisdom and knowledge concerning some things so that you can put your focus more towards what your purpose is for being here.

At Christmas time you see some people walking around with up to two buggies full of toys, now that's foolishness under the sun because they'll end up broken the day after Christmas anyway. You are rounding up more toys in the buggies then you are SOULS for Christ. And that's what it should be about.

Rounding up souls for Christ so that they may receive the gift of salvation and all the other gifts that comes along with the new birth in Christ.

Just as the angels in heaven rejoices every time a soul is born again into the kingdom of God we should rejoice also. We should rejoice with exceeding great joy as the wise men rejoiced over the birth of Jesus, although by the time they reached Him he was somewhere around two years old. Why they depict Jesus lying in a manger with Mary and three wise men standing around, I don't know.

According to Matthew 2:11 by the time the wise men reached Jesus, He was a young child and was living in a house. We also have to take into consideration distance and travel time of these men, who could have been a number of who knows how many men. Read Matthew 2 carefully.

Knowing that these wise men were observers of the stars, God broke through their misguided system of astrology to make the great event known by showing them a sign in the sky that would lead them to the child. They rejoiced at His birth and brought gifts of gold, frankincense, and myrrh.

As I look at the word "star" and the astrologers it reminds me of how some saved folks look to the stars for guidance. God is not controlling their lives, the zodiac is. They're not trusting God. They are trusting in their lucky numbers for the future. Astrology is a study of the stars in the belief that they influence the course of human events. The word astrology is associated with magicians, sorcerers, and soothsayers. All of this zodiac stuff falls up under witchcraft.

Some make it a daily routine to read their horoscope to get a glimpse of what their day or week will look like. And then there are saved folks walking around asking folks, what's your sign? You better release yourself from that stuff and put your faith and trust in God for your life.

So if you want to celebrate the birth of Jesus what better way to do it is by bringing in souls so they may enter into the "new birth" and receive the ultimate gift of salvation. It is the best present ever. And not only that but you are rewarded with a heavenly reward for each soul that you win to Christ. For each soul you bring to God, the angels are keeping a record. When the time comes for you to ask anything in His name, whether it is spiritually or earthly, He will surely tell the angels to pull out your records and He will honor your request accordingly. Sometimes He will answer immediately and at other times in His own timing.

So if you want to offer a gift at Christmas offer the gift of salvation. Jesus was a Light unto the Gentiles, John was a burning and shining light and we as children of God are to be the same all year round. Many souls are in the valley of decision. Let your light shine that they may be drawn into the marvelous Light of salvation.

The birth of Christ is not about going out splurging on things that you really can't afford. Here you are running up your credit cards trying to buy a gift for Auntie Brenda Sue and Cousin Ila Denise. You got a list longer than your grocery list and Christ is no where to be found on it. And you know why? It's because Christ is not in all of that foolish spending. Christ is about salvation. When the New Year rolls around you find yourself in financial distress trying to call the debt consolidators and credit counselors. The words to describe your situation now are "financial bondage." And that is not of God. God said in His Word to owe no man anything.

The spirit of giving is something that God requires of His people anyway and not just at Christmas time. As we give we should give from the heart. Don't give expecting something in return. There are some people who will say I got to get you something since you got me something. They hadn't thought to get you something until you popped up with a gift for them. They haven't grasped a hold of the principles of giving yet. You have reached inside of your heart and bought them something and now they feel motivated to get you a gift. Now that's not giving from the heart.

Why wait until December 25th to recognize the birth of Jesus Christ and the giving of gifts? We should acknowledge the birth of Christ every time a soul has been born again because he has crossed over from darkness into the marvelous Light, which is Jesus and has received the free gift of salvation. And we should always maintain a spirit of giving especially to the homeless and those who are in need.

Why wait until Thanksgiving to give thanks unto God for all He has done? Ephesians 5:20 tells us to give thanks unto God everyday. Give thanks unto Him everyday for the things He has done and give thanks in advance for the things He is getting ready to do. Give thanks unto Him for those things you have asked for that have not manifested in the natural because its all in His timing that you will see them come to past. In the meantime thank Him and praise Him.

Giving thanks always (continually) (nonstop) for all things unto God and the Father in the name of our Lord Jesus Christ. Let us maintain a spirit of thanksgiving all year 'round. Let us offer up the sacrifice of praise to God continually, that is the fruit of our lips giving thanks to his name. Hebrew 13:15.

A Message To The Godly

HALLOWEEN

Lastly, let's look at Halloween also called All Hallows' eve, a holy or hallowed evening, as we know observed on October 31st, the eve of All Saints' Day, honoring dead saints. We know that the word *"hallow"* takes on the meaning of the words *"holy or sanctify"*. I don't care how much they dissect the word *"Halloween"* by breaking it down; there is nothing holy about this evil observance. Halloween is a pagan festival that goes back to the Celtic and the Anglo-Saxon times honoring Samhain, the Celtic lord of the dead. The Druids were the priests and teachers of the Celts who headed the customs such as bobbing for apples, bonfires, burning sacrifices, fortune telling, and wearing costumes. This Celtic celebration marked the beginning of the season of cold, darkness, and decay. Now, that sounds very eerie.

And then the Romans joined in and we already know that they are bonafide pagan worshippers. The pagan observances influenced the Christian festival of All Hallows' Eve, celebrated on the same date. I see nowhere in the Bible where God told us to honor dead folks. Jesus told a man once to let the dead bury the dead but you, man, go and preach the gospel.

According to the Bible I am to honor God. He says to honor thy mother and thy father. He says to give honor unto whom honor is due and you have to be careful in how you do that because God is a jealous God. Ecclesiastes 9:5 tells us that **the dead knows not any thing, neither have they any more a reward (here): for the memory of them is forgotten.** The saddest thing about this occasion is Christians take part in some of the Halloween customs. They say its okay to dress up as long as you are portraying a positive image. For instance an angel, shepherd boy, bozo the clown or even Mickey Mouse. The devil has tricked them already. There are some churches that will allow the kids to go trick or treating as long as they don't dress up in a costume, it's not going hurt anything they say. Some churches host Halloween parties but they give it a different name having carnivals and games and some go as far as decorating the church premises with Halloween décor. No matter how much you try to polish it up on a positive side you are still partaking in this devilish pagan oriented observance when you adopt the customs. God is not about demons, superstition, scaring people, jack-o-lanterns, and wearing costumes. There's too much costume wearing going on in the church already.

In these last days the church need to be aware of some of the secular observances they take part in and start doing some research on these things. As you can see most of them have pagan origins. God is trying to awaken the church out of her deep sleep and get His church ready. God is about SOULS. That's all.

BROAD AND NARROW

The Bible tells us in Matthew 7:13, **Enter through the strait gate; for wide is the gate and broad is the way, that leadeth to destruction, and many there be which go in thereat;**
14th **Because strait is the gate, and narrow is the way, which leadeth unto life, and few there be that find it.**
Here we have a gate. Once you enter through this gate the way is either broad or narrow. God says in

Deuteronomy 30:19, **I call heaven and earth to witness this day against you that I have set before you life and death, blessing and cursing: therefore choose life, that both thou and thy seed** (descendants) **may live:**
You choose which path to travel on. God was merciful enough to let us know that the narrow way would be beneficial to us and the broad way leads to destruction. The broad path is what many travel on. It is enticing. It is broad in that it is diverse and has a lot of deceptive things to offer. It is highly plagued with deception. This path is not strict. It is not strict at all. On this path you can do anything you want to do and live however you want to live.

On this path people are lead to believe that they are on the right path to God when actually they are not. The devil doesn't care who he uses to mislead these people. He has tricked people into thinking they can live any kind of way and still go to heaven. On this path they say all souls go to heaven. They dispute the Bible having departed from the faith. They say there is no devil. They say the devil is something you conjure up in your mind. Instead of saying, I am a god: they say I am God. They say hell is a figment of one's imagination. They say there is no God. They credit Darwin's theory of evolution.

The devil is the leader on this broad path, but the followers can't even discern him. They can't discern the spirit of error from the spirit of truth. The spirit of truth is false to them. Reason being is because they don't want the truth. They will turn around and ask you, are you sure you're saved? John the Baptist preached repentance and they said he had a devil. They said Jesus cast out devils by Beelzebub, attributing the Spirit's work to satan. You see there is a lot of ignorance along this path.

273

The spirit of error comes to them in sheep clothing. He appears to be righteous on the outside but on the inside he is false. False prophets, false teachers you name it. Out of his mouth he is saying Lord, Lord, but not everyone who says Lord, Lord shall enter into the kingdom of heaven. Only those who do the will of the Father. Misleading people is not doing the will of the Father. It is getting you a Woe in front of your name.

On this path all kinds of false information from false leaders is being eaten up. As the Bible so plainly puts it, they are giving heed to seducing spirits and doctrines of devils. When truth is presented unto them they will label it as a strange doctrine and will question your role as a Christian. On this path, right is wrong and wrong is right. People are acceptant to any thing offered out there. They will accept anything to keep from having to live by God's standards. They open up their minds to believe all of this garbage that is floating around in society.

The narrow way is too strict for them. You see, on the narrow path you can't do what you want to do and call yourself a child of God. You have to abide by the Ten Commandments, statutes and laws. God has set guidelines for His children to live by. And is He asking much? No. On this narrow path you will find the truth, the whole truth and nothing but the truth. And some people don't want that. On the narrow path you will find true love, true joy, true peace and true happiness. On the broad path it is imitation only. On this narrow path of truth you will get called everything but a child of God. Don't worry about it because the Bible says Blessed are ye when men persecute you and say all manner of things against you.

The narrow path leads to life through Jesus Christ. Jesus says in John 14:6 **I am the way, the truth, and the life: no man cometh unto the Father, but by me.** This passage says No man comes unto the Father but by whom? Jesus. He says in John 11:25 I (Jesus) am the resurrection and the life. If you believe in Jesus and when you die physically you shall live on spiritually and eternally. And who ever live physically and believe in Jesus shall never die spiritually and physically. This narrow path will lead you to every promise God has given in His Word. On this path you have security, healing, prosperity, comfort, power, spiritual gifts, eternal life, just to name a few. Hey, God has a lot to offer!

Let's take a minute and go back to the broad way. Begin to picture Hollywood and the term "Broadway" in reference to the street name. Here you have the glitter, the bright lights, diverse lifestyles and beliefs, fancy cars, offers, entertainment, deception and just plain fun. All of that excitement doesn't even last. At some point it leads to unhappiness, depression, drugs, murder, and suicide. Bottom line is it leads to destruction. It is one thing to be rich and famous and living according to the principles of God. And it is another thing to be rich and famous and not covered under the blood of Jesus Christ. It will destroy you being rich and not having Jesus in your life. People are trying to take alternative routes to God. There are no alternative routes to God. Since you can't read my lips I ask you to read my writing: JESUS IS THE ONLY WAY TO GOD.

Man has created unto themselves many paths, but God has only set before us one gate and two paths to choose from once we get to that gate. Simple and plain, God has set before us the way of life and the way of death. The broad way leads to curses and death and the narrow way lead to blessings and life. All paths do not lead to God. There is only one way to God and that is through Jesus Christ. To sum it all up there is only **one Lord, one faith, and one baptism.** Ephesians 4:5

DECEPTION

Today the devil is bringing a lot of deceptive things into this world to distract people's attention away from God and if you are not spiritually discerning then you may very well find yourself becoming deceived.

I Timothy 4:1 says, ***Now the spirit speaketh expressly, that in the latter times some shall depart from the faith, giving heed to seducing spirits, and doctrines of devils;***

2nd ***Speaking lies in hypocrisy; having their conscience seared with a hot iron.***

There are all kinds of doctrines out there; doctrines of devils, seducing spirits, false teachings, etc. and therefore you got to know your Bible. In this day and time you need to be in a place in God where you will be able to discern the spirit of error and the spirit of truth.

One religion that is high on the rise is the New Age religion. It is not of God. It is a false doctrine. It is a counterfeit gospel that tries to imitate the true Gospel. This religious movement is tied to the Babylonian church mentioned in Revelation. God says don't be carried away by every wind of doctrine. Don't buy into false doctrines that teach you anything other than the Word of God that will damage your spiritual walk. God says in I Thessalonians 5:21, ***Test all things with the Word of God.*** Go to the Word of God and see what He says.

God is not concerned about what denomination or religion you belong to. He is concerned about SOULS. So often the question is asked, what denomination do you belong to? Or what religion do you belong to? And so often my response is, I am a child of God. Being a Pentecostal, Catholic, Methodist, Baptist, don't mean anything. For God has called all unto holiness and repentance. He says to be ye holy for I am holy regardless. As far as God is concerned, religion is nothing if it don't follow after the principles of God.

Religion comes up with its own beliefs and practices. They deceive their followers into thinking that their way is the only way to God. Some religions don't adhere to the things of the Bible. They don't want to eat the whole roll, so they dip and dab. They don't want to obey the whole Truth so they take some and leave some. They add to and take away from the Bible when God has warned in Revelation 22:18,

For I testify unto every man that heareth the words of the prophecy of this book (Bible), If any man shall add unto these things, God shall add unto him the plagues that are written in this book:

And if any man shall take away from the words of the book of this prophecy, God shall take away his part out of the book of life, and out of the holy city, and from the things which are written in this book.

There are some that believe that the Bible has been tampered with. The only thing that has been tampered with is the human mind. The first thing that the enemy attacks is the human mind. He's doing a three-ring circus act with the mind. He figure if he can get to your mind then he can have you thinking and perceiving every which way but the way

God intended for you to follow and understand.

The bottom line is all scriptures were given by inspiration of God unto men who wrote the Bible. God was right there with them. There's no way they could have gone wrong. Whether there be missing books, chapters, etc., I believe God allowed just what He wanted to be in the Holy Bible for us to live by.

Once again, if you believe that all religions lead to God, then you are deceived already. The only way to God is through the Gospel of Jesus Christ and the repentance of sin. Mind control, yoga, and meditation will not lead you to God. Buddha cannot lead you to God; he's just a nonliving nothing. Allah is a god all right, but he can't get you to the one and only True living God Almighty of Abraham, Isaac and Jacob. Muhammad can't lead you to God; he is a dead man. God is not dead. Jesus came to this earth in the flesh and is still not dead. He is alive.

No man can come to the Father except by Jesus Christ first. I don't know why people think they can get to God some other kind of way. Jesus is the way, truth and the life. God has highly exalted Him, and given Him a name, which is above every name. And He only sits on the right hand of God. Mark 16:19. Jesus was chosen and foreordained before the world was even formed; He was made manifest for our sakes.

SALVATION AND GOOD WORKS

Religion differs in what salvation is and how it can be gained. Some think you can obtain salvation through good works. Ephesians 2:8 lets us know that by grace ye are saved through faith and that not of yourselves: it is the gift of God. And verse 9 says not of works, lest any man should boast. These scriptures let us know that works cannot save. We are created in Christ Jesus that we may do those good works that God predestined for us.

As you can see good works goes along with salvation. Unsaved people can do good works, but what good is it if he doesn't acknowledge Christ in his life. A good person can do good works; however, what good is it if he does not have Christ in his life. Just because you send a million dollars to a charity or to a disaster stricken city does not guarantee you a seat in heaven. What good is it anyway if you don't have salvation? We obtain salvation through faith in Jesus Christ in believing that He died for our sins and through Him we receive forgiveness of sin and eternal life. As I mentioned before, Jesus is the only way we can obtain salvation. Acts 4:12 lets us know this. *Neither is there salvation in any other; for there is none other name under heaven given among men, whereby we must be saved.*
And then Matthew 1:21 says *and she shall bring forth a son, and thou shalt call His name JESUS: for He shall save His people from their sins.*

So if you think Krishna or Shiva is the way, or singing in a state choir or passing out food to the hungry will give you salvation; then my prayer is may your blinded eyes be opened that you may receive the knowledge of the Truth. And invite Jesus Christ into your heart that ye may gain salvation and eternal life through Him.

A LOOK AT RELIGIONS

There are certain religious sects that go door to door misinterpreting and wrongfully applying the Word of God. They are far from the Truth. They have missed God already. They quote scriptures off the top of their heads and have no understanding of them. That's why God tells us to study to show ourselves approved. This religious sect disputes just about everything in the Bible as well as other groups. They resist the truth that you feed unto them. They have been brainwashed and taught by the commandments and doctrines of men. Their minds are already corrupt and reprobate concerning the faith.

I Timothy 6:3 tells us that if a person teaches otherwise and don't teach according to the gospel of Jesus Christ that he is proud, knowing nothing. He has an unhealthy fondness for controversy and disputes and strife about words that result in envy, strife, railings, and evil surmisings. God says to stay away from such. Stay away from those that argue concerning the Law. They will ask you questions and try to make you look like you don't know what you are talking about; however, the Word tells us how to handle these people. It tells us to answer not a fool according to his folly, lest he be wise in his own conceit. In their own eyes they think they are right no matter what. It will take the power of the Holy Ghost to change them. Isaiah 5:21 says, **Woe unto them that are wise in their own eyes, and prudent in their own sight!**

There is one religion that teaches that the term *"rapture"* is when UFOs are coming down to rapture people off the earth. You see how satan is doing a great big circus act with people's mind? The term UFO means unidentified flying object. UFOs are associated with demonic forces. One thing I can say is God does not need beam-me-up scottie spaceships to pick His people up off the earth. God doesn't need any help. And there will be nothing unidentifiable about Jesus appearing in the clouds. All will see Him and will know who He is.

Some teach that God is both man and woman. That is not so. Saying God is woman is like saying He is gay. There is nothing feminine about God. God created the first man and woman. Saying that God is both man and woman is saying He is flesh and blood. God is not flesh and blood. John 4:24 tells us that **God is a Spirit.** God is a Spirit being. He is a Supreme Being. He is God.

There is a religion that teaches that once you die you will become reincarnated. You will come back as a dog, cat, etc. I must say that once you die you're not coming back as anything. I wouldn't trade eternal life to come back to this sinful world if I had the chance. That's not the way God set it up. Even if you go to hell you're not coming back. Ask the rich man who knew Lazarus. The term *"reincarnation"* means a rebirth in a new body. The only reincarnation I know of is when this old body of mine will be changed into the image of Christ at His coming. The scripture says that we shall all be changed in a moment, in the twinkling of an eye, at the last trump: for the trumpet shall sound, and the dead in Christ shall rise first. And we that are alive and remain will be caught up together with them in the clouds to meet the Lord in the air. It didn't say anything about any beam me up scottie spaceships picking anybody up. This is a supernatural event wrought by the hands of God himself.

Some religions use myths to describe the creation of the world. Being that God has put the Bible in front of us, He does not need any other kind of help. The creation speaks for itself. I Timothy 1:4 tells us **to neither give heed to fables and endless genealogies, which minister questions, rather than godly edifying which is in faith: so do.** A myth is nothing but a false belief that is designed to deceive and mislead people. There is nothing mythical about the things of God.

There are some religions that put more emphasis on their leader. Anytime you see a religion that gives more reference to their leader and their leader is the most dominant figure in their group, then you can very well say that he is their god.

There is a religious cult out there that worship God with snake handling and drinking poisonous venom. They are lying on the Holy Ghost saying that the power or anointing of the Holy Ghost moves upon them to perform this type of ritual. They are lying on the Word of God saying that it mentions that the Apostles and the disciples performed snake handling. They make no mention of being knowledgeable to the fact that the snake represents satan and God cursed the snake back in the Garden of Eden after he beguiled Eve.

They wrongfully apply the Word of God and take the scriptures all out of context. They go to Mark 16:17 which says ***And these signs shall follow them that believe;***
18th ***They shall take up serpents: and if they drink any deadly thing, it shall not hurt them.***
Therefore they handle the snakes in their hands and do their little ceremonial dance. And they take it upon themselves to drink venom. They are doing these things to show their faith in God. But God does not operate like that.

And then they use Luke 10:19 which says ***Behold, I give unto you power to tread on serpents and scorpions.*** And right there at their services they lay out snakes on the floor endangering the lives of others attending the services. They even bring their children to these services. This religious crap is not of God.

There is a spiritual interpretation to both of these scriptures and they are far from it. The word *"serpent"* in both scriptures pertains to the evil forces backed up by the devil himself that have a stronghold on people and keep them in bondage. And we as children of God have the power to rebuke these evil spirits that come to kill, steal and destroy people lives.

The scripture that best fit these people in this religious cult is Ephesians 4:18. **Their understanding is darkened, being alienated from the life of God through the ignorance that is in them, because of the blindness of their heart.** What they are doing is blaspheming against the Holy Ghost and tempting God when He says in Matthew 4:7 **that thou shalt not tempt the Lord thy God.** I don't know what god these people are serving but he sure isn't the God of Abraham, Isaac and Jacob.

"I AM GOD"

Nowadays, people are looking within themselves calling themselves "GOD." I hear a lot of that going around. So much for the little *"g"* they are going for the big *"G."* What they need to do is start looking within themselves doing a reality check and come off of that high they are on. That same boastful, pride spirit got Lucifer in trouble with God. God has not changed. He is still the same God as He was then. Jesus said in Luke 10:18, **I beheld satan as lightning fall from heaven.** Now that's quick action. Just as quickly as He gave satan His just desserts by kicking him out of heaven, He'll swiftly give you what's coming to you.

People are boasting on the airwaves, behind the pulpit, on Christian TV, in the Internet chat rooms etc., proclaiming to be somebody they are not. They say, "I am God," instead of saying, "I am a god. There is a distinct difference. Therefore we need to be careful. Yes, the spirit of God dwells inside of us and we are created in His image, but that does not mean we can look within ourselves and say I am God. There is only one God, but there are many gods.

If any man consider himself to be God, then speak another world into existence and see if it appear. Far too long man has played God. For example cloning, artificial insemination. Perhaps the false teachers are showing the people and misinterpreting John 10:34 and Psalms 82:6 that says **Ye are gods: and all of you are children of the most High.** A big "G" has replaced the little one. II Chronicles 2:5 says, **Our God is greater than all gods.** You see that little "*g*"? That's where you stand. You cannot put yourself on the same level as God. God is superior to man. We are His servants. The Bible describes us in scriptures as "little children." But, no, that's not enough for you. Why not put yourself under subjection to God and humble yourselves before Him as "little children."

"I AM JESUS CHRIST"

As we have approached the end of the age, I hear preachers, teachers, etc., saying "I am Jesus Christ" or "I am Christ." God warned us in His Word that this would happen. Matthew 24:5 reads, **For many shall come in my name, saying I am Christ; and shall deceive many.** A little further on into the chapter it says **There shall arise false christs, and false prophets doing great works insomuch that, if it were possible, they shall deceive the very elect** (the church). They are wolves in sheep clothing.

284

But, them that know God can discern between the spirit of error and the spirit of truth. Have you ever heard someone preaching and all of a sudden they blurt out, I am Jesus Christ. I've heard it. Note that a lying spirit has crept in and caused that person to take a wrong turn, therefore he needs to back up and regroup. And some have become so immune to saying that, they are just straight up false anyway.

In the Bible you will find that I Corinthians 3:23 says, ***And ye are Christ's; and Christ is God's.*** Some of you need to go back to school and take English 101 all over again. We need to pay close attention to the punctuation marks here. People have deleted the apostrophe "s" and slid the "s" next to the "t". ***And ye are Christ's.*** This shows ownership that you and I belong to Christ. It is not saying, And ye are Christs. Lord help us today. Some of you have about ten different Bibles in front of you when you only need one. Just because the scripture says, Thou art the Son of the living God (referring to Jesus) and the scripture says that we are the sons of the living God (referring to His children) does not mean we can call ourselves Christ. Yes, we have the mind of Christ according to I Corinthians 2:16 and we are all one in Christ according to Galatians 3:28 and we are to walk in His footsteps. But, that does not mean for you to walk around proclaiming you are Jesus Christ or Christ and calling yourself the Saviour.

People are getting mixed up here and that is the trick of the enemy. All of this mix up is starting from whomever they are following. They follow the leader. You've heard the saying, "gone where no man has gone before. Well, some of the Bible scholars, teachers, preachers, etc., are taking the scriptures somewhere they shouldn't. They are playing Bible Scattergory. They have the scriptures all out in space launching whatever meaning they want to hook on to it. And they are playing too much Scripturenary, misinterpreting and wrongfully applying the scriptures.

If any man thinks highly of himself to be able to say he is Jesus Christ then take a trip to Jerusalem. When you get there find you a cross to fit your size in stature. Next, bear that cross upon your shoulder and carry it up a hill. Let the people put a crown of thorns upon your head and watch the blood drip down your face. Let them drive nails through your hands and feet to secure you to that cross. Feel the pain and blood streaming down your body. Listen to them as they scorn you and throw stones at you. Let them pierce you in the side and whip you. Listen to the crowd cheering, crucify him, crucify him. You see God couldn't find one man on earth who would sacrifice himself for the sins of the world but yet we have so many people saying, "I am Jesus Christ".

NONTRINITARIANS

There are religions that deny the Trinity. Trying to leave out the Holy Ghost. Even the Webster dictionary has sense enough to acknowledge the Trinity as being the Father, the Son, and the Holy Ghost. Webster doesn't seem to have a problem with the Holy Ghost being the third person of the Godhead, so why do you? Denying the Holy Ghost is denying God His personality. The Holy Ghost is the Spirit of God. The Holy Ghost possesses the same attributes of God being omnipresence, omnipotent, omniscience, truth, holiness, and wisdom. I heard a preacher on the radio just as big and bold say there is no Trinity. He lacked wisdom and understanding.

The Bible says if any of you lack wisdom let him ask of God. I John 5:7 says **For there are three that bare record in heaven, the Father, the Word (Jesus Christ), and the Holy Ghost and these three are one.** What is so confusing about that? They each bear witness one to the other. These three work hand in hand with one another in unity just like the body of Christ should be. The Holy Ghost represents power. The word *"trinity"* itself means a set of three. This unique set of three so happens to be one. When you leave out one then you have broken off the union. In Acts 5:3 and 4 you will see His association with God when Peter asked Ananias why has satan filled your heart that you should lie to the Holy Ghost. The 4th verse says you have not lied to men but to God.

The devil is the author of confusion. He is the one that has people minds erring from the Truth and not wanting to receive that which is written in the Bible. He has people twisting the scriptures, doubting the scriptures, omitting scriptures, and believing how they want to believe. Another evidence of the Trinity is found in Matthew 28:19. **Go ye therefore, and teach all nations, baptizing them in the name of the Father, and the Son, and of the Holy Ghost.**

Here you have God in three persons. Christ commissioned the disciples in this verse to fulfill their work together in the name of the Father, the Son, and the Holy Ghost. The same goes for the church today. We need the Holy Ghost to fulfil the work of the Father that is carried out in the name of Jesus. It is by the power of the Holy Ghost that dwells inside of the believer that he or she is able to fulfill the mission to win others to God. You can't just throw the Holy Ghost away. He is vital. You can't leave Him out. Yes, He is a person and should be

287

referred to as a "he" and not an "it". You cannot separate the three persons of the Godhead and call it a *"Jesus only"* thing. When you do that you deny God. And I leave you with II Corinthians 13:14 that reads, **The grace of the Lord Jesus Christ, and the love of God, the communion of the Holy Ghost, be with you all. Amen.** This is yet another proof of the Trinity.

SPEAKING IN TONGUES

Since we are talking about the Holy Ghost, lets go into the area of speaking in tongues. Speaking in tongues is the outward manifestation of the Holy Ghost present in a believer's life. Some teach that if you don't speak in tongues you don't have the Holy Ghost. That is not true. When you are filled with the Holy Ghost that is the Spirit of God being manifested inwardly as well. The characteristics of a Spirit filled person are Christlikeness (fruit of the Spirit), worship and praise, submissiveness and service. Other manifestations of the Holy Ghost being inside of you are the gifts of the Spirit, power, teaching, learning, dedication and prayer. The Holy Ghost filled person strives to be obedient. The Holy Ghost inside of you comforts and encourages. A Holy Ghost filled person will follow the lead and guidance from the Holy Ghost. Being filled with the Holy Ghost means being controlled (directed) by the Spirit of God, whereas the baptism of the Holy Ghost is a covering or protection upon a person's life to do work in a certain ministry. It is the pouring out of the Spirit's power in missions and evangelism.

People are teaching that speaking in tongues is not of God and that it is of the devil. This is what you call blaspheming against the Holy Ghost and that is a very dangerous thing to do. Mark 3:29 tells us, ***But he that shall blaspheme against the Holy Ghost hath never forgiveness, but is in danger of eternal damnation.***

A name for speaking in tongues is called *glossolalia* in which it is said not to be truly a language. Social scientists have dissected this word down to the vowels and consonants saying that not enough was used to make a language, as we know it.

Another word *"xenoglossia"* is the utterance of an existent foreign language by one whom has no knowledge of it. Until God brought it to my attention I had no idea whatsoever that there are people out there that research *"tongues."* Social scientists are trying to come up with some type of explanation for what they call the speaking in tongues and healing phenomenon.

There are some churches that teach techniques on how to receive the Holy Ghost. The only way I know to receive the manifestation of tongues is by getting on my knees in prayer and tarrying and allowing the Spirit to give me utterance. You may not receive the manifestation the first time, but don't give up. Try again. That's where tarrying comes in. You got to wait on God. And remember everything is in God's perfect timing. Read Acts 2.

There have been accounts of people speaking in tongues in another language being heard by others that recognized the language as their own.

I Corinthians 14:2 says ***for he that speaketh in an unknown tongue speaketh not unto men, but unto God.*** When a person is speaking in tongues, his spirit is in direct communication with God. Speaking in tongues is a heavenly language. God knows exactly what he or she is saying. It is not for you to understand, but it is for that person's edification.

Some of the things of God may be a little too hard for the mind to absorb. They are a mystery. It is hard for the carnal mind to fathom. If we walk in the spirit we would be able to perceive the things of God. The carnal mind cannot perceive the things of God for they are foolishness unto him and makes no sense.

There are some that say healing is not for the today church; it was for the early Christians. Yet God has made several promises of divine healing to His people in scriptures. For instance, Exodus 15:26 says I am the Lord that healeth thee. I Peter 2:24 tells us that by Jesus stripes we are already healed. And yet I can attest to the fact that healing is for today because God healed me of cancer. It surely didn't go away by itself.

BELIEVE IT OR NOT

There are people out there that don't believe Jesus was God in the flesh. But John 1:1 clearly tells us that in the beginning was the Word, and the Word was with God and the Word was God. If you look a little further down to verse 14 it tells us that the Word (Jesus) was made flesh, and dwelt among us, (and we beheld his glory, the glory as of the only begotten of the Father), full of grace and truth.
They can't perceive the fact that Jesus is God still. Therefore I must take you to Matthew 1:23 which says **Behold a virgin shall be with child, and shall bring forth a son (Jesus) and they shall call his name Emmanuel, which being interpreted is, God with us.**

There are some that don't believe Jesus is the Son of God. Some try to discredit Jesus but God has already exalted Him above every name. Even the devil believes Jesus is the Son of God for he trembles at that name. At the name of Jesus the devil knows he has to flee. Read Matthew 8:28 and 29. The demons addressed Jesus by saying, **What have we to do with thee, Jesus, thou Son of God? Art thou come hither to torment us before the time?** Now that is something how the devil believe and yet there are human beings out there that don't believe. The devil got people looking for God in all the wrong places thinking they got to go through all of those rituals and practices to get to God.

The devil has played on the minds of many people. Many are serving all kinds of gods but James 2:19 tells us that even the devil knows that there is only one God. He once lived in heaven until God had to kick him out. He has people fooled. He has their minds alienated and their eyes in blindfolds.

TOUCH NOT, TASTE NOT AND HANDLE NOT

There are doctrines that tell you if you eat pork; you'll go to hell. The touch not, taste not, handle not religions. Since when has whatever you touched, tasted, or handled has anything to do with your salvation. These practices do not honor God and has nothing to do with salvation. Don't beat some one in the head because he or she eats or don't eat certain foods. What you eat has no bearing whatsoever on you getting into the kingdom of heaven. For the kingdom of heaven is not meat and drink; but righteousness, and peace, and joy in the Holy Ghost. Meat commendeth us not to God: for neither, if we eat, are we the better; neither, if we eat not, are we the worse.

Some religions command that you wash certain things before you eat or whatever. Leaves me to wonder what will you do if you are out in the middle of the desert with limited supply or no water at all? Will you starve until the rain comes, so you can wash up or will you bend the rules and eat?

THOU SHALT NOT WEAR

Religion has plagued people's wardrobe telling them what they can and cannot wear. Some religions require their followers to put a covering on their head. The Bible tells me that a woman's hair is her glory. Since a woman's hair is her glory then she needs to show it off. Some religions have their followers walking around looking like multiple twins with the same outfit on. They don't even look happy. They are just going along with the program trying to find God. You need to loose these people and let them wear the latest labels as long as they dress in modest apparel. What do you think the manufacturers are here for?

Some religions go deeper discouraging people from wearing certain colors. Black is a color and so is white. Just because Sister Style wears white does not mean she is going to heaven and just because Sister Style turns around and put on black does not mean she is demonic and is going to hell. Color has nothing to do with salvation. Give the people a break and come off the colors. Let them enjoy life as we are told to in the Book of Ecclesiastes.

Years ago, the old school had God's people under bondage with that "dress issue." Instead of having people running to God and remaining, they had people running away from God. Why? Because they went all out in left field and put more emphasis on what you can and cannot wear instead of being concerned about the soul. They condemned a lot of people to hell because they wore pants. They couldn't wear earrings and they couldn't wear makeup. That was nonsense then and it is nonsense today. Get out of people's jewelry cases and powder rooms and let the Holy Ghost work on them? Your job is to win them over to Christ. Your job is not to run them away.

The old school even went as far as to say that you could not attend functions that the world attends. Say for instance, sporting events, theatres, etc. That was and still is straight up bondage. Now wisdom has kicked in and said let your light shine that men shall see your good works, but how will they see if you are cooped up inside the four walls of the church. You think the world is coming to the church, no, you have to get out there and compel them to come. God is a versatile God and He may use you to witness to someone at that basketball game. He may use you to speak a word to that stranger sitting next to you in the movies.

Matthew 9:10 tells us that Jesus ate with the publicans and sinners. And yes the Pharisees criticized Jesus. But Jesus responded by saying They that are whole need not a physician, but they that are sick. You see Jesus had compassion for all people. He had a heart for the lost that were in desperate need of spiritual help. Jesus did not invite the self-righteous attitude to rest upon Him as so many do today. His main concern was SOULS. We need to follow in His footsteps.

As far as this "dress issue" is concerned there is a way to teach modest dress especially to newborn babes in Christ who are fragile to begin with. As a person grows into the knowledge of Christ, the Holy Spirit will speak and deal with that person as well and will finished what you have already planted and watered.

STUCK ON THE PAST AND
STUCK ON STUPID

There are religions that can't seem to move forward because they're still stuck on the past and can't seem to forgive and forget. They are just full of hate. There are groups out there that preach, if you ain't white you ain't right. They say God intended for each race to be separated and not mingle. They must be relating to their god satan because the God I know tells me to love one another as Christ has loved me.

Another religious group wants to establish a separate territory of their own either on the North America continent or elsewhere for those whose parents were descendants of slaves. In other words what it all boils down to is they want to be separated from a particular race or races. They try to act like they want unity; however, underneath their skin they are full of hate.

This group can't seem to let go of the past. They have been complaining for years about the white man this and the white man that. And one reason why they don't see change is because they are not obeying what God Almighty has written in the scriptures.

They have lost focus on God. They are looking at past situations and present situations that have produced hate and unforgiveness and God cannot bless in the mist. The God that I serve tells us to love one another and to forgive one another so that the Father who is in heaven may forgive us also. We must live in unity and love. And it is to be expressed far beyond just one's own race. It must go over into other races no matter what they have done to a particular race in the past. We still have to love and this includes loving our enemies as well.

This religious group need to seek the true God Almighty who came down here on earth in none other person but Jesus Christ and Jesus Christ only. They need to demonstrate God's divine nature by showing forth the fruits of the Spirit, which are love, joy, peace, longsuffering, gentleness, goodness, faith, meekness, and temperance. Hate and division is not of God.

As I reflect back on a dream (described in detail further down into the chapter) of the countless number of souls that I saw standing before the throne of God. These were people of all nationalities and races from all over the world. God is about SOULS. God is about giving the free gift of salvation through His Son Jesus Christ. It's not about the color of your skin and your religious practices and rituals. It's about SOULS. The white man can be forgiven just like the black man. The Asian man can be forgiven just like the Black man and so on.

God would that no man should perish but have everlasting life. God is no respecter of persons. The reason why I say that is because this same group believes that the Negroes are the most in need of mental resurrection, I guess because they suffered years of slavery. There is no race on this earth that need more of something than another race. We are all equal in the eyes of God. God is not looking at color; He is looking at the soul.

The mind is brought back to life through repentance of sin and the blood of Jesus Christ. When you acknowledge Jesus Christ into your life you become a new creation. It's like starting all over again. You receive a new mind, a new way of thinking and a new personality. With this new mind in Christ Jesus you let bygones be bygones. You let the past stay in the past and be forgotten. You learn how to forgive so that your heavenly Father will forgive you also. With this new mind in Christ you don't stay stuck on stupid holding on to past issues and that's because a mental resurrection has taken place. A healing of the mind has transpired through the blood of Jesus Christ.

As for physical resurrection, there is no biblical proof that a particular race will be resurrected first. The Bible tells us that the dead in Christ shall rise first, whether they are Hispanic, Negro, Jew, Caucasian, etc., and those who remain shall be caught up to meet Him in the air.

We better learn how to mix and mingle and get along down here on earth. There will be no division in heaven. God did not plan for a certain race of people to be resurrected first. He just said the dead in Christ shall rise first. He didn't give a race preference. All will be given a chance to receive salvation and upon receiving salvation through Jesus Christ, they will reign with Him no matter what skin color they are.

ANGEL WORSHIP

Some religions teach the worship of angels. Jesus created the angels to magnify God, to serve as messengers of God, to protect us, and to minister unto us. There is scriptural proof in Revelation 19:10 that lets us know that we are not to worship angels. As you read this scripture John was instructed by an angel not to worship him, but instead to worship God. It read as follows: ***And I (John) fell at his (angel) feet to worship him. And he (angel) said unto me, See thou do it not: I am thy fellowservant, and of thy brethren that have the testimony of Jesus: worship God: for the testimony of Jesus is the spirit of prophecy.*** We are not to worship angels. I know if we are not to worship angels we are also not to worship Mary.

There are religions that give reference to the statue of Mary, being totally ignorant of Exodus 20:3 and 4. Thou shalt have no other gods before me. Mary did not die on the cross for your sins. Jesus did. Thorns were driven through His hands and not Mary's. Blood was dripping down His body, not Mary's. We are to worship Jesus, the Savior.

HELL

Some are tricked into believing there is not a hell. I must tell you that hell is about as real as you sitting here reading this book. Hell is not a figment of one's imagination. Hell is real. Hell existed way before you did. Hell is satan's kingdom. It is the abode of his angels. Hell is the eternal home of people who have not repented of their sins. The Bible mentions hell in several scriptures.

The rich man who lifted up his eyes in hell and looked afar off to see Lazarus sleeping peacefully in the bosom of Abraham, asked Father Abraham to let Lazarus go back to earth to warn his relatives that hell is real. As you can see, he was aware of his horrible surroundings. I strive to do everything in my power to keep from going there. And what may that be? That is to live right.

PURGATORY

All souls do not go to heaven. If you have not repented of your sins then you are on the path to hell and destruction. There is no in between point. Your living soul will either go to heaven or hell. There is no way for you to make amends for the sins you have committed after you have died. And neither can the prayers of the living help you once you are dead. God did not create purgatory. It is a lie and a trick from the pits of hell. Once you die, that's it. You will either receive eternal life or eternal punishment. There is no such thing as temporal punishment once you die.

Purgatory is the state wherein souls through suffering pay their debt of temporal punishment and are thus enabled to enter heaven. I don't think so. How you live your life on earth will determine your eternal destiny. The churches that involve themselves in this type of teaching should be ashamed of themselves holding holy masses praying for dead people who they say is in this state of temporal punishment. They are praying and asking God to accept the merits of Christ to makeup for the shortcomings of these people. God doesn't even waste His time listening to that type of prayer.

Prayer cannot help a dead man once he is gone. We are to pray for them while they are living. We should be praying that God deliver our friends and loved ones or that they may come into the knowledge of Jesus Christ before its too late. Whatever sins he or she committed while on earth must be put under the blood of Jesus Christ while they are living.

There is no such thing as dying in holiness with unforgiven sins. If you die in holiness that means you have been forgiven of your sins and is in right standing with God and therefore have the green light to enter into heaven. If you died in your sins you must suffer eternal punishment of damnation and you therefore have the green light to enter into hell. So, get your mess covered under the blood of Jesus Christ while you can because once you die it's too late.

So we have all of these religions I've mentioned in this chapter with all these beliefs. If a religion does not line up with the Word of God then it is vain. It is pointless, empty, ineffectual and fruitless. When I study some of the different beliefs I wonder how ignorant can people get. There is a spirit of ignorance that has plagued the minds of people. They are ignorant to the fact that there is a God. They are ignorant to the fact that God has given us the Ten Commandments to live by. They are ignorant to the fact that God inspired men to write the scriptures and that we are to use them as a guide for our everyday living. I find that people who go off into their own doctrines and believe what they want to believe are people that don't want to abide by the Truth. They don't want to obey the principles of God.

We as children of God must know the Bible and when people approach us with something that sounds stupid, we will be able to go to the Bible and see what God has to say concerning the matter. Sometimes you don't even have to go to the Bible because you know right off that what they are speaking is not of God. We know that God's Word is truth and that God cannot lie. Galatians 1:9 tells us **if any man preach any other gospel unto you than that ye have received, let him be accursed.**

MYSTICAL ACCOUNTS OF HEAVEN

There are several that have given mystical accounts of heaven. Most of these accounts have happened on the hospital bed wherein these people have claimed to have died and went to heaven and came back. A couple of accounts includes floating around in heaven or being in some type of glass bubble. Now floating around gives me a sense of wandering around, being somewhat lost and being inside of a glass bottle is like being in bondage all over again.

There are accounts of people being guided into the gates of heaven by whatever religious figure prominent to their religious belief. We already know that all religions do not lead to God and that there is only one way to get to Him and that is through Jesus Christ. Things like this happens to deceive people to make them think they are on the right track. If Buddha or Shiva meet you at the gate I guarantee you they are not escorting you to God.

As far as being greeted by dead relatives, as for me, I'd prefer to by pass all of that because I want to see the Master. I want to go straight to the Source. I don't mind entering into the bright light because light itself represents Jesus. I don't mind being escorted by an angel but he has to take me straight to God. I want to go straight to the Creator, God himself, the mastermind behind my life who inspired me to write this book.

When you hear of different accounts of heaven, I Corinthians 2:9 should jump out at you. ***But as it is written, Eye hath not seen, nor ear heard, neither have entered into the heart of man, the things which God hath prepared for them that love him.*** That's pretty much self-explanatory.

Some of these people are in their weakest state and are heavily sedated with medicine (drugs) which can cause them to have trances during which they claim to have supernatural knowledge and experiences. Take a look at the word *"pharmacy"*. You will find that the word *"sorcery"* which is the practice of magic comes from the same Greek word (pharmakia) as our English word *"pharmacy,"* which has to do with the use of drugs, medicine, spells, and potions. In all reality people take medicine to rid them of their pain or sickness and so often it works like magic. Swallow the pill and I'm healed. It's gone.

Some saved people are hooked on medicine more than they are hooked on the healing power of God. What in the world are they going to do when the Antichrist comes on the scene? You're so busy trying to get raptured out of here. The Bible tells us that the Antichrist will take his position before the coming of Jesus. And you have adopted blind eyes and deaf ears to the reality of the scriptures. You don't want to accept the truth. When he comes on the scene you won't be able to buy or sell. There are home remedies out there that work and there are herbs out there that works. Instead of running to God for advice you run to the medicine cabinet. It's like an addiction. How do you spell relief? Some spell it P-H-A-R-M-A-C-Y while others spell relief J-E-S-U-S. How can you be effective in the kingdom of God all drugged up?

I once read an article that said taking medicine for life's more common aches and pains often does more harm than good. Taking drugs for minor aches can lead to ulcers and re-injury of sore muscles. Here you are taking medicine for one thing and it effects other organs in your body leaving you diagnosed with another disorder. That is not God. Here is an excerpt from my book *Let the Holy Spirit Embrace You with Poems of Inspirations* titled *God's Remedy:*

Wisdom and knowledge to make these drugs
From God they did not get
They spend countless hours in laboratories
Numerous pills they do dissect
Wisdom from God is first pure
For I am perfect I make no mistakes
A lot of My people are taking man made drugs

301

And My Word they will not take
For My Word is medicine unto your flesh
And in them you will find life
But My people rather go broke buying medicine
Taking every pill in sight
What will you do when the Antichrist appears?
Trust Me now because his time is drawing near
For you will not be able to buy nothing
unless you take the mark
So, put your trust in Me
That's where you need to start
For it is I who has the power to make one whole again
Look to Me as your Physician
And know that your God can.

So for all of you who say that God made medicine, we must remember that God is all-powerful and He doesn't need any help. If God made medicine it would cause no side effects. He intended for the leaves of every tree to be medicine to us. Read it in Ezekiel 47:12. **And the fruit thereof shall be for meat, and the leaf thereof for medicine.** You'd be amazed at the healing properties found in fruits and veggies. What worked back then still works today. Let thy will be done on earth as it is in heaven. It is the will of God that man uses the leaves of every tree (herbs) for healing and not man-made medicine. I'm not saying it is wrong to take medicine, however I can show you God's intent for mankind in Ezekiel.

Just because you take medicine don't make you any less than the person that does not take it. And because God promised He would never leave you or forsake you He will be in the operating room to guide the surgeon hands because the surgeon doesn't see what God can see. Just like they didn't see the abnormal tissue they had left in my body that turned cancerous over a short period of time, but God used that to get me to where I am today. Had not God stepped in when He did the next step would have been chemo and radiation. But the grace of God didn't allow that. The grace of God taught me how to appreciate what He has already given unto us in Genesis 1:11,12,29 and at the same time bringing to my attention the healing foods in the Bible. Genesis 1:29 reads, ***And God said, Behold, I have given you every herb bearing seed, which is upon the face of all the earth, and every tree, in the which is the fruit of a tree yielding seed; to you*** (mankind) ***it shall be for meat.*** If we stick with the Biblical principle of eating then we can enjoy a long healthy life. Old Testament people are our examples.

The grace of God taught me how to eat right and what to stay away from (Leviticus 11). We must remember our body is the temple of God. We must take good care of it. God has taught us already how to maintain it. If we grab a hold of the principles of healthy eating, then it would alleviate having to be cut on and popping all of those drugs into our bodies and continuous visits to the doctors. You won't be all drugged up on the table hallucinating and talking about entering into the light and seeing dead relatives who told you to go back because it's not your time. According to Daniel 12:2 when you die you are sleep until you become resurrected at the coming of Jesus.

I'm not knocking medicine or physicians because in all reality they are needed because man has strayed away from God's true intent in Ezekiel and Genesis. True enough they had physicians back in the Bible days. But what did they use to heal the people? Medicine remedies included the application of bandages (Isaiah 1:6), oil (James 5:14), roots and leaves (Ezekiel 47:12), wine (vinegar) I Timothy 5:23 and salves (Jeremiah 8:22). Sin is so much more rampant now. The more man sinned the more they refused God's will. The more they refused God's will, their knowledge concerning things came through hard thinking and reasoning on their own.

People that make medicine spend countless hours in laboratory dissecting pills and some of them are off into other religions. Most of them don't even believe in God. They obtain their knowledge of medicine through reasoning and through experimenting. Prescribing drugs is nothing but an experiment and a moneymaking venture. They experiment on humans. If one drug don't work then they'll try something else on you. In some cases they experiment on animals to prove whether or not it is safe for you to take. There is a distinct difference between a human being and an animal.

God has already laid out everything in the Bible that would save us from wasting time in the labs. Healing foods and remedies are right there in the Bible. Wisdom from above is pure. It is simple, clean, spotless, untainted, and perfect. If God made medicine it wouldn't cause all of this other crazy stuff to go on inside of your body. I've heard of being drunk in the Spirit, but the side affects that accompany these drugs are not the work of the Spirit. I know God does not want His people to depend on medicine, but instead to have faith in Him.

When you talk faith on that level some people will call you deep. God allows people to get to this level to let others know that it can be achieved. I am reminded of the scripture O the depth of the riches both of wisdom and knowledge of God: how unsearchable are his judgments, and his ways past finding out. There are deeper depths and higher heights to attain in God. What better way to attain them is through experience. God shows Himself to His people and will aid you in your thinking. Or else you are on your own. He shows Himself to us in nature and conscience, providence and especially in the Bible. There are things to learn about Him far beyond the Bible. And only He can provide the wisdom and understanding of the things that pertains to Him.

After God miraculously healed me of cancer about four years ago I have not taken medicine. The reason being is because I know that if He is powerful enough to take cancer out of my body then He is powerful enough to take away any other sickness or pain that comes upon my body. All I have to do is have faith and trust in Him, pray and wait on Him. If I don't wait on Him and go ahead and take the medicine, then how will I know what took the pain away, God or the medicine? As I said before God does not need help. He is all-powerful by himself. If you don't have the type of faith it takes to see God move then you have no other choice but to rely on medicine until you reach a certain level of faith. There are times when medicine will take the pain away and there are times when it will trigger a harmful effect to other parts of the body. And that is not God. God does not inflict. Satan inflicts. Ask Job and then go back to the definition of *"pharmacy."*

God honors our faith in Him when it comes to depending on Him for healing as well as other things. We must go to God in prayer concerning all things for His guidance. Sometimes these things come upon us to test us. It may be due to a sin issue that requires repentance (James 5:13-16). It may be that God is trying to get us to walk in power and lay hands on ourselves. Surely He wants us to trust Him. When we stand on His promises and wait on Him, He can't help but move on our behalf. No matter what the illness is, He will in no way fail to keep His promise. He has already said in Exodus 15:26, I am the Lord, that healeth thee. And He means just that.

As we go back to the different accounts people have given concerning heaven, God is bringing back to my remembrance a vision He had given unto me. In this vision, I could see for miles wide and miles in length, the countless number of souls dressed in white standing before the throne of God worshipping Him. And then the vision went blank and God brought it before me again and this time it was as though I was lifted up high upon a balcony and I could look over and see the same vision over again.

According to Revelation 22:3, in my eternal state, I will not be cooped up inside of some glass bottle or floating around in heaven like a lost child. Once I am in heaven, I will be His servant. I shall serve Him who sits on the throne in worship for I shall see Him as He is. And then if you go over to Revelation 7:15 it reads as follow: ***Therefore are they before the throne of God, and serve him day and night in his temple: and he that sitteth on the throne shall dwell among them.***

Heaven to some is described as a state of mind, a delusion, an idea or wishful thinking. I know heaven is none of these things. Heaven is real. It is a place and a home for all God's children. Jesus clarifies that in John 14:2, ***In my Father's house are many mansions (translated "abode"): if it were not so, I would have told you. I go to prepare a place for you.*** *3rd **And if I go and prepare a place for you, I will come again, and receive you unto myself: that where I am, there ye may be also.***

PHILOSOPHERS

We as Christians must be careful not to let our minds be taken captive by the philosophy of this world concerning the truths of life and the universe. Remember, in God is hidden all treasures of wisdom and knowledge. The wisdom of this world is foolishness with God. Man's wisdom is teaching you things contrary to the Bible. Man's wisdom is telling you that you came from an ape. When the Bible tells you, in the beginning God created man and woman and heaven and earth. And the earth was without form, and void; and darkness was upon the face of the deep. And the Spirit of God moved upon the face of the waters. Now why can't man swallow that?

Philosophers are thinkers who ask deep questions. They are still trying to figure out how the world was formed. It's hard for their minds to even fathom the fact that a Supreme Being actually looked out into the waters and said, Let there be light and there it was. And God said, Let there be a firmament (heaven) in the midst of the waters and it appeared.

And further down to Genesis 1:26, God made man in His image. Everything about the universe and life itself is centered on its Creator, God. There is proof out there and yet men argue against what the Bible says concerning these things. Man has the audacity to question God's intelligence and power to have created all things.

God says in Colossians 2:8 ***Beware lest any man spoil you through philosophy and vain deceit, after the tradition of men, after the rudiment of the world, and not after Christ.***

We as Christians should not listen to these things and neither give them any thought. Remember to keep the faith.

The world can't perceive the things of God. The natural man receiveth not the things of God for they are foolishness unto him. There are people out there that can't grasp a hold of the fact that a child was born of a virgin. They can't accept the fact that Jesus was God in the flesh and to top it off the Bible says they both are one. Again, Matthew 1:23 tells us behold, a virgin shall be with child, and shall call his name Emmanuel, which being interpreted is, God with us. Instead of believing what the Bible says, they go on to try to come up with their own explanation of things and try to discredit the Bible.

Where is the wise? Where is the scribe? Where is the disputer of this world? Hath not God made foolish the wisdom of this world?
God says that the wisdom of the wise men shall perish and the understanding of the prudent men shall be hid. God is getting ready to take over. He said He will proceed to do a marvelous work amongst His people.

We as God's people must use our spiritual weapons against the philosophy of the world. II Corinthians 10:4 says, **For the weapon of our warfare are not carnal, but mighty through God to the pulling down of strong holds.**
5th **Casting down every imagination (reasoning) and every high thing that exalteth itself against the knowledge of God, and bringing into captivity every thought to obedience of Christ;**

The Bible warns that there will be scoffers in the last days walking after their own lusts. These people have not been truly redeemed. They speak against the creation, the Flood; they speak against the coming of Jesus, they deny that there is a God. They listen not to the wisdom of others. They willfully overlook and forget facts of the Bible. There is plenty enough proof out there to destroy their theories, but they ignore them. They frequent the airwaves with their false teachings and prophesying lies concerning end-time events. They write books and some of these books are heavily indulged in. Not being spiritually discerning at all.

Wisdom is available unto all to learn but many refuse godly wisdom. In Proverbs 1:22, God has something to say to scoffers and others that divert the Truth. *How long, ye simple ones, will ye love simplicity? And the scorners delight in their scorning and fools hate knowledge?*

23rd *Turn you at my reproof: behold, I will pour out my spirit unto you, I will make known my words unto you.*

24th *Because I have called and ye refused; I have stretched out my hand, and no man regarded;*

25th *But ye have set at nought all my counsel, and would none of my reproof:*

26th *I also will laugh at your calamity; I will mock when your fear cometh;*

27th *When your fear cometh as desolation, and your destruction cometh as a whirlwind; when distress and anguish cometh upon you.*

28th *Then shall they call upon me (God), but I will not answer; they shall seek me early, but they shall not find me:*

29th *For they hated knowledge, and did not choose the fear of the Lord;*

30th *They would none of my counsel; they despised all my reproof.*

31st *Therefore they shall eat of the fruit of their own way, and be filled with their own devices.*

We must teach our children the real truth concerning the universe and life so that they may not be deceived by the philosophy of this world. We must get to our kids before they do. There is so much information out there that can deter their minds away from the Truth. My son came home and told me that his science teacher told the class that there is no such thing as the bottomless pit. That's science for you. I thank God he knows what the Bible says concerning the bottomless pit as well as other things that they are teaching in the schools contrary to the Bible. We need to anoint our children each morning before they go off to school.

DISOBEDIENT CHILDREN

Since we are now on the subject of children, let's go inside the home. When God says to get our house in order what better place to start other than our home. How will you be able to do a work for God when your own home is in a wreck? One characteristic that has intensified as we draw near to the coming of Jesus is disobedience to parents. The Bible says to train up a child in the way he should go: and when he is old he will not depart from it. Children across the nation are running the household today. And guess what, the parents can't do anything with them! And guess what else? Some of these parents are saved, sanctified and filled with the Holy Ghost. Now, that just doesn't set right. There are many ghosts out there, but the Holy Ghost I know represents power.

The Bible tells us that after that the Holy Ghost is come upon you ye shall receive power. Do you know what it is going to take to say, satan get thee under my foot or get thee behind me and see him actually do that? Or satan, I rebuke you, flee in Jesus name and he actually flees? It is going to take power. We need to use that same power in our homes against satan who is trying to destroy our children.

The Bible says that satan is walking to and fro upon the earth seeking whom he can devour. Now I as a child of God better know that I got power over him like the Bible says I do. If I don't begin to know and learn how to use that power, he'll try to walk all over me. The closer we get to the end; satan is going to lash out some strong demons.

Satan don't care what position you hold in the church, if you got kids he is coming after them to try to harden their hearts and deter their minds away from God. Some of the worst acting kids come out of five-fold ministry households. The devil works extra hard on them because He knows that they being of that blessed seed are our future prophets, evangelists, teachers, presidents, politicians, you name it. He is warring with their minds. He knows his time is just about up, so he's sending out his lieutenants, commanders and chief captains on them.

The Bible already lets us know that the antichrist himself will make war with the saints and he will wear out the saints of the Most High. And you can't even handle these little day to day demons satan has assigned to you and your family. Don't you know this is to get you into practice for the things ahead? And now is the time to walk in power knowing that you have it like God said you have it.

So, we see satan is warring with our young people and why is there so much room for him to do that? Saved or unsaved, we can truly look at the parents. Some parents' attention is focused on everything else but the child. Some of you spend more time running

311

around for the church more than you spend time with your spouse and children. It's what you call family neglect in most cases. We must know that God comes first before all things, then the family and lastly the church.

Here your child is struggling with the issues of life, etc. and you are busy trying to get recognition in the church. You are trying to be everything in the church and you are trying to be in just about every auxiliary there is. You don't have time for them. If you don't spend time with them satan will. He will show them what they can get into. The world offers more for these young folks to get into than the church. They must be kept busy. If we don't give them the attention they need and communicate with them, satan will. He will give them a so-called family that will listen to them and will deter them farther away from God. The church got to stay at least one step ahead of the devil in all things.

Something is wrong when you are in a 200 member church with fifty youths and only two or three can be accounted for as actually on their way to achievement or has already achieved with a good head on their shoulder setting an example for others. While others are walking around the church being rebellious with no goals, trying to be cool talking about that's da bomb or this or that is "tight" or "cool" only to find out later in life they weren't so cool or all that after all. Some of them are so rebellious they bring bad on themselves by dishonoring their parents.

I've heard of dysfunctional families in the unsaved household but men and women of God we have an upper hand on the situation by putting the dysfunctional spirit in the family under the blood of Jesus Christ. And allowing the Holy Spirit to lead us and guide us concerning our children. Its going to take the anointing to be able to handle them and to be able to know the right words to say to them and get desired results. When we try to handle things our way and not God's way they can be drawn farther away from us. There are ways to raise your kids up without them feeling like prisoners. When you become too strict on them that makes them even more rebellious. Unwanted pregnancies, dropouts, drug use, gang involvement, etc. will occur.

Our local churches should have classes in parenting skills, communication skills and time management for parents and ongoing activities and classes for the children. For instance, youth services, youth conferences, youth outings, you name it. If we don't come up with classes and ongoing activities for them the world will. The things that the world is teaching them are not lining up with God's guidelines for our everyday way of living.

Some of you act like your kids are grown. The world has influenced the way in which they dress. And you then allow them to come to church dressed any kind of way. The boy is wearing pants hanging off of his waist, tinted hair, plaits or braids in his hair and an earring in his ear as if he is grown. The girl is wearing tight whoochie momma clothes, tinted hair and too much makeup as if she is grown already. They come into the house of God with no church etiquette whatsoever. They have that "I don't wanna be here" attitude. Little ones are cutting up in church and the older ones act as if they haven't been taught why it is that we go to church in the first place.

Your children are a reflection on you. The way they act and the way they dress is a reflection on the parents. You're not running them: they are running you. You have the nerve to say you'll let the Holy Spirit work on them. Well, the Holy Spirit is suppose to be inside of you already and you as the parent of that child who is still living under your roof is to work with that child yourself under the guidance of the Holy Spirit.

Here you are trying to preach a message on family values and people are not receiving it because they are looking at your family. The wife got a bad attitude and the husband has no control whatsoever in the household. People know your house isn't in order. Here you are trying to preach modest dress, etc and your family is walking up in the church looking like they are ready to go step into a nightclub. Now what kind of example is that? You see when you hold a title or a position in the church people watches you and everything that represents you.

Some of you all situations with your kids are real bad and therefore you may have to make a sacrifice and fast for your child or children. When you see your child began to change, whether it be in attitude or in the way they dress, say for instance, walking in your house looking like a gangbanger or an occult worshipper, you better go on you a fast and pray hard. That is the only way you will see results. They go not out but by prayer and fasting says Matthew 17:21. You can stop the devil dead in his tracks and rebuke him off your child.

You have kids in your house that don't want to be saved. They have no interest in God. They don't want to go to church. They don't want to live by your rules. You are allowing them to bring ungodly things in your house and you saved parent know well that God's Spirit cannot dwell where evil abides. They are enmity against each other. The reason why you feel the presence of evil in your house is because you have allowed junk to take up residence. You should have enough Holy Ghost draining off of you to the point where your children, your husband, or your wife will respect you. Yes, some of you let your ungrown kids have their way in your house.

Some of them get involved in the occult, some gangs, and others drugs. Right under your roof. Why you, saved, Holy Ghost filled, fire baptized can't control them is baffling. Some kind of way you are trying to destroy yokes and trying to cast out devils in other people lives, but can't seem to take control over the devil that is controlling your house.

There is no such thing as my son or daughter is out of control and I can't handle them. That's like saying the God that you proclaim has no power. The more you let your kids whether they be big or small, old or young have their way, the more ole slewfoot will use them to drain you, put gray strands in your hair and drive you crazy. God has told us many times in Ecclesiastes to enjoy life. It is a gift from God. You can't even enjoy life because of your children. You have to lay your foot down and tell your children as for me and my house we are going to serve the Lord. Hold those family Bible studies. Get that Word circulating in your house for it is powerful. Although they may stray away as they get older, the seed will already be planted in them. They will not forget it.

And if they are still in your house and don't want to abide by the rules then they need to get out on their own. If they are that grown, they need to get out on their own. The only thing you can do is put them in God's hand and go on with your life. But as long as they are in your house you are due respect and honor. They cannot continue to stay in a Christian environment and cause havoc especially when there are younger siblings in the household being brought up into the knowledge of God at an early age. Children being disobedient to parents is just a sign of the end-time, but we as parents are not to let them rule. We must begin to stand up. And know that we got victory over anything the enemy brings our way. God is calling for His people to get their house in order. God has plans and He is in no way going to let anything stand in the way of them. We must take heed to this call.

WAKE UP

As the Lord reveals things to me and gives me what to write, it saddens me in my spirit to see how God is not being taken serious and how the church is playing church. His grace and mercy is being taken for granted, not only by the church world, but the secular world also. All I can do is wonder in my spirit, God, when will the church wake up? When will the world realize you are GOD? When will the church realize your purpose for the church? When will they catch on to the fact that you are GOD?

God is King and Master and we are His servants. Meaning that we are suppose to carry out His orders and functions that He has given each and every one of us to do. When will we realize that God is concerned about SOULS? That's all. And when will the church realize God is trying to use them to win these souls into the kingdom of heaven so that they do not perish.

THE LOST SHEEP

There are times when the Lord will lead me to turn on the TV. Sometimes the talk shows will let you see how badly of shape people in other parts of the world is in. Whether these people are faking it out or what I don't know. It's sad to see these people so lost and deceived by satan himself. I do know that in all reality these things do go on in the world today.

The world is crowded with dysfunctional people and dysfunctional families that are bound by generational curses who need emotional, spiritual and mental healing. These are the same people that God wants to use us to win into His kingdom. These are the ones that society has told that they need to see a counselor or a shrink, when in all reality they need to be introduced to the real counselor Jesus Christ.

They need to know the answer to their life and problems is in Jesus Christ. These are souls that are on the path to destruction and God wants to give them a chance to repent. They are part of the harvest of souls that God wants us to reach, but we must first get our house in order. These people have some serious strongholds on them and we got to let God prepare us for the work.

I am remind of a poem God had given to me titled, *God Can:*

What's wrong with people
Who go on TV talk shows?
They're all confused and don't know where to go
They go to all kinds of counselors,
Putting their trust in man
Not even realizing that God can.
Have they even heard of God
Or know what He can do?
And that if you have a problem
God is whom you can take it to.

These people are caught up in unheard of sin. Sin on top of sin on top of sin. Sin is running rampant and has been since the beginning of time. I thought the people in the Bible days were bad. This generation today is about the most wicked and perverse generation that ever existed. Do we not know that according to Hebrew 12:29, *that **our God is a consuming fire?*** Do we not have the fear of God in us knowing that God sees all and knows all? It is by the mercy and the grace of God that this world has not yet been consumed by fire. It's getting there.

According to II Peter 3:10, **But the day of the Lord will come as a thief in the night; in the which the heavens shall pass away with a great noise, and the elements shall melt with fervent heat, the earth also and the works that are therein shall be burned up.** Ignorance and sin will no longer abound.

GET BACK ON TRACK

According to Galatians 5:21 a lot of things you find so hard to give up cannot make it into the kingdom of God. They will cause you to miss God. They will cause you to miss out on the coming of

318

Jesus Christ. Sin is enmity against God and it stinks in His nostrils. God wants you to sell out. He wants total surrender. He don't want part of you, He wants all of you. Proverbs 6:16 list six things that are an abomination unto God; take a look at them.

A proud look, a lying tongue, and hands that shed innocent blood, a heart that deviseth wicked imaginations, feet that be swift in running to mischief, a false witness that speaketh lies, and he that soweth discord among brethren.

Ephesians chapter five lists those things that should not be named among the saints and those things hath no inheritance in the kingdom of God. They are as follows: fornication, uncleanness, covetousness, filthiness, foolish talking, and jesting. If we gave reference unto God always like the Bible commanded us to, where would there be any room for carnality?

Romans 8:6 tells us, **To be carnally minded is death; but to be spiritually minded is life and peace. Because the carnal mind is enmity against God: for it is not subject to the law of God, neither indeed can be.**

God wants us to get our spiritual walk together. He wants us to get our house in order. Stop thinking you're saved and get it right. Stop acting like the Pharisees and the Sadducees. God is calling for sanctification among His people. You become sanctified through His Word. Lose yourself in His Word on a daily basis.

I Thessalonians 5:23 says, **And the very God of peace sanctify you wholly: and I pray God your whole spirit and soul and body be preserved blameless unto the coming of our Lord Jesus Christ.**

Sanctification involves walking and having an association with Jesus. He will sanctify you through His Word, through His blood, Hebrew 13:12, and through His spirit, I Peter 1:2. Through sanctification you are consecrated, your outlook is different, you are set aside, you think different, you are dedicated, holy and perfected. God wants us to put on all the fruits of the Spirit in Galatians 5:22. These includes, love, joy, peace, long-suffering, gentleness, goodness, faith, meekness, and temperance. If you walk in the spirit, then you won't fulfill the things of the flesh. Try doing what Ephesians 5:19 says, Speaking to yourselves in psalms and hymns and spiritual songs, singing and making melody in your heart to the Lord. Be like David in Psalm 34:1 when he said, *I will bless the Lord at all times: his praise shall continually be in my mouth.* Praise Him for His goodness and worship Him for who He is. Give thanks unto Him for the things He has done. Praise is the key to unlock the kingdom of heaven.

I Thessalonians 5:17 says, *Pray without ceasing.* Spend quality time with God in prayer. Pray while you're driving, pray while you're cleaning house, etc. It is important to stay prayerful.

I Timothy 2:15 says, *Study to show thyself approved unto God, a workman that needeth not to be ashamed, rightly dividing the word of truth.* Study the Bible for spiritual growth. Fasting helps your spirit man and helps keep the flesh under subjection.

Hebrew 10:25 says, *Forsake not the assembling of yourselves together, as the manner of some is exhorting one another: and so much the more, as ye see the day approaching.*

Some people think they don't have to go to church to be saved. As you go along this walk with Christ, it is not easy; therefore God has set leaders in the church to keep watch over you. Under this leader you will get fed the Word of God. Once you decide to surrender all, the devil will be on your trail real tough and you will need that fellowship of strength and encouragement from your sisters and brothers in the Lord. Find you a church where the power of God is being manifested through the gifts of the Holy Spirit. Colossians 3:16 says, **Let the word of Christ dwell in you richly in all wisdom: teaching and admonishing one another in psalms and hymns and spiritual songs, singing with grace in your hearts to the Lord.**

Now, if we live according to all these scriptures, tell me where will there be time for us to fulfill the things of the flesh? Again, God is looking for a holy generation, a holy people, separated from the world. Again, He says, "Be ye holy for I am holy".

If you desire an intimate relationship with God, you must sacrifice those things that are taking your attention away from Him. Get rid of those idols. He wants your undivided attention. You must get into His Word with fasting and prayer. Then God will speak to you. He refuses to talk over your gossiping, He refuses to talk over your TV, He refuses to talk over anything that is not nourishing your spirit man because He knows that you will not be able to hear or recognize His voice.

You have to spend quality time with Him. God says, He is a jealous God and that we are to have no other gods before Him. He's not only talking about graven images. He's talking about those things you put before Him; they have to be put aside. Prayer, fasting, and reading His Word is the key to a closer relationship with God. Through prayer, fasting, and feasting on God's Word comes many, many revelations that God wants to share with you.

As you may well notice by now, the word "fasting and prayer" has been mentioned quite often in this chapter. That's because it is essential in our Christian walk. It is not only for your benefit, but that others may get blessed through you as well. God wants us to view fasting as a means of dying out our flesh and with the sole purpose of helping others by making a difference in their lives also.

In Isaiah 58:6 God lets us know the reason for fasting.

6th *Is this not the fast that I have chosen? To loose the bands of wickedness, to undo the heavy burdens, and to let the oppressed go free, and that ye break every yoke?*

7th *Is it not to deal thy bread to the hungry, and that thou bring the poor that are cast out to thy house? When thou seest the naked, that thou cover him; and that thou hide not thyself from thine own flesh.*

To be able to do verse six and seven and come out with power to get results you must fast and pray. We Christians do not need to enter into the new Millennium powerless. We do not need to go into the new Millennium laying hands on people who are bound by satan only to find them yoked back up again the following day. The devil awaits some of them at the door as soon as church lets out.

Jesus was an example for us to follow. He showed us by example what we have to do to successfully accomplish the will of God. Even Jesus himself fasted and prayed. He was flesh just like you and me. It didn't take Jesus two hours to cast out a spirit. He didn't have to get on His knees and wrestle or play tug-o-war with a spirit with sweat dripping down His forehead asking for a thirst quencher.

Jesus stood straight up with power and authority and looked that thing in the eye and said only two to five words. For example He would say, flee, come out or get thee behind me or be thou loosed and the spirit would flee with no hesitation whatsoever. He spoke to sickness far away without having to be there and it fled.

Some of God's people don't even have enough power to rebuke a headache, etc., off of them. It is an oppressing spirit and if you could see into the spirit realm you would see an imp just pounding away at your head, etc. Sometimes an affliction, etc., is allowed for chastisement or it may be something you have to go through before God use you for a specific purpose or it may be that God is trying to get you to walk in Acts 1:8.

He tells us in Matthew 17:21 that these things goeth not out but by fasting and prayer. Jesus went on forty-day fasts. Here we are today can't make it past two hours without eating. And think we can go to church on Sunday and say "loose him." My word of advice to you is, do not tell the devil to loose him unless you are fasted and prayed up. He is going to loose something all right and it'll be something you can't get off of yourself. It's time out for the popcorn fasting and prayers considering the things that the church will be faced with ahead.

Speaking of Jesus fasting the way He did. There are some churches that go on extensive fasts and still come out powerless. It is mainly because they are going about it the wrong way and for the wrong reasons. If you lend yourself to that much fasting, physically blinded eyes got to come opened, the dumb must speak, the dope dealer will stop selling, wheelchairs will be going back to the suppliers, the pimp will stop pimping, and the hearing aids will be trashed and so on.

With the kind of things that are coming upon this earth we are going to need power. Power to get results. Power to speak to that rock and see it turn to water. Power to speak to that stick and watch it turn to bread. Again, Jesus is our prime example and God has given instructions in Isaiah as well as other scriptures concerning fasting.

The churches of today are much like the seven churches mentioned in Revelation chapters 2 and 3. Today we have the lukewarm church, the form of godliness church, the cold dead church, the idolatrous church, adulterous church and in them you have the hypocrites, the self righteous, the benchwarmers, robbers of God, Pharisees and Sadducees, etc. And God had a message for them all.

This section of Visions of God's Coming Judgment titled "A Message To The Godly reminds me of the seven churches because it is a message God told me to give to His people today; the church. He brought the seven churches to my attention at the very end of this chapter.

Let us, church, allow God to have His way in our lives, so that we may be the church without a spot or blemish that Christ will return for.

Let us be like unto the church of Philadelphia.

PRAYER OF REPENTANCE

Dear God,

I believe in you and I believe that Jesus is your Son. I believe that He died on the cross for my sins and He rose again. I confess with my mouth that I am a sinner, and I ask you to please have mercy on me and forgive me of my sins. I ask you to come into my heart and make me a new person. Save my soul from death eternity and accept me as your child. Renew my mind and give me a new walk and a new talk. Cleanse me from all unrighteousness and make me into the vessel you would have me to be so that I can be ready to meet Jesus when He comes.

I choose this day to serve you wholeheartedly. I thank you for having mercy on me. From this day on, I accept you as my personal Savior.

Amen

If thou shalt confess with thy mouth the Lord Jesus, and shalt believe in thine heart that God has raised Him from the dead, thou shalt be saved.
For with the heart man believeth unto righteousness; and with the mouth confession is made unto salvation.
Romans 10:9-10

GENESIS ONE

The Bible says in the beginning God created
But man with his own theories don't seem to appreciate it
They are still trying to figure out how the world began
Have they ever read the Bible or held one in their hands?
Evolution says we derived here some other kind of way
I'd rather believe the Word of God
than believe what man say
In the beginning God made you and I
Are you going to believe the Word of God?
Or will you continue to believe a lie?
The lie today is we came from a monkey or an ape
How much of this nonsense will you continue to take?
The spirit of atheism has swept through this country
How do they think they are breathing?
Or how they got up this morning
It is by the grace of God that you are here today
Don't be deceived by the devil thinking you got here some
other kind of way
For everything that exist today God created
So start giving Him the credit and begin to appreciate it!

Genesis 1, Genesis 2:7 and Psalms 104

GOD'S WARNING

Hale (hell) Bopp will return again
It won't take as long as astronomers claimed
This particular comet is Bible prophecy
It's God's judgment upon the world
for refusal to take heed
Take heed to God's Word
and turn from their wicked ways
Ignoring the fact that we are living in the last days
Doing all kinds of abominable things in the sight of God
Turning a deaf ear to Him, not adhering to His call
This particular comet is in the palm of God's hands
It is part of His judgment to be poured out on mankind
Remember it didn't fall to earth
like some were expecting it to
That's because God has a special assignment
for it real soon
It's going to creep up out of nowhere
on this world out of the blue
With no warning whatsoever
and people won't know what to do
Behold a vision of the earth keeps appearing unto me
This world catastrophe is closer than we think
Even the people in the cult got deceived, O, what a fate!
The Bible says suicide is murder
that will send you to Hell's Gate
Hell is real and God Almighty too
When He warns you to repent,
that's what He expects of you
In another vision the word "asteroid"
has appeared to me twice
It has something to do with the comet in the northern sky
John seen it in Revelation as a star falling out of the sky
It caused all kinds of destruction,
it even affected the water supply
People hearts will be failing them
for the destruction it will bring
I thank God I am covered under the blood of Jesus
I don't have to worry about a thing

Let us not forget the mountain burning
as it went into the sea
It was nothing but a meteor, oh yes, it's Bible prophecy
Take a look at the people in the Bible days,
like Sodom and Gomorrah
They'll tell you when God says repent,
it's best not to wait until tomorrow
Even the people of Nineveh,
if they were here they would probably say
Why put off for tomorrow, what you can do today?
And the people of Noah,
they were doing all kinds of wicked deeds
They ignored the warnings of God
and refused to take heed
They and more people got first hand experience
of what God's wrath is like
And so will the world today if they don't get right
These people can tell you it's best
to take heed to God's warnings
When God says, destruction is coming,
you had better believe it's coming
Take heed to the warnings God's people
are giving unto you
It is only given unto them to know the mysteries of heaven
And to know exactly what to do
For there is nothing hid which shall not be manifested
Neither was anything kept secret,
but that it should come abroad
Who shall escape the wrath of God?
Only the righteous indeed!
They feared God and repented of their sins
In other words they took heed.

Revelation 8

THE CONFIRMATION

As I began to question God
About the visions He had given me
God being the all-knowing God of my thoughts
Confirmed it in a dream
In this dream I was a passenger in a car
And to my surprise I looked up in the sky
Two moons with the letter "Y" in them
And earth I saw nearby
One moon in particular had the letter "Y"
And at the same time a cross in it
Signifying "Yes" this destruction will happen
And the people must repent
Behold the confirmation among confirmations
The Lord has given unto me
Concerning a mystery
A Bible prophecy.

Revelation 8 is near upon us!

RIDER ON THE WHITE HORSE

The man on the white horse
Faithful and True
He was the One that delivered you
He lifted you up through the heavenly skies
He was taking you to the place where you shall abide
Daniel 12:35 says even the wise shall fall
But, at the coming of Jesus, you'll be standing tall
Hold on to the faith and endure to the end
Faithful and True one day I shall send
Yes, you were caught up through the clouds
What a great feeling!
You will make it, dear child,
That's what God was revealing
For you are chosen and seated in high places
You are victorious; you're going to make it
So, look up my child
For your redemption draweth nigh
This is a divine message from on High

October 2, 1998
Revelation Dream given on September 20, 1998
Confirming scriptures:
Revelation 19:11 and Daniel 11:35

THE CASHLESS SOCIETY
A Revelation Dream

The cashless society is drawing near
God gave me a dream, it seem so real
As we rode down the street
Businesses were closed everywhere
Things were quite different
You could feel it in the air

> Wait a minute! What am I doing here?
> I'm supposed to be raptured up
> That's what man has taught for years
> For years and years
> They've said we won't see these things
> But, God got a hold of me
> And gave me a revelation dream

The cashless society is well on its way
Exactly when will it happen God did not say
But look at the headlines,
People are losing money today
Look at Japan, Russia, Pakistan
Oh, well, America it's coming your way

> Never in my life had I found money before
> There was a wallet with money inside lying on the floor
> No need for it now the cashless society was in affect
> Jesus had not come to get His people just yet

I remember it being very gloomy outside
God's glory was no where in sight
His Spirit was no longer here
Nothing at all seem to have life

> We were now embarking on something
> That the Bible said would come to pass
> . We were now living in a society
> That no longer used cash.

II Thessalonians 2, Genesis 6:3, Isaiah 55:6

September 2, 1998

THE POWER OF GOD IS WITHIN YOU

The power of God is within you
You can tell the devil what to do
He has no authority whatsoever
To walk all over you
Power in His Word and power within
God did not leave us defenseless
We don't have to put up with what the devil dish out
Oh no, it's very senseless
We overcome him by the word of our testimony
And the blood of the Lamb
Resist the devil and he'll flee from you in Jesus' name
If you had three choices and the devil made a show
Eenie, meenie, minie, moe,
devil you most certainly got to go
I belong to Jesus and in Him I got power
I don't belong to you anymore
No not in this day and hour
Flee, get thee behind me and get thee under my foot
Those are the commands we need to use
To give the devil a boot
At the name of Jesus he trembles and he pedals
If you could see him in the spirit realm
You may want to give him an Olympic gold medal
There is power in the blood of Jesus
And it started on Calvary
All I got to do is believe
And know it is inside of me
The devil is real and he ain't playing
He has but a little time left
He will not cease to leave God's people alone
And besides, you haven't seen nothing yet
Daniel 7:25 says,
He's going to wear out the saints of the Most High
Some of us may be tortured, imprisoned,
And killed for our belief in Christ
Another passage in Daniel says
That satan made war with the saints
A saint is a person living an upright life
So you're either a saint or an ain't

Daniel saw you and you and you
In the tribulation period
Power you must draw from God now
Because we're getting nearer and nearer it
Daniel seen it all my friend for he didn't miss a beep
For he was a prophet full of wisdom and knowledge
And many things he did see
He saw enough to let us know
We better know that we got power
We're surely going to need it in that selfsame hour
So if you're not walking in power
I suggest that you start now
Because the devil will keep on riding you
And he will keep on beating you down
If you got the Holy Ghost
You're suppose to have some power
We're getting ready to embark on a time
When there will be some very dark hours
Read Acts 1:8 and begin to walk in it
Cause what you're going through with the devil now
Is only just the beginning.

February 24, 1999

THE WORLD IS IN TROUBLE WITH GOD

The world won't be here much longer
Just look around you and see
The wrath of God is about to be
poured out upon the seas
Blood and bloody waters and bloody lands
For your eyes to behold
Just like in the Book of Revelation
As we are told
They are doing all kinds of abominable
things in My sight
They have become open with their sins
No longer do they try to hide
They have forgotten their Creator
The laws and commandments I've laid down
Ignoring the fact that God is serious
He is not playing around
They have forgotten I created the world
And formed man in My image
Just as quickly as I put them here
I have the power to quickly diminish
Sin, sin is tearing this country apart
They must repent from the bottom of their heart
They have provoked God to anger long enough
No need to pray for mercy, for their time is simply up
You must be protected with seal of God
Or you won't be able to escape
the things that John saw
Many things, many things are about to
come upon this earth
If you have the seal of God, you don't have to worry
The Bible says in those days shall men seek death
And it shall not find them
And they shall desire to die
and death shall flee from them
Oh, blessed are they who have obeyed
the commandments of God
For only they will be able to escape
what John in Revelation saw.

THEY WANT SIN ON A SILVER PLATTER

They want sin on a silver platter
With you Lord I know it is not so
They want sin on a silver platter
When you have said in your Word "NO"
They want sin on a silver platter
They want you to give them a pat on the back
They want sin on a silver platter
They want you to say it's okay to do this and that
For sin is enmity against God
Umm, do you think that even matter?
No, they want to hold on to their sin
And put it on a silver platter
If you compromise you jeopardize
The things God has in stored for you
Thinking you can have God
And at the same time do what you want to do
For sin in any shape, form or fashion
Cannot enter into the Kingdom of Heaven
Neither will sin continue to reign on this earth
And take its place on a silver platter.

October 10, 1998

*What shall we say then? Shall we continue in sin that
grace may abound? God forbid. How shall we, that are
dead to sin live any longer therein?*

Romans 6:1-2, Isaiah 59:2, Romans 6:12-13

THE WORK ACCOMPLISHED

Putting this book together was quite an experience for me. What started out to be a four-page tract turned out to be a three hundred-page book. Many things, many things I did encounter and that is to be expected when you are doing a work for God. I knew I had to keep my focus on God. God had given me revelations on top of revelations and visions on top of visions and instructed me to write them plain upon the tablets for all to see. When God gives you something to do you best be on your P's and Q's and get it done.

Lives are at stake; I had to keep reminding myself. God is trying to get a message across and He's holding me responsible for what information He has given me. Many hindrances and obstacles came my way. The enemy will use whomsoever weak enough to let Him use them to try to cease the work of God. He will use your sister or brother in the Lord, your family, etc. he doesn't care. But God reminded me that I am on the wall and I can't come down. I am doing a great work for Him.

The Lord took me to the story about Nehemiah building the wall. It was very encouraging. Surely there will be Sanballats and Tobiahs in the midst. Those two headed up every attack against the wall being completed. The work was attacked by mockery, by conspiracy, by extortion, by compromise, by slander and by treachery. When you are doing a work for the Lord you have to stay in prayer and maintain surveillance at all times because the attacks will come. When you are doing a work for the Lord many sacrifices will have to be made on your part because God's work takes priority over all. You really don't have time for foolishness and carnality. Time is running out. A lot of things I had to put on the backburner because this book had to get completed. What people fail to realize is God is God and when it comes to souls, He is serious. It is He who holds the keys to life and death and not man.

A lot of things we need to put on the backburner have nothing to do with winning souls. What the church needs more of today is Simon Birches. Simon had a tremendous amount of faith and spoke the truth in boldness. Simon had a mind to work. He boldly stood up and asked the preacher and congregation, what does God has to do with coffee and donuts? He's right. What does God has to do with all these traditions and functions the church places in front of winning souls into the kingdom of God? Even he knew that God was not a God of tradition. He set out in his mind to find out why God put him on this earth. God has a purpose for each person He placed on this earth. Simon wanted to find out God's purpose for him while on earth. And when he found out what his purpose was in life, he fulfilled it and fulfilled it well. Even in the midst of a set of parents who didn't want him and people who mocked him and talked about him, he kept his focus on God. When it all came down to the end he had to end up helping his enemies and saving lives.

Amid all the obstacles and hindrances the work of Nehemiah and the others got accomplished. The scripture says that when all the enemies heard that it was finished, and all the heathen about them saw it, they were much cast down in their own eyes: for they perceived the work to be wrought by the power of God. When God ordains something no devil in town can stop it. If your work is not being attacked by the devil you better find out if what you are doing is of God or not. When all hell breaks loose in the midst of your work, smile because that is your cue that you are doing something right. As for Simon by the time he saved all those people, they too knew that He was truly sent by God. By the time you finish reading this book, you too will come to realize that it is a work wrought by the power of God.

For those of you who are on the wall, keep in mind that time is of the essence. Stay prayerful and keep a watchful eye because the devil will stop at nothing to try to get you to come off the wall. The demons are trembling because you are doing a work that will cause hell to decrease and the kingdom of heaven to increase. Remember that you are doing a great work for the Lord and you can't come down for any reason whatsoever. Keep your eyes on God and know that great is your reward in heaven.

The Author

Upon receiving the visions, dreams and revelations in this book, the Lord took me to Habakkuk 2:2,3 and it reads:
And the Lord answered me, and said, Write the vision, and make it plain upon tables, that he may run that readeth it.
For the vision is yet for an appointed time, but at the end it shall speak, and not lie: though it tarry, wait for it; because it will surely come, it will not tarry.

As I began to type my manuscript God opened my eyes concerning this book. As you will note how computers have the capability to do grammar check, word count, etc. I took note that at the end of each chapter, as I would do a word count, a readability statistic box would appear. My attention came to Fleisch Kincaid grade level. For each chapter in this book I did a grade level check and readability ease score. I began to see how God in His awesome power orchestrated this book to be set up starting on a 5th grade reading level on up. Even a child can go through this book with reading ease.

In all reality there are adults out there that are reading on such a level or lower and God knows that. He said to "write it plain on tables" in other words to write it simple on tablets in simple language for all to be able to understand what He is talking about. God is so caring and considerate that He thought enough to send you a message that is not brought unto you in complicated language as such as been in times past. Too many are missing the mark because men have been teaching, etc., using great swelling words and people can't comprehend what is being said. The Lord also brought to my attention as I did my word count that He had 50,000 words to say unto the godly and only 15,000 to say to the ungodly. Why is that? The church needs to get their house in order.

All in all when God says, write it plain on tablets, He means just that. He wants you to understand what He is saying unto you and when you finish reading with understanding, He expects action on your part. This book may make you run and it's perfectly okay to run and tell the visions. However, upon finishing this book, *don't run from God, but run to God instead.*

Special Recognition

A very warm and heartfelt thanks goes out to my pastor and first lady of Aurora Co, Bishop Johnnie Smith, Jr. and Lady Julia Smith. Thank you for being the good shepherd God has called you to be, for your love and guidance and for blessing us to be a part of the vision God has given unto you. May God continue to bless your ministry in exceedingly abundance and know that He is smiling upon you.

The Jacksons

ABOUT THE AUTHOR

Kimberly Vinson-Jackson was born and raised in Macon, Georgia. She was brought up in holiness at an early age and strayed away over the years, only to be lead safely back to the cross by the mercy and grace of God. She is blessed with good health, her wonderful husband, Phillip and three beautiful children, Brandon, Kierra and Shalandria.

Her home church is Joy Tabernacle Holiness Church in Aurora, CO where she served as a Deaconess, a Sunday school teacher and was involved in the Children's Church ministry until God moved her and her family onward to the Atlanta area.

Since renewing her vows back to God, He has truly been involved in every aspect of her life. He is her Healer: her Provider, her Protector, her Deliverer, her Friend, her Counselor, her Teacher and her night and shining armor. She has a mindset to please God. The very key to her every blessing and success is *"obedience"* to God. God has done far more exceedingly and abundantly in her life as He has promised in His Word.

Upon blessing her with a unique gift of writing, God has birthed into her *Divine House Ministries*, a book ministry of inspirational writings that reaches out to all people. He has called and anointed her to minister spiritual and physical healing to a sick and dying world.

As she received visions and dreams from God concerning the future, He commissioned her to write what she saw in *Visions of God's Coming Judgments*. Over a period of seven months in the year of 1997, God gave unto her poems of inspirations that you can enjoy in her first book titled, *"Let the Holy Spirit Embrace You with Poems of Inspirations"* with *"Hidden Treasures of Wisdom and Knowledge"* being her second poem book. And thirdly, *"Visions of God's Coming Judgments"* this book she declares is one of her greatest accomplishments in life presented unto you in God's perfect timing. She is told by the Holy Spirit, "Many things shall you write. This is just the beginning of more to come!"

READER'S AISLE

If you have enjoyed *Visions of God's Coming Judgments,"* I would like to encourage you to read another book written by the author entitled *"Let The Holy Spirit Embrace You with Poems of Inspiration."*

This book of poems is truly inspirational and God-given. As you read, the words speak straight to your heart. As I read, on various days, each day seemed to be just the food and encouragement I needed for that day. As you read, *"Let the Holy Spirit Embrace You with Poems of Inspiration,"* please open your heart to receive what God would have for you. Some of these poems have the *praise and worship* sincerity of the Psalms. Others have the *teachings* of the Proverbs. Others yet seem to have the *leading and instructions of the epistles.* As I read, my mind was challenged to consider the awesomeness of our God, Jesus our Savior, and the precious presence and power of the Holy Spirit. I urge you to read these poems seeking God's power to minister to you. I also thank God for the willingness and obedience of Sister Kimberly Jackson. I encourage her to continue to allow the Spirit of God to speak to her and through her that others may be blessed.

Evangelist V. L. Spencer

Plus another poem book is coming!
Hidden Treasures of Wisdom and Knowledge
Order any of these copies today by contacting us at
Divinehous@aol.com

For more information on ordering
additional copies or to contact the author,
write to:

Kimberly Vinson-Jackson
Divine House Ministries
P.O. Box 374140
Decatur, GA 30037-4140

Or e-mail us at
Divinehous@aol.com